The Last Confederate
Ship at Sea

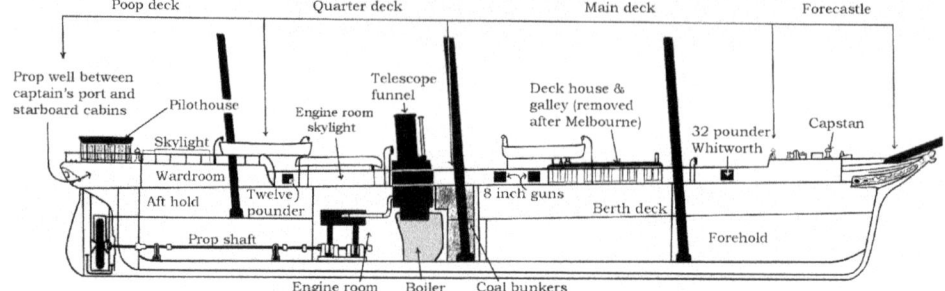

CSS *Shenandoah*

Built at Glasgow by Alexander Stephens & Sons, and launched August 18th, 1863, as the *Sea King*, fully rigged as a clipper ship with auxillery steam engines. Capable of sixteen knots under full sail with propeller hoisted, and ten knots under steam.

The Last Confederate Ship at Sea

*The Wayward Voyage
of the CSS Shenandoah,
October 1864 – November 1865*

PAUL WILLIAMS

McFarland & Company, Inc., Publishers
Jefferson, North Carolina

ALSO BY PAUL WILLIAMS

Custer and the Sioux, Durnford and the Zulus: Parallels in the American and British Defeats at the Little Bighorn (1876) and Isandlwana (1879) (McFarland, 2015)

LIBRARY OF CONGRESS CATALOGUING-IN-PUBLICATION DATA

Williams, Paul, 1946 March 14–
    The last Confederate ship at sea : the wayward voyage of the CSS Shenandoah, October 1864–November 1865 / Paul Williams.
        p.   cm.
    Includes bibliographical references and index.

    ISBN 978-0-7864-9857-4 (softcover : acid free paper) ∞
    ISBN 978-1-4766-1995-8 (ebook)

    1. Shenandoah (Cruiser) 2. United States—History—Civil War, 1861–1865—Naval operations, Confederate. I. Title.

E599.S5W66 2015
973.7'57—dc23   2015003220

BRITISH LIBRARY CATALOGUING DATA ARE AVAILABLE

© 2015 Paul Williams. All rights reserved

No part of this book may be reproduced or transmitted in any form or by any means, electronic or mechanical, including photocopying or recording, or by any information storage and retrieval system, without permission in writing from the publisher.

On the cover: Recaulking the *Shenandoah* (Naval History and Heritage Command); *left to right* Master's Mate Cornelius Hun (Naval History and Heritage Command); Lillias Lewene Nichols (courtesy Charles Nichols Blanchard); James Iredell Waddell (Naval History and Heritage Command)

Printed in the United States of America

McFarland & Company, Inc., Publishers
  Box 611, Jefferson, North Carolina 28640
  www.mcfarlandpub.com

Acknowledgments

This book has been twenty-five years in the making, my research into the *Shenandoah* having commenced in 1990. A special thanks to Sharon Hollingsworth of North Carolina for her excellent research assistance over the last few years.

A special thanks also to Charles Nichols Blanchard of Searsport, Maine, for sharing his family history, and Clark Nichols, Paige Lilly and the staff of the Penobscot Marine Museum, Searsport (1991); Judy Macdonald of the State Library Melbourne Victoria (1990); Barry Crompton of the Civil War Round Table of Australia; the Museum of the Confederacy, Richmond, Virginia; Naval History and Heritage Command, Washington D.C.; Victoria Police Museum, Melbourne, Victoria; National Library of Australia, Canberra, ACT; Angus Curry and other helpful folk and friends who offered relevant texts and information in a variety of ways.

Contents

Acknowledgments	v
Prologue	1
1. Tears Stood in His Eyes	3
2. To Prevent Her Doing Wrong	5
3. Captain Blood	12
4. You Be Damned	20
5. Never Return to Europe	28
6. She Will Thank Me Even More	45
7. A Most Scandalous Romance	56
8. A Piratical Vessel	68
9. I Was Not a Prisoner of War	81
10. How Dramatic!	87
11. I Will Fight for My Ship	93
12. I Want My Dinner, Lord	113
13. Utterly Worthless	120
14. Fiery Sparks	125
15. A Sensation of Freedom	140
16. Some Motive That Would Not Bear Explanation	145
17. An Evil Genius	150

18. Mercilessly Defrauded 160
19. The Crinoline Under Which Thou Hast Kindled
    an Incendiary Fire 171

Appendix: Victims of the Shenandoah 181
Chapter Notes 185
Bibliography 193
Index 197

Prologue

On October 19, 1864, the Confederate cruiser *Shenandoah* was commissioned at sea after sailing from London, England. Her mission was to "sink, burn and destroy" all ships carrying the Federal flag during a cruise of up to fifteen months.

Lieutenant Commanding James Iredell Waddell carried orders from Commander James Dunwoody Bulloch. These included the following:

> I am inclined to think that when you have performed the work assigned you the best disposition you could make of the *Shenandoah* would be to sell her, either somewhere on the west coast of South America or to adventurous speculators in the Eastern seas. Thus would be realized a partial return of the cost of the cruise, and the ship would never return to Europe, where, as Confederate States property, her presence might give rise to harassing questions and complications.

Despite these instructions, James Waddell sailed the *Shenandoah* from the North Pacific to distant Liverpool, the only Confederate vessel to circumnavigate the globe. No satisfactory explanation has been given for this action, and many other questions remain unanswered.

This book has been written to tell the story behind the cruise of the *Shenandoah*.

1

Tears Stood in His Eyes

On August 2, 1865, the Confederate raider *Shenandoah* came in contact with the British bark *Barracouta* in the Pacific Ocean between the Sandwich Islands (Hawaii) and the Mexican mainland.

A boarding party was sent across, and soon returned with recent newspapers. The cruiser's commander, James Waddell, read final proof that the American Civil War was over. Confederate President Jefferson Davis had been captured on May 10, and the last shots fired a few days after that.[1] Waddell's ship had captured or destroyed thirty-eight United States merchant vessels during a ten-month cruise, and twenty-five of these had been taken since the war's end. All vessels still at sea under Confederate colors had been declared pirates; a hanging offence. With a heavy heart, Waddell ordered the *Shenandoah* decommissioned as a man-of-war, her big guns dismantled and stored below, her Enfield rifles discharged.[2]

The question now was what to do next? Waddell's orders had recommended the ship's sale in the Pacific region. From the outset a return to Britain had been virtually ruled out due to the vast distance from the North Pacific, and to avoid "harassing questions and complications."[3] The British had been accused by the United States of collusion in launching rebel ships.

A conference was held with senior officers, and the decision was made to hasten to a neutral port before a Federal warship could catch them on the high seas. Earlier in the year, they had carried out repairs in Melbourne, Australia, and the port of Sydney on the same continent was even closer. The course was set, and for twenty-four hours the ship moved southwest towards the neutral port of the British Empire. Waddell hoped to sell the ship as recommended in his orders,[4] but if a sale was not possible, he would surrender her to either the British or American authorities.

But the captain appeared on deck the following morning. "Tears stood in his eyes and his voice was thick," recalled Midshipman John Mason. "I was truly sorry for the poor man."[5]

The distressed captain informed his officers that he had changed his mind about their destination. They were now to embark on the long, perilous voyage to an English port in the Atlantic Ocean to avoid "throwing a lot of young officers on shore without money in a port thousands of miles from home." Most officers, however, decidedly wished to take their chance with an Australian port rather than a Federal cruiser and a hangman's noose. Two officers, appalled by the decision, approached Waddell and asked him to reconsider, but he "had made up his mind to go to Liverpool," he informed them. And he would "be d—d if he did not take her there."[6] But Liverpool was three months and seventeen thousand miles away.

James Iredell Waddell, a man who returned to Britain for "the honor of my country's flag and the welfare of 132 men." But another man claimed "some motive that would not bear explanation" (Naval History and Heritage Command).

Despite the objections, the *Shenandoah* remained on course for the Atlantic Ocean.

A British colony in the South Atlantic, Cape Town, South Africa, was suggested, but this too was ignored despite earnest petitions from most officers. Waddell would later write, "The officers set a bad example to the crew. Their conduct was nothing less than mutiny. I was very decided with some of them. I had to tell one officer I would be captain or die on the deck."[7]

Federal warships had terminated the Confederate cruisers *Alabama* and *Florida* through bloody conflict. The war's conclusion meant more warships were now released from blockading duties and free to track him down.

Against such opposition, why had Waddell come to such a decision, and why was he distraught having made it?

2

To Prevent Her Doing Wrong

Southern Indian Ocean, December 29, 1864:

> The squalls of snow and hail during that gale were frightful. On the 29th December, the wind moderated as rapidly as it had risen, and was then nearly at south, bringing along with it an occasional squall of fine rain, and leaving an ugly cross sea that seemed undecided how and where to expend itself. It broke against the sides of the *Shenandoah*, sending fine spray through the open seams of the hull into the berth deck. James Waddell[1]

"Sail ho" was heard from the lookout; a vessel far to the cruiser's stern. Waddell ordered his ship to hold her luff to allow the stranger to approach and communicate. He was concerned she would slip by and quickly outdistance the cruiser's guns. "Everyone having a spyglass or lorgnette watched eagerly the approaching and unsuspecting visitor, whose hull was painted white and green." The *Shenandoah* hoisted false British colors, and a faded Stars and Stripes ascended in reply, "which caused a stifled outburst of delight."

"Providence seems to have smiled upon our endeavors," recalled Midshipman John Thompson Mason, "For this last fellow came right into the lion's mouth."

The *Shenandoah* had already captured or destroyed eight United States vessels since departure from London the preceding October. She was now voyaging towards Melbourne, the capital of the British colony of Victoria, on the south coast of the vast, mostly unexplored continent of Australia.

"She continued to approach," recalled Waddell. "Raised a blackboard, a familiar way in which one vessel enquires of another her longitude." A blank was loaded into a twelve-pounder gun, and the Yankee ship passed close by the *Shenandoah*'s stern. "We fired a cartridge, hoisted at the same time our own colors," wrote Executive Officer William Whittle.[2] But the bark plowed on with billowing canvas in a good position to make her escape. The cruiser's deadly Whitworth rifled guns were cleared for action; a live shell might change her skipper's mind. Losing faith, however, the Yankee ordered his mainsail hauled up before a lethal shot could be fired, and the helmsman brought the bark into the wind. She heaved to in a gesture of surrender, her colors lowered.

Sailing Master Irvine Bulloch, Master's Mate John Minor and a party of men armed with revolvers and cutlasses rowed to the bark, went aboard, and informed the captain that his vessel was a prize of the Confederate States government. She was the *Delphine* of Bangor, Maine—en route from Gravesend, England, to Akyab, Burma—with seventeen people and a cargo of rice-cleaning machinery on board. Her captain was thirty-two-year-old William Green Nichols, of Searsport. Also on board was his twenty-six-year-old wife, Lillias Lewene Nichols. "I suppose you are going to steal my canary birds," she exclaimed, "so you had better take them at once!"[3]

Bulloch declined the lady's offer and told her husband to gather the ship's papers for examination. With the first mate, Edward Jones, Bulloch and Nichols returned to the *Shenandoah* where Jones remained on deck while Captain Nichols was taken into the wardroom to be questioned. When told his ship was to be destroyed, Nichols protested, "It may cause the death of my wife to remove her. The report of the gun has made her very ill."

Midshipman Mason recalled that Captain Waddell was "an exceedingly tender-hearted man and believes everything one tells him and seemed almost disposed to bond the vessel."[4] Tenderhearted, perhaps, but not totally naive, Waddell referred Nichols to the ship's surgeon, Dr. Charles Lining, who wrote, "I heard his account of the sickness, came to the conclusion that she was not as sick as he made out, but that he wanted to make her a handle by which to get off." Assistant Surgeon Frederick McNulty was sent over to check the condition of the apparently frail lady, but found a

Sailing Master Irving Bulloch declined Mrs. Nichols' kind offer to steal her canaries, but took the ship instead (Naval History and Heritage Command).

"brave cultivated woman" in good health. When asked if she were ill she laughed and said, "No."[5]

Captain Nichols was instructed to transfer his wife to the *Shenandoah* along with their six-year-old son Phineas, stewardess Mary Lingo, and her husband Edward, the steward. The women and child were transferred from the condemned bark by rowboat. Lillias Nichols was swung aboard the *Shenandoah* in a bosun's chair, her two caged canary birds in hand, to reveal an attractive, tall, buxom, brown-eyed brunette.

"A finer looking woman I have seldom seen," noted Dr. Lining.[6]

As the captives were shown to the "ladies chambers"—the captain's starboard cabin—Mrs. Nichols made a fateful encounter. "Welcome on board the *Shenandoah*," said Captain Waddell.[7]

> Mrs. Nichols asked in a stentorian voice if I was captain, and wished to know what I intended doing with them and where they would be landed. "On St. Paul, madame, if you like." "Oh no; never. I would rather remain with you." I was surprised to see in the sick lady a tall, finely proportioned woman of 26, in robust health, evidently possessing a will of her own, and it soon became palpable she would be the one for me to manage, and not her husband. A refractory lady can be controlled by a quiet courtesy, but no flattery.[8]

Midshipman Mason agreed with Captain Waddell's assessment. He referred to her as a "pretty woman but rather a strong minded one I should judge from the present appearances and I rather think she wears the breeches."[9] Lieutenant John Grimball recalled, "A woman of some culture, attractive in appearance and very decided."[10]

It was Lieutenant Francis Chew, however, who made the most acute observation: "And so we have the trouble of another woman on board." An understatement, as it would transpire. It seems unlikely that Mr. Chew ever learned how much trouble Mrs. Nichols' arrival had really caused.

Livestock and personal luggage were transferred to the *Shenandoah*. This included Mrs. Nichols' numerous books, but it came as no surprise that her piano was left behind. The captain and two mates were paroled, and the other seamen placed in irons. Six of the *Delphine*'s fifteen seamen were released when they signed for service on the *Shenandoah*, a welcome addition to the cruiser's short-handed crew.

By 11:00 p.m. the *Delphine* was prepared for destruction—a blow to Mrs. Nichols' husband, brother and father. Each owned a one-eighth share, along with her builder, Eliah Metcalf. All were members of a consortium of eight who owned her.

Master's Mate Cornelius Hunt wrote a melodramatic account of the bark's demise:

Night closed around us before the first forked tongue of fire, issuing from the companion-way of the fated barque, warned us that the destroying element had commenced its work. Rapidly the flames gathered headway, casting a fierce, lurid glow over the heaving bosom of the ocean; from doors, windows and hatchways they burst forth like the vengeful spirit of destruction, wound up the spars, stretched out upon the yards, swiftly enveloping shrouds, sails, and halyards in one splendid, fiery ruin; and standing out, strongly revealed against the darkening sky, the burning vessel surged and tossed, a holocaust to the God of War.[11]

The *Shenandoah* sailed away from the burning hulk, a possible beacon for Federal cruisers, and the destructive glow slowly faded. "At four next morning, when I went on deck, the burning wreck was still in sight from aloft," noted Lieutenant Chew.

The following day, Mrs. Nichols' irate disposition gave way to a composed acceptance of her new situation. She even "laughed and talked" at tea, the only meal she attended that day. But she took exception "to some remark" about Waddell having done his duty by burning the *Delphine*. The volatile lady became sarcastic and "flew out once when she asserted that the Captain *did know* he'd done his duty," recalled Charles Lining.[12]

Little wonder Mrs. Nichols was concerned for "where they would be landed." The War of 1812 had seen her grandfather's crew sent to Dartmouth Prison, Nova Scotia, after his schooner *Belfast* was captured by a British privateer off Martinique. Born in Searsport on July 4, 1838, she was the daughter of prominent sea captain and shipbuilder Phineas Pendleton II and Wealthy Carver. The Pendletons, Nichols, Carvers and Blanchard families were a notable shipbuilding dynasty. Family members often intermarried, and on September 29, 1857, she wedded William Green Nichols, a second cousin, in Boston. Their son Phineas was

Lillias Lewene Nichols' arrival triggered a series of clandestine events which had a profound effect on the *Shenandoah*'s ultimate voyage (courtesy Charles Nichols Blanchard).

born two years later, and another child, Hannah, was born in 1862, but died shortly after birth.[13]

As the days passed, both Mrs. Nichols and her melodious canaries cast a sensual ambiance over the ship. The birds "sang delightfully all day," recalled Midshipman Mason. Young Phineas, called "Phinny" by his mother, played with goats taken from the *Delphine*.

John Mason recalled:

> Amongst other trophies we received from the *Delphine* was two pigs and two goats, one of them a young kid that gives a great deal of amusement. The pigs who were put in the same pen as ours did not seem to relish the idea of being obliged to mess with rebels, or perhaps our good Confederate pigs were insulted at being obliged to take in the Yankees; at any rate they kept up a tremendous noise last night and this morning in the mid watch I went forward and noticed them being apart in the pen; the Confeds on one side and the Yanks on the other.

As Mrs. Nichols' demeanor calmed, the blustery wind and clouds also faded away to a clear blue sky. James Waddell reflected on his current circumstances:

> Thirty-first of December closed the year, the third since the war began. And how many of my boon companions are gone to that bourne from whence no traveler returns! They were full of hope, but not without fears, when we last departed. They had fallen in battle in defense of their homes invaded by a barbarous enemy.[14]

Atlanta had fallen to General Sherman the previous September, and General Lee was unable to break Grant's vice-like grip on Petersburg, still under siege. The "barbarous enemy" was closing in rapidly. The last months of the Confederacy were at hand, but those on board the *Shenandoah* did not realize this at the time. Executive Officer Whittle noted that the *Delphine*'s steward Edward Lingo wished to be paroled "as he did not want to be put in the Federal army when he got back." But Lingo was from Missouri, a slave state that remained with the Union, and the parole was refused. Whittle "considered him nothing but a traitor." In regard to Mrs. Nichols, however, "Our lady passenger's becoming more sociable and really seems to think that we are not a parcel of piratical barbarians." Perhaps it was the ambiance cast by Mrs. Nichols that made Whittle brood over his family and a sweetheart he had met only once. "How much would I not give to see the dear ones at home again, and my own darling Pattie. God protect them I pray."[15]

"I have just had the distinguished honor of playing a rubber of whist in the Captain's cabin with himself, the First Lieutenant and the Assistant Surgeon," recalled Midshipman Mason. "It is positively prohibited for officers to play cards on board ship, but in the Captain's cabin it is allowable as the 'skipper' is monarch of all he surveys." It was the last day of 1864 and brandy bottle was produced.

Glasses were raised and a toast drunk to sweethearts, wives and 'success to the Cause.'"[16]

January 1, 1865, saw the *Shenandoah* sailing on a tolerably smooth sea, "the first fair and delightful day that we have had since we have been in the Indian Ocean," wrote Dr. Lining. The captain read the Articles of War to his crew, then "The new year was welcomed," recalled Waddell. "By the hoisting of a flag which had never before been unfurled to the breeze, and the *Shenandoah* had then been in commission two months and eleven days, and had destroyed or ransomed more property than her original cost."

Captain Nichols, Waddell recalled:

> expressed shame for having introduced the condition of Mrs. Nichols' health to save from destruction his vessel, and said enquiringly, "I did not think a lie under the circumstances was wrong." He told me after he sailed on that voyage his little son called attention to the tenth verse, twenty-seventh chapter of the Acts of the Apostles, Paul's dangerous voyage.[17]

This seems somewhat ironic as on February 2 the *Shenandoah* dropped anchor off St. Paul, a small island formed by an extinct volcano. The crater had been breached and flooded which formed a bay flanked by steep cliffs. It had once been part of the French Empire, but even they had renounced their claim to the desolate outpost in 1853.

Charles Lightoller, the second officer who survived the *Titanic* disaster of 1912, would be shipwrecked here in 1889. In his autobiography, Lightoller speculated that pirates may have used St. Paul's caves to stash treasure, but if so Lieutenant John Grimball and his armed party missed the booty. They found only two French fishermen and some provisions ashore.[18] The Confederates came back on board the *Shenandoah* with some eggs, fish, a few chickens and a penguin. A piece of rag was pinned around the bird's neck appearing to be a shawl, and all laughed as it waddled across the deck, "Like an old woman for all the world," exclaimed Mrs. Nichols.

"She had tamed down somewhat, and I rather admired the discipline she had her husband under," recalled Waddell. Mrs. Nichols' relationship with the man under her "discipline" was strained, however. She blamed him for the premature surrender of their ship—the *Shenandoah* being short-handed and ill equipped to give chase under the weather conditions that day. "If she had been in command the *Delphine* would have escaped—she said so," recalled Lieutenant Grimball.[19]

Captain Nichols was "very melancholy," reported Midshipman Mason, "and refused to be comforted." Little wonder, as his share of the vessel carried no insurance. The destruction wrought by rebel cruisers had made premiums excessive. Had Nichols altered his course by quarter of a point that morning, Lieutenant Francis Chew pointed out, he would never have been taken. "That shows how much you know about it," replied the disgruntled captain. "That is just what troubles me; I did alter my course that very morning exactly one quarter of a point, and that was the only reason why I was captured."[20]

Charles Lining's 31st birthday fell on January 6, "one of the most beautiful days I ever saw—bright, clear, warm while in the sun." Perhaps the highlight of the day was the pleasure of "a long talk with Mrs. Nichols," her family photograph album the subject under discussion. But the charm of the tête-à-tête was disrupted by an intrusion. Lining recalled that the "infernally jealous" Captain Nichols "never allows me to talk to her that he does not come poking around." Annoyed with the arrival, Lining thought Nichols a fool, "obliged to suspect his wife, to have to keep his eyes on her to prevent her doing wrong."[21]

It seems that Captain Nichols had little faith in his wife's devotion.

3

Captain Blood

Ninety-five years later, James Waddell's memoirs were published for the first time. Edited by writer and historian James D. Horan, they were on sale to the general public in book form.

But a reading of Waddell's original in the *Official Records* and the published Horan version reveal a number of alterations and omissions in relation to Lillias Nichols.

Waddell originally wrote that Mrs. Nichols "had tamed down somewhat, and I rather admired the discipline she had her husband under." James Horan changed this to, "had somewhat softened in tone, and we admired her for the discipline she observed towards Mr. Nichols."[1] A blatant reversal of the facts.

Waddell's description of Mrs. Nichols had a sentence cut midstream, the following deleted: "and it soon became palpable that she would be the one for me to manage, and not the husband. A refractory lady can be controlled by a quiet courtesy, but no flattery." Horan's version and the original memoir then continued in sync.[2]

Also removed was Waddell's description of the Nichols family leaving the ship in Melbourne. This included: "On the following morning soon after daylight I was aroused by voices in the adjoining cabin, and I heard Mrs. Nichols say: 'If these sextants and chronometers were mine I guess I'd make him give them to me.'" Another put down of William Nichols, and the word "him" exposed anger with Waddell personally. Mrs. Nichols had been obliged to sign a parole after being promised that she was "not a prisoner of war." Included in this cut was Lillias leaving the ship yelling, "I wish that steamer may be burned!"[3]

Thus anything with Waddell flaunting Lillias Nichols' dominance over her husband, and her being in a distressed emotional state after being "tamed down," was either rewritten or removed. The deleted words, "tamed down," and "controlled by a quiet courtesy," could also be interpreted by some as seduction.

But Horan included: "On the following morning soon after daylight the prisoners deserted taking their luggage with them much to my comfort."[4] Waddell was apparently happy to see Mrs. Nichols go.

And when Waddell referred to female prisoners: "For the fact was I felt a compassion for the women, because they would be landed I did not know where. The thought of inflicting unnecessary severity on a female made my heart shrink within." Horan replaced this with "We all felt a compassion for these poor women, and we had no idea of retaliating upon them for the injuries which General Hunter, Sheridan, Sherman and their kind had inflicted on our unhappy countrywomen."[5] Thus Horan expunged this disclosure of Waddell's personal compassionate feelings towards women in his charge.

The original wording and the altered version, both readily available, can be compared with ease today.

My curiosity regarding the relationship between James Waddell and Lillias Nichols was aroused by a series of incidents and documents that came to my notice while carrying out research in 1990 for a novel and screenplay based on the ship's stay in Melbourne. My original concept was for a plot to destroy the ship, but the emphasis shifted as research progressed.

The very fine Penobscot Marine Museum is located in Searsport, Maine, where Lillias was born in 1838. She passed away in the same town, aged 94, on April 7, 1933. I wrote to the museum staff inquiring if they knew anything about her. They did, and I was delighted to exchange letters with the museum librarian, Paige Lilly, and Clark Nichols, treasurer.

Clark wrote to me on December 6, 1990:

> I am old enough to have known Lillias. Back in 1926 my family rented a house across the street from Lillias on Water Street for the summer ... spent endless hours playing baseball while Lillias watched from her rocking chair on the porch. I don't think she thought much of our ability. We would occasionally have some lemonade with her when the weather was hot. The house still exists but it is not the house she lived in as a child ... the original portrait of William and Lillias is in the Searsport home of one of the trustees.... We will be glad to meet you at the museum sometime next summer.... The museum undoubtedly has additional information from which you can gain material for your novel and screenplay.[6]

I traveled to Searsport in June of 1991 and settled into The Home Port, a fine old 1860 mansion providing accommodation for visitors, originally the home of Captain John Nichols.

During my stay, I was introduced to Charles Nichols Blanchard.[7] His grandmother Clara was Lillias' younger sister, passing on two years before her in 1931, and he, like Clark Nichols, had known Lillias in the autumn of her life. A devotee of his seafaring ancestors, Charles kindly invited me to visit his home that very evening to discuss his family's history. He and his wife, Mildred, were living in their summer house near Penobscot Bay, winters being spent in another home a little farther inland. An ex-army officer, Charles had received awards during World War II for developing advanced aircraft loading systems onto freighters. Following the war he was vice president of the stevedore firm Turner and Blanchard of New York, and upon retirement moved to his family's ancestral home of Searsport. A pillar of the community, he served as chairman of the school board and on the board of selectmen.

Charles produced family documents, letters and photos as we talked for some time. The family's vessels were often named for family members, and William Nichols had commanded the bark *Lillias* before the *Delphine,* named after one of Lillias' younger sisters.

Charles' grandmother Clara, Lillias' sister, had married Captain William H. Blanchard in 1863. They had five children over the next 20 years, and Scott Blanchard was the last, born on the bark *Frank Pendleton* in 1883. Scott eventually married Lewene Alexandre Nichols,[8] born in Searsport in 1890 and named after Lillias Lewene Nichols. They had two children, Scott Jnr. and my host, Charles Nichols Blanchard, born in 1922. Charles recalled Clara's funeral at Searsport in 1931. He had travelled with his mother from his birthplace, New York City, and they visited Lillias—usually called Lill or Lilli within the family.

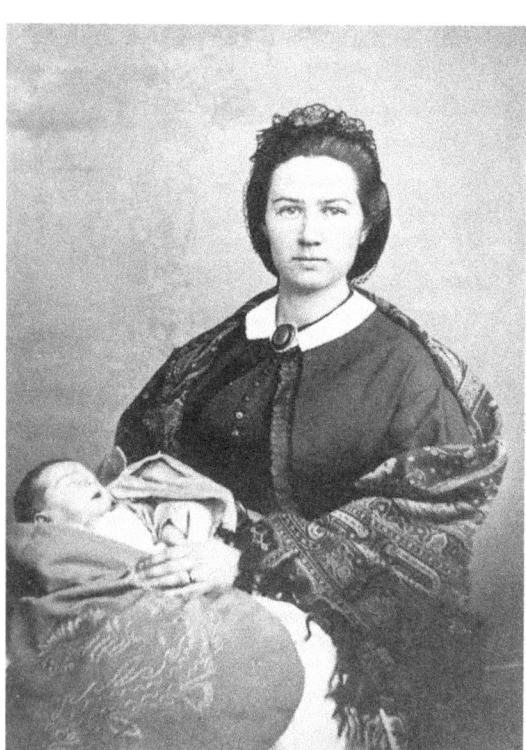

Clara Blanchard, the sister of Lillias Nichols. In 1991 her grandson, Charles Nichols Blanchard, divulged the origin of Waddell's memoirs being "doctored" before publication in 1960 (courtesy Charles Nichols Blanchard).

Having established a good rapport, I made a tactful suggestion that perhaps there was more to the relationship of Lilli Nichols and James Waddell than history records. Hesitant at first, he agreed, with some reluctance, to reveal some startling facts, skeletons in the family closet, so to speak. Fate seemed to have brought me to his doorstep, and Charles revealed the following story, a piece of fascinating history.

Following Lilli's death in April 1933, a diary had been found in her home by her grandchildren, Lillias Pendleton Nichols and John McCready Nichols. Her son Phineas had died in 1911.

Lilli's writings exposed a love affair with James Waddell. It commenced onboard ship and continued on land after debarkation in Melbourne. The pages also revealed the saving of a Yankee ship at her behest, and an anguished separation when the lovers parted.

In one aspect this was not a surprise as, based on my examination of the facts, I had assumed a love match had taken place. But the saving of a Yankee ship had escaped my notice.

The diary had been left where it could be easily found, so the forthright Lilli Nichols wanted her story told. By 1933 there were few who could be seriously affected by such disclosures, she outliving both her own children and Waddell's only child.

There was no intention, however, to make the contents public, but someone talked, probably Lilli's grandson, and rumors quickly spread through the Penobscot Bay communities. A lengthy story about Lillias and the *Shenandoah* had appeared in the *Bangor Daily News* in honor of her 94th birthday, July 4, 1932, so her Civil War capture was well known.[9]

Some recalled reading their parent's copies of Master's Mate Cornelius E. Hunt's memoir, *The Shenandoah; or the Last Confederate Cruiser*, first released in 1867, shortly after the destructive voyage, and reprinted in 1910. The only book solely about the cruise at the time of Lilli's death, it had been widely read in New England seafaring communities grievously damaged by rebel cruisers. Of the 255 ships taken, 30 had come from Penobscot Bay.[10] Some residents in 1933 had recent family involved, as was Lilli herself. Copies were pulled from dusty shelves and fingers pointed at one line in particular: they "indulged in the most scandalous romance at our expense after they got on shore."[11]

Hunt was talking about the Nicholses disparaging the ship's officers after leaving the *Shenandoah* in Melbourne. In light of the diary revelations, however, some wondered if the master's mate knew more than he revealed.

In an amazing twist of fate, the pirate movie *Captain Blood* was released in 1935 when the rumors were still fresh. The cruise of the *Shenandoah* and the adventures of Mrs. Nichols had strong parallels with the Errol Flynn blockbuster, which first established the actor as a major film star.

During the story an enemy ship is recognized but allowed to escape to a safe port. "You'll never know how close you came to not getting there," says Errol Flynn. Apart from this, the movie's early plot bears no relation to the

Shenandoah, but in the last act the beautiful actor Olivia de Havilland is taken prisoner by the handsome rogue who, when approaching the enemy, flies false colors. And of course, despite initial hostility, the pirate captain wins the heart of his lovely prisoner. On land, the home government collapses. The crew think they will hang because of the ship's proposed destination. Mutiny is threatened.

"This is what comes from sailing the seas with a lovesick madman!" says the gunner when told Port Royal is their destination, a hangman's noose awaiting them.

Thus the captain has to win the crew over, and, sure enough, they arrive safely; Liverpool in reality for James Waddell and Port Royal in fiction for Errol Flynn.

The film was a huge hit, eagerly watched in places with a sailing ship heritage like Searsport. The population of about 2,000 included many relatives and friends; a small community where everyone knows everyone; ripe for the rumor mill. Before you knew it, jokes about "Errol Waddell" and "Lillias de Havilland" flew not only around Searsport but other seafaring communities on Penobscot Bay, Lilli's birthday article well remembered. Here was a story too good not to repeat, and repeat. *Captain Blood* provided great publicity for the indiscretions of Lilli Nichols.

Errol Flynn then appeared as himself in the Technicolor short *Pirate Party on Catalina Isle*. Alongside him was his wife, Lili Damita. "With a girl like Lili at home, no wonder the captain hates the sea," says the narrator. Olivia de Havilland became established in many local people's minds as "Lillias de Havilland," then appeared in a whole string of romantic films with "Errol Waddell" over the following years: *The Charge of the Light Brigade, The Adventures of Robin Hood, Four's a Crowd, Dodge City, The Private Lives of Elizabeth and Essex, Santa Fe Trail* and *They Died with Their Boots On*.

Shortly after *Captain Blood*'s release, film star Mary Astor also made a scandalous contribution. The explicit "thrilling ecstasy" love affair contents of her diary were leaked to the press as she fought a custody battle. The Astor scandal was huge and Searsport saw comparisons drawn. The story was only replaced on the front pages by yet another, bigger scandal—King Edward and his Yankee lover, Mrs. Simpson.

Then, of course "Lillias de Havilland" appeared as Melanie Hamilton in the greatest Civil War romance of all time, *Gone with the Wind*,[12] her arms around her gray-clad hero, Ashley, when he returns from the war. In *Strawberry Blonde* she played a demure nineteenth-century woman who shocks James Cagney with her supposedly "liberated" views regarding sex without marriage, while "Errol Waddell" appeared in the very appropriate *Adventures of Don Juan*. Due to legal action Errol's off-screen sex life had become legendary, giving rise to the "in like Flynn" metaphor. Thus the rumors never went away.[13]

Errol kept the stories alive with more swashbucklers through the 1950s, such as *The Master of Ballantrae, Crossed Swords* and *The Warriors*. Olivia contributed with *The Proud Rebel* where a Yankee woman gets involved with an ex–Confederate played by Alan Ladd. In the plot, scandalous gossip spreads about the unmarried couple, reflecting events in Searsport. Director Michael Curtiz, who did *Captain Blood* twenty-three years earlier, continued to feed the rumor mill with this piece of work.

Film is a powerful medium, and anyone doubting this effect need only consider the recent moves for Scottish independence, a direct result of the 1995 movie *Braveheart*, which provided the catalyst.

Writer and historian James Horan approached Lilli's granddaughter. He told her of his plans to write a novel about the CSS *Lee*, based on the *Shenandoah*. Were the rumors true? Lillias Jnr. denied all and asked Horan to help quash the matter by excluding any romantic inference whatsoever. He agreed and only included Lilli's pet canary, her son and husband. Conspicuous by her absence is any mention of Lilli herself, apart from a vague reference to women from the *Delphine* meeting the captain. An unrelated fictional romance does appear, but in London before setting sail. His novel *Seek Out and Destroy*[14] came out in 1958, the same year as *The Proud Rebel* movie.

Then the family heard that Waddell's memoirs were to be published for the first time, and on sale to the general public. Lilli's diary had revealed all, so what would Waddell have to say? Seafaring Searsport would find many buyers for such a book, especially those who had heard the rumors and spread them to the next generation.

Errol Flynn died in 1959, aged 50, but it was as though fate had decreed that this publication should come out to take Errol's place in 1960. It was, however, to be an *edited* version. But who was the editor? None other than James Horan, the writer of *Seek Out and Destroy*.

Charles Blanchard's mother, Lewene, was third cousin to Lillias Jnr.—born five years later—and she had also been distressed by this blot on the family's name. These two ladies approached the helpful Horan, and asked him to assist quashing the "Errol Waddell" and "Lillias de Havilland" legend. He agreed to help the ladies out with a bit of "creative" editing, thus the changes to Waddell's original memoir by Horan as seen at the beginning of this chapter.

But why should James Horan wish to protect the reputation of Lillias Nichols? Because in doing so he also protected James Waddell. He went even further and wrote that Waddell:

> was proud and he refused to tarnish his honor or that of his ship by serving his own and the crew's interest at the cost of disobeying his country's orders, which were to return to Liverpool and surrender to British authorities ... Waddell had the choice

of disobeying his orders and saving his own neck, or obeying and risking execution by a country already in the white heat of lynch rule because of the murder of its beloved President.[15]

But, in fact, the captain's instructions advised the ship "never return to Europe," and even Waddell never claimed he was following "his country's orders." So why did James Horan wish to protect the reputation of James Waddell? Because the 1960s liberation of sexual attitudes had yet to come, and the married captain was known to have been a fine man "radiant with kindness" who captured or destroyed thirty-eight vessels, without loss of life, and ultimately ordered the last shot fired, the last flag lowered; in all, an exemplary record.

Years after the diary's discovery Charles' mother told him of what had occurred, and Charles, in turn, passed the fascinating story on to me that summer evening. "It's the first time I've told anyone about this," he said, possibly because I was the first person to ask. But he felt I should be rewarded with the truth after realizing what had taken place and traveling all the way from distant Australia. Charles' mother, Lewene, had died three years before, aged 97, so he felt it would now do no harm for the story to be revealed in a romantic novel so long after the event.

Lillias Jnr., however, had inherited the family genes. She was still alive as we talked in June 1991, aged 96, thus I was only given this information on the grounds that Charles' specific revelations not appear in the novel. I did, however, cheat slightly by having the diary appear as part of the romantic story. Published by Hodder & Stoughton, Australia, *The Shenandoah Affair* was released in 1992, a semi-fictional narrative of the *Shenandoah*'s stay in Melbourne and the love affair between James Waddell and Lillias Nichols.

Lillias Jnr. died on November 23, 1991,[16] thus she passed on, without my knowledge, before publication. A risqué novel, it may not have been appreciated by someone born in 1895, especially as it revealed a relationship she had sought to conceal.

I hoped to contact James Horan for his side of the story, but learned he had died in 1981, aged 67.

Lilli's two grandchildren had no offspring, so her branch of the family died out with the passing of Lillias Jnr. in 1991. The diary, now missing, may well have been destroyed, as was Mary Astor's in 1952. Executive Officer William Whittle's revealing journal only came to light in the 1980s during an attic clean-out.

The cousins' efforts were in vain in the long run, of course, but their efforts bore fruit in the short term. Those eagerly buying Waddell's memoirs for some proof would have been sorely disappointed to read: "had somewhat softened in tone, and we admired her for the discipline she observed towards Mr. Nichols."

Along with the cuts and changes, the hint of anything suggestive had been removed. This would certainly have created doubts in prying minds.

How ironic was it that cousins Lillias and Lewene Nichols should, by concealing the truth, provide proof of the affair of Lillias Lewene Nichols? A case of truth being stranger than fiction.

The parallels between *Captain Blood* and the *Shenandoah* events are readily seen with a viewing of the film. Also, *The Proud Rebel* and *Pirate Party* movies, at time of writing, can be viewed on the Internet. Lilli's diary may be missing, but the significant results are not; the alterations and deletions from Waddell's original memoir. This can be read online in the *Official Records of the Union and Confederate Navies* and compared with the altered 1960 Horan version, *CSS Shenandoah; the Memoirs of Lieutenant Commanding James I. Waddell*, available online.[17]

I was shown through Lilli Nichols' house in Water Street, a picturesque two-story colonial dwelling, white with blue shutters. In a local church I saw a stained glass window dedicated to the memory of her parents. The tall Nichols' family headstone in the Elmswood cemetery is inscribed *Lillias L. Pendleton*, her maiden name, possibly a reflection on her marriage. Her sisters' headstones carry their married names, so the use of maiden names was not a family tradition. Lilli was the last of her immediate family to pass on after Hannah, William and Phineas, all inscribed. Baby Hannah also has a separate headstone in the Bowditch Cemetery on Pendleton Road.[18]

4

You Be Damned

The Southern Indian Ocean was far from the theatre of war. How a Confederate warship came to be approaching distant Australia in December of 1864 might well be traced to events on February 4, 1861. In Montgomery, Alabama, delegates from the states seceding from the United States met, the result being the Provisional Constitution of the Confederate States of America. The new government was empowered to provide an army and navy, said President Jefferson Davis, the Commander-in-Chief.

The Confederacy was devoid of armed forces in the true sense of the word, but had already started assembling munitions, men and vessels should the newly elected president of the United States, Abraham Lincoln, refuse to allow them to leave the Union peacefully.

The first state to adopt an Ordinance of Secession had been South Carolina, on December 20, 1860. Moored in Charleston Harbor was the U.S. revenue cutter *WM Aiken* of ninety tons, armed with a forty-two pounder pivot gun, and in fine trim. Seized by the state authorities along with the steam cutter *Grey*, they became the first vessels of the navy of South Carolina, the embryonic Confederate States Navy.[1]

Lilli Nichols' father had been one of those New England skippers who had delivered rock for the construction of Fort Sumter, strategically built on a man-made shoal in Charleston Harbor. It was here, on April 12, 1861, that the simmering differences between the northern and southern states over various slavery issues finally came to a head. Cannon boomed along the shoreline as Confederate forces under General Pierre G. T. Beauregard opened fire on the Yankee stronghold.

A few days later the garrison surrendered, the Stars and Stripes hauled down; the battered brick ramparts occupied by the victorious rebels.

Further north, Richmond, Virginia, was still in the Union, but bands played

Dixie's Land and *The Bonnie Blue Flag* as a joyous throng marched on the state capital building. The Yankee flag was pulled down to be replaced with the Confederate Stars and Bars, and a hundred-gun salute shook the ground in honor of Fort Sumter's surrender. Virginia seceded within the week, and Richmond soon became the Confederate capital.

A different mood would have prevailed had the crowd been given a glimpse of the same Richmond streets, four years hence, desolated by fire and famine, their glorious Cause a memory in the dust.

But now the South waited with tension to see the North's response. Would the South be allowed to leave the Union peacefully or would there be war? The answer came quickly with Abraham Lincoln's call for 75,000 volunteers, and his proclamation of a naval blockade on Confederate ports. The news was greeted joyously by hotheads in the South who had been spoiling for a fight, while more sober souls, realizing the South's limited ability to wage a sustained war, shook their heads with apprehension. The United States' heavy industry, capable of producing shot, shell, rifles, railway locomotives and the other materials of war, was almost wholly located in the North. The Tredegar Iron Works in Richmond was the only Southern foundry capable of producing heavy cannon.[2]

The naval outlook was equally bleak for the emerging nation. The Confederacy had few facilities for building ships of war, and no capacity for producing large and powerful marine steam engines. The only Southern naval shipyard of substance was at Norfolk, Virginia.

Naval officers, however, it had in abundance, as 320 resigned their commissions from the United States Navy. Lieutenant James Iredell Waddell of North Carolina received word of the war's outbreak when the USS *John Adams* docked at St. Helena while en route from Hong Kong to New York. "I had determined if the North made war on the South to go South and assist those people," he recalled, and he wrote his letter of resignation[3]:

To the Hon.
The Secretary of the Navy:

Sir:
   The people of the State of North Carolina having withdrawn their allegiance to the Government, and the State from the Confederacy of the United States; and owing to these circumstances, and for reasons to be hereafter mentioned, I return to his Excellency the President of the United States, the commission which appointed me a Lieutenant in the Navy, with other public documents, asking acceptance thereof.
   In thus separating myself from associations which I have cherished for twenty years, I wish it to be understood that no doctrine of the right of secession, no wish

for disunion of the States impel me, but simply because, my home is the home of my people of the South, and I cannot bear arms against it or them.

                    I am, Sir, respectfully,
                    James I. Waddell

Little did Waddell realize when he wrote this in November of 1861 that he would ultimately command the last fighting unit of the Confederacy on land or sea.

Only four days after the surrender of Fort Sumter, Confederate President Jefferson Davis offered letters of marque to Southern ship-owners prepared to turn privateer and sail under Confederate colors. They were to plunder the mercantile marine of the United States. Privateers had been used by the Americans to great advantage in their two conflicts with Great Britain—the Revolution and the War of 1812[4]—and at least twenty privateers were soon at work off the eastern coast doing the same work for the Confederacy.

The *New York Herald* of August 10, 1861, protested that $20,000,000 worth of property had been lost to these "highwaymen of the seas." The worst was not the loss of ships, claimed the paper, but the destruction of American commerce: "Now no Northern vessel will get a charter or can be insured for any reasonable premium. English bottoms are taking all our trade."[5]

Lincoln's initial response when imposing the blockade was a threat to treat captured privateer crews as pirates, but a promise from the rebels to match hanging for hanging saw a revised decision to treat them as prisoners of war.[6]

The success of the rebel privateers was short lived, however. The Union government purchased and built ships to augment its navy and the blockade was tightened from Virginia to Texas. This discouraged privateers' attempts to bring captured prizes into southern harbors, and neutral nations banned prizes from being sold off in their ports. With the profit motive removed, there was little incentive for privateers to take to sea.

The rebel government formulated new plans for commerce raiders owned by the Confederate States Navy. Their task would not be to capture, but to burn and sink Federal shipping. If enough damage was caused, Yankees ship-owners may pressure the Federal Government to allow the South to go her own way.

In June of 1861 the steam sloop CSS *Sumter,* commanded by Captain Raphael Semmes, ran the blockade from the mouth of the Mississippi. In the next six months she brought her five guns to bear on eighteen U.S. merchant ships. Seven were burned and the others, for various legal reasons, ransomed for their value to be paid at the end of the war. Finally trapped by Federal warships in the harbor at Gibraltar, Semmes abandoned his ship and traveled to England where he collaborated with Commander James Dunwoody Bulloch, of Georgia. This thirty-eight-year-old officer had been charged with the task of utilizing

Britain's shipyards as a provider of warships for the Confederacy. An expert seaman of over twenty years experience in both naval and merchant vessels, Bulloch also had the tact and prudence required for dealing with the British government which, while not recognizing the Confederacy as a sovereign nation, did recognize it as a legitimate belligerent power. Under Queen Victoria's Neutrality Proclamation of May 1861, British subjects could not break a lawful blockade, equip any craft as a ship of war or privateer, or give passage to troops or military stores for either side.[7]

Many British skippers made a mockery of this. They frequently ran the blockade, bringing not only badly needed war supplies to the South but also tea, coffee, silk and other luxuries for those who could pay. On the return trip they would carry cotton and huge profits were made. Approximately 80 percent of attempts were successful, but about 1,500 blockade runners were captured or destroyed in the course of the war.

Shortly after his arrival at Liverpool, June 1861, Bulloch initiated contracts for two cruisers to be equipped with both sail and steam. The first, the *Oreto*, barkentine rigged, would ultimately become the CSS *Florida*. The second, known simply as the *No. 290*, would win everlasting fame as the CSS *Alabama*. Bulloch then purchased a fast steamer, the *Fingal*, packed her hold with munitions, took personal command, and successfully ran the blockade into Savannah, Georgia. This vessel, unable to return to sea because of the tightening blockade, was soon modified into one of a new breed of warship, an ironclad ram, and renamed CSS *Atlanta*.

The French and British had pioneered the construction of ironclads, but the Civil War saw a turning point in history. When the Confederate ironclad *Virginia*, built up from the remains of the burned out USS *Merrimac*, steamed into Hampton Roads on March 8, 1862, she quickly sank the wooden warships *Cumberland* and *Congress* with the loss of 240 Union lives; the worst day in the history of the U.S. Navy. The Confederate vessel received superficial damage with the loss of only two lives despite taking 98 hits. One survivor from the USS *Congress* was an African-American sailor by the name of John Williams who, no doubt, would have been astonished had he known that before the war's end he would be sailing under Confederate colors onboard the CSS *Shenandoah*.

Next day the *Virginia* was confronted by the *Monitor*, a revolutionary, low profile Federal ironclad which had arrived during the night. An example of changing times, she had a revolving turret containing two eleven-inch guns. For hours the two ironclads fought, solid shot and exploding shell doing little damage, and neither vessel gained the advantage. At the end of the day they withdrew, the battle inconclusive, but the ultimate death of the wooden man-of-war was now assured. The *Monitor*'s design, however, lacked seaworthiness, eventually being lost in a storm, and the *Virginia* was soon blown up to avoid capture when Norfolk fell to the Federals.

Naval men with an eye to the future hailed the new vessels with enthusiasm, but souls with a more romantic view of sea craft felt differently. A postwar newspaper article about the *Shenandoah* provided the basis for James Waddell's own feelings, as they appear in his memoirs:

> The worst of the iron plated vessel is that the black, ugly armor has no such vitality and cannot be christened with the pretty old-fashioned names which helped the sailor's superstition out, we cannot answer for such hideous monsters. They are created out of dull mineral from the bowels of the earth, and should they not all come to grief like the Monitor, the blacksmith will some day turn them into pots and pans, iron railings and boilers. But the timber of the wooden ship grew in the sunlight, it waved in the forest and heard the wind sing, before bending to the breeze under topsails.[8]

The ironclad warship was not the only naval innovation first put to the test during the Civil War. On February 17, 1864, the USS *Housatonic* was rent by a large explosion, and sank rapidly to the bottom of Charleston Harbor. This ship had the dubious distinction of being the world's first victim to a combat submarine, the *H. L. Hunley*. This cigar shaped, iron vessel was powered by six men who manually rotated a propeller shaft. Her skipper controlled submersion by elevators on each side. The torpedo was delivered on the end of a long spar at the ship's bow, but the unfortunate pioneer submariners did not return from their historic venture, the sub lost with all hands.

But clumsy ironclads and submarines were not yet suited to commerce raiding on the high seas. Speed was what counted, so the lean and beautiful timber sailing ship with auxiliary steam had not yet had her day.

As the ironclads fought their historic duel, James Bulloch returned to Britain in another blockade runner and finalized preparations to launch the Confederacy's new raider. Sailing from Liverpool on March 22 as an unarmed merchantman to circumvent Britain's neutrality laws, the *Oreto* met another steamer at the Bahamas. Guns and munitions were swung aboard, then she underwent a name change to CSS *Florida*. She came under fire from three Federal gunboats while running the blockade into Mobile and, her crew decimated by yellow fever, received considerable damage, as described by James Bulloch:

> The fore-topmast, and fore-gaff were shot away, all the boats were cut to pieces, the hammock-nettings were nearly all swept off on one side, the main rigging was adrift, and she was hulled in many places. One 11-inch shell had passed clean through her just above the water-line, and another had entered the captain's cabin, fortunately without exploding.[9]

Fully manned and fitted out, however, the *Florida* made her escape on the night of January 15, 1863, and commenced a destructive career which made her very name bring a shudder to Northern skippers of the merchant marine.

The U.S. Consul at Liverpool, Thomas H. Dudley, was determined not to let Bulloch's second and larger cruiser slip out as the *Florida* had done. His spies and double agents accumulated proof that the *No. 290* was intended for service as a Confederate cruiser. But fate played a strange hand to save the rebel ship. The Queen's advocate who received Adam's proof had gone insane, and any action was delayed.[10]

Bulloch received word that the British authorities were about to move. On July 29, 1862, the *No. 290* slipped into the Mersey for a "trial run" out to sea. She never came back, and was supplied from another vessel bearing guns, munitions and supplies. On August 24 the *No. 290* was commissioned as the CSS *Alabama*, Captain Raphael Semmes in command. For the next two years the *Alabama* haunted the Atlantic and Indian Oceans, capturing or destroying sixty-four Yankee ships.

In June of 1864 the *Alabama* put in at Cherbourg, France, but found her exit thwarted by Captain Winslow of the USS *Kearsarge,* and the two ships met beyond the three-mile limit. Thousands gathered on the heights of Cherbourg in clement weather to watch the fight. This included the artist Manet who captured the event on canvas with oil paint and brush.

The *Alabama* was the first to fire, but not the last. For over one hour the two vessels circled each other. Shot and shell were exchanged, but the Confederate ship was badly damaged and holed from repeated hits. Her executive officer John Kell recalled:

> It became necessary to clear the deck of parts of the dead bodies that had been torn to pieces by the 11-inch shells of the enemy. The captain of our 8-inch gun and most of the gun's crew were killed.... Going to the hatchway, I called out to Brooks to give the ship more steam, or we would be whipped.
>
> He replied she "had every inch of steam that was safe to carry without being blown up!"
>
> Young Matt O'Brien, assistant engineer, called out, "Let her have the steam; we had better blow her to hell than to let the Yankees whip us!"[11]

The young and trim Matt O'Brien, when in uniform, a sword by his side, looked more like a dashing cavalry officer than an engineer. He would become chief engineer on the *Shenandoah*, but his bravado was to no avail on this occasion. Inrushing seawater doused the *Alabama*'s furnace fires.

The wounded were put into lifeboats and men jumped overboard as the *Alabama* settled by the stern, and then sank. Nineteen men died with her. The *Kearsarge* lowered boats to pick up survivors. When brought alongside the rebel sailors saw protective anchor chains draped over the Union vessel's sides concealed by light timber casing, now largely shot away. Raphael Semmes and others were rescued by the English steam yacht *Deerhound* and made good their escape.[12]

With the U.S. Navy's blockade on southern ports very few warships were available to protect the sea-lanes. This resulted in the capture of over 255 craft on the high seas. But the ships destroyed by commerce raiders actually did less damage than the fear they created. To avoid both capture and increased insurance rates, at least 700 other U.S. vessels were sold to foreign interests, usually British. The disappearance of their merchant fleet caused fury in the United States, and it was not until well into the twentieth century that a full recovery was made.

James Bulloch contracted with Laird's shipyard at Birkenhead, England, for the construction of two ironclad rams mounted with double revolving turrets, each carrying two 9-inch guns. They would be state of the art warships capable of breaking the blockade and, it was hoped, holding New York City to ransom. Charles F. Adams, the American Minister to Britain, advised British Foreign Secretary Earl Russell that delivery to the Confederacy could possibly lead to war between the United States and Britain. Bulloch then had ownership of the ironclads transferred to a French firm that was supposedly buying them for the Khedive of Egypt. But this fooled no one, especially Charles Adams, who reiterated the possibility of war.

British Prime Minister Lord Palmerston was angered by Adam's attitude and wrote to Earl Russell, "It seems to be that we cannot allow to remain unnoticed his repeated and I must say somewhat insolent threats of war." He suggested Russell reply in civil terms, "You be damned," as they were going to seize the ironclads in any case, he claimed, and did not wish to appear humbled by "Yankee bullying."[13]

The ships were purchased by the Admiralty at a handsome profit to the Confederacy, and eventually raised steam as the British warships *Scorpion* and *Wyvern*.[14]

France became Bulloch's new hope and he contracted for the building of six new ships, but the Gallic rooster proved to be as troublesome as the British bulldog. A demand was made for the vessels be sold to powers other than the Confederacy. The persistent Bulloch, however, managed to retrieve one ironclad from Denmark. The CSS *Stonewall* set sail to wreak havoc with the blockading Union fleet, only to arrive in Cuba and learn the war was over. The ironclad was eventually sold to Japan and saw spirited action as the *Kotetsu*.

Most British aristocracy made no secret of their support for the Southern Cause. They identified with a rural gentry fighting for independence from an aggressive Yankee government starving Britain of cotton with its "damned blockade." By mid 1862 the supply of cotton was down by two-thirds, and mill workers in both Britain and France became unemployed and desperate. They relied on charity for the most basic subsistence. Influential members of the government advocated war with the United States if they did not relax the blockade. Many considered the war as good as won by the South as the Federal army had been given bloody repulses at Bull Run, Wilson's Creek and Ball's Bluff.[15]

Those most badly affected by the cotton shortage, the mill workers themselves, however, showed a remarkable degree of sympathy with the Union. Many looked upon slavery and the Confederacy as the cause of the problem. Charles Adams, wrote, "The great body of the aristocracy and the commercial classes are anxious to see the United States go to pieces, while the middle and lower class sympathize with us," and "see in the convulsion in America an era in the history of the world, out of which must come in the end a general recognition of the right of mankind to the produce of their labor and the pursuit of happiness."

5

Never Return to Europe

In August of 1864 James Bulloch received a letter from Confederate Secretary of the Navy, Stephen R. Mallory:

> The enemy's distant whaling grounds have not been visited by us. His commerce constitutes one of his reliable sources of national wealth no less than one of his best schools for seamen, and we must strike it, if possible. If you can do no better, can you not send in so safe and secret a manner that your action will not be known until their blows are felt, two clipper sailing ships, lightly armed with judicious officers, against this commerce?[1]

Following the fiasco of the Laird rams, construction of new warships was out of the question, as was the purchase of warships already afloat. Agents for the Union government scrutinized all such transactions in detail. The British government, sensitive to political pressure from the United States, was now far less convinced that the South would win the war. July of 1863 had seen General Lee's Army of Northern Virginia bloodily repulsed at Gettysburg, and Vicksburg fall to General Ulysses S. Grant. This placed control of the Mississippi River in Union hands. Grant had since been promoted to Commander-in-Chief of the Union forces and he now besieged Petersburg, Virginia—the key to the Confederate capital Richmond—and General William T. Sherman's troops skirmished their way towards Atlanta, Georgia—a vital railway and manufacturing center in the deep south.

But the South saw itself far from beaten. President Jefferson Davis considered the various battle plans his generals proposed for counter-attack to crush the Yankee juggernaut.

In response to Mallory's request, James Bulloch set about his task with characteristic zeal, but the acquisition of one vessel only for the proposed assault on the Yankee whalers was deemed practical. Some time before Mallory's request,

Bulloch had already "caught sight of a fine, composite, full-rigged ship, with something more than auxiliary steam power." The Clyde-built steamer *Sea King*, 1,160 tons was fully rigged as a clipper, carrying a cloud of canvas, and was known to have logged sixteen knots—one of the fastest ships afloat. Capable of ten knots under steam, her single screw could be lifted to reduce drag underwater, and her telescopic funnel could be reduced to half height, allowing an improved flow of wind to her sails. Her frame and lower-mast sections were of iron, her hull of rock elm below the water line and East Indian teak above. She was long and narrow, being 220 feet by 35, but her decks were spacious enough to carry guns. Built in 1863 by Alexander Stephens and Sons of Glasgow, she was chartered by the British government as a troop transport to help quell a Maori uprising in New Zealand. From there she sailed to Hankow and Shanghai, then returned to England with a cargo of tea.

"You will be gratified to learn this good fortune in finding a ship so admirably suited to our purpose," Bulloch wrote to Mallory. Although unsuited to open combat with a Federal cruiser, there was ample field for "cutting up his commerce" and "destroying his transports." Bulloch commented on the difficulty of enlisting seaman, but "every possible effort will be made to overcome all obstacles, and if the ship gets safely out to sea she will be called the *Shenandoah*."[2]

Bulloch's preparations were clandestine. Union spies were on the alert. As with the *Florida* and *Alabama,* the plan was for the *Sea King* to sail from London as a merchantman. Peter S. Corbett, an English captain who had skippered blockade runners, would initially command her. He carried a letter with

Commander James D. Bulloch, Waddell's commanding officer, excluded information as "merely confidential between ourselves" from his memoirs, including "never return to Europe" (author's collection).

authorization for a sale of not less than 45,000 pounds. This legal sale to the Confederacy would take place on the high seas outside British jurisdiction. She would sail with the two small twelve-pounder guns she still carried from her days as a troop transport. Once at sea she would meet another vessel with large guns, munitions, stores and Confederate officers on board. This included Lieutenant Commanding James I. Waddell. For this task Bulloch procured the screw-steamer *Laurel,* then carrying passengers and freight between Liverpool and Ireland.

First Lieutenant William Conway Whittle, the cruiser's executive officer, was to sail as a supposed passenger aboard the *Sea King.* A red-headed, clean-cut, unfashionably clean shaven twenty-four-year-old, Whittle appeared to have a promising future. An Annapolis graduate, the young midshipman had received praise for his part in the 1860 capture of a warship while U.S. naval vessels were supporting the Mexican government, the country rent with rebellion.

Whittle resigned from the U.S. Navy, and was soon appointed a lieutenant in the Confederate service. He received more praise when he ran the Federal blockade while in temporary command of the CSS *Nashville.* These successes seemed to give the young Whittle a very positive view of his place in the world. He often signed his name, "Wm C. Whittle, Lieutenant and Lieutenant Commanding C.S. Steamer *Nashville.*"[3] He was a young man impatient for permanent command.

The ambitious lieutenant saw action against Yankee ships at New Orleans, but was taken captive when the *Landis* surrendered. Exchanges of prisoners were made between North and South, and Whittle was released in August of 1862. After frustrating inaction, he was posted to France where he was eventually ordered to London as first lieutenant on the *Shenandoah.* He knew James Waddell socially, regarding his wife "with the affection of a brother," and in his journal referred to Waddell as a "friend." This would appear, however, to have been a disadvantage. It gave Whittle an undue familiarity with his commanding officer, and contributed to a contentious relationship once at sea.

On October 6, 1864, William Whittle received instructions from James Bulloch which could well have been taken from the pages of a dime novel, very popular at the time:

> Sir:
> You will proceed to London by the 5 o'clock p.m. train today and go to Wood's Hotel, Furnival's Inn, High Holborn. Take a room there and give your name as Mr. W. C. Brown if asked. It has been arranged for you to be in the coffee room at the hotel at 11 o'clock a.m. precisely tomorrow, and that you will sit in a prominent position, with a white pocket handkerchief rove through a buttonhole of your coat, and a newspaper in your hand. In this attitude you will be recognized by Mr. Richard

Wright, who will call at the appointed hour and ask if your name is Brown. You will say "Yes," and ask his name. He will give it and you will then retire with him to your room, hand him the enclosed letter of introduction, and, throwing off all further disguise, discuss freely the business in hand. Mr. Wright will introduce you to Captain Corbett, with whom you are to take passage to Madeira, and you will arrange with him how to get on board without attracting notice.... Say that I desire him to carry you to Madeira, and explain how he is to communicate with the Laurel.... It is important that the *Sea King* should not be reported, and you will request Captain Corbett not to exchange signals with passing ships, or at any rate not to show his real number. The object of your going out in the *Sea King* is to acquaint yourself with her sailing and other qualities and to observe the dispositions of the crew. You can also inspect the internal arrangements, and discuss with Captain Corbett the necessary alterations, and you can learn the stowage of the provisions and other stores, and even pick out the best positions for the magazine and shell room. Perhaps the construction of these might be actually begun under the superintendence of Captain Corbett.... When you reach Madeira and the Laurel joins company, you will report to Lieutenant-Commanding Waddell, and thereafter act under his instructions.[4]

Bulloch finalized preparations for the *Sea King*'s departure, and the *Laurel* was supposedly sailing to Havana with freight and passengers. The freight was, of course, the armaments and supplies for the *Sea King*, and the passengers were officers of the Confederate States Navy, some of whom had been on board the *Alabama* for her last fight.

On October 8 the *Sea King* sailed from the Thames estuary. But Union spies had got wind of Bulloch's scheme and American Minister Charles Adams had the warships *Sacramento* and *Niagara* cruising offshore. The *Niagara* had captured the CSS *Georgia* the preceding August, but both Yankee skippers now failed to identify their prey. The *Niagara* chased and seized a Spanish vessel suspected of carrying Confederate contraband by mistake.[5] The *Sea King*'s crew were oblivious to their ship's real nature in the belief they were sailing legitimately for Bombay. The seamen would, no doubt, have been horrified to realize there was the possibility of being shelled by American warships.

The following morning the *Laurel* sailed from Liverpool commanded by Lieutenant Ramsay, an Englishman in the Confederate service. Her crewmen were also unaware of the voyage's true purpose. The Confederate officers on board had transferred from a steam tug brought alongside dressed as civilians.

Four days after the *Sea King*'s departure, the American bark *Delphine* sailed from Gravesend, a town on the south bank of the Thames about twenty-five miles east of London. Those on board may well have admired the sleek lines of the *Sea King* as she slid past on the river current, and perhaps William Whittle noticed the Yankee bark, a potential victim, little realizing the fate of both craft would be drastically linked in the months to come.

Five days after sailing, the *Laurel* arrived at Madeira, the Portuguese island off the coast of Africa, where she lay at anchor for another four days. During the night the *Sea King* arrived, signals were exchanged, the *Laurel* raised anchor and followed the new arrival to Las Desertas, an uninhabited island nearby. The two ships were lashed together and Confederate officers, including James Waddell, came on board the *Sea King*. The crews worked all night to transfer the *Laurel*'s cargo, but some of the stores burst open. This revealed ammunition, alerting an already suspicious crew to a covert operation they knew nothing about.

Captain Corbett called the crews of both vessels aft and James Waddell, in "full Confederate uniform" now made himself known. "Men, I am an officer in the Confederate navy, authorized to take command of this ship." He said his mission was not to fight except in an "urgent case," but he was going to sink, burn and destroy ships flying the Federal flag. As each vessel was taken they would be valued and half the value divided amongst the crew as prize money when the war ended. He offered 15 pounds bounty in gold and 7 pounds per month wages, half payable to the men's wives in England if they so desired. The wages were high, he said, and they would be asked to serve for six months.[6]

A bucket full of sovereigns was placed on the deck as an inducement. The men muttered amongst themselves and the officers moved around encouraging them to enlist, but much to Waddell's disappointment only twenty-two men

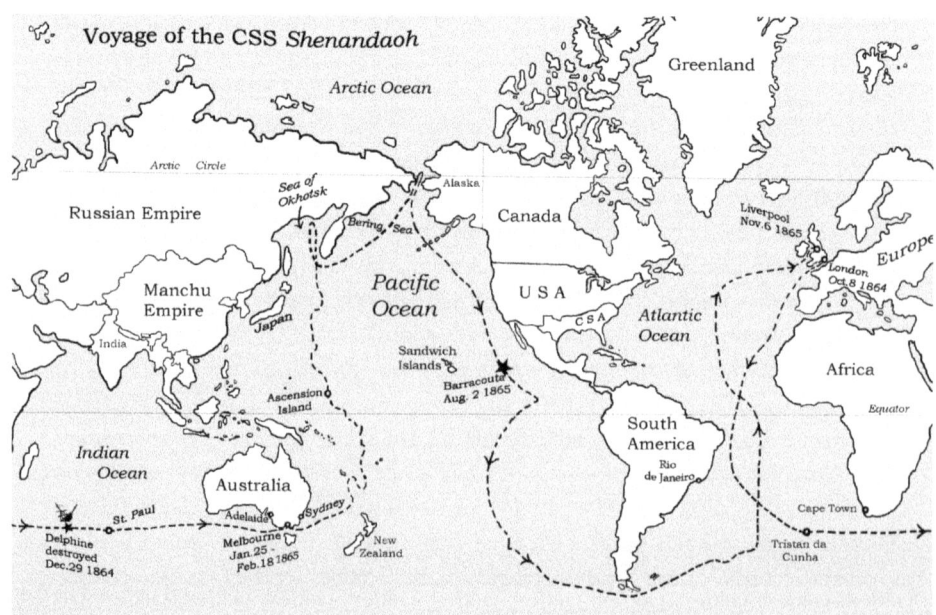

from both ships were adventurous enough to sign up. With twenty-four officers, it meant a total complement of only forty-six men. One problem was "an engineer in whom great reliance was placed to influence the firemen to ship ... belied all his promises, and actually did his best to dissuade the men in his department from remaining,"[7] wrote Bulloch, who had estimated recruiting "an effective force of seventy-six souls, a sufficient number to navigate the ship with ease and safety, and even to fight the guns."[8] These seamen, however, were to be augmented by sailors from captured vessels. The *Alabama* had carried one hundred and forty-nine men in her last battle.

Seamen who declined the offer to enlist accepted Corbett's offer of transport home on board the *Laurel*. "I have never seen such a set of curs in all my experience at sea,"[9] recalled Ramsay with disgust.

Ramsay and Corbett both advised Waddell to put into port and await the arrival of more seamen. Waddell, however, not easily deterred, wisely decided to confer with his officers. To sail with so few men without first gauging their confidence could well be suicidal. Encouraged by their enthusiasm to stay at sea, he decided to take his chances. The ship was renamed CSS *Shenandoah*, after the Virginian valley which had seen much fierce fighting, and the Confederate flag was raised.

> My feeble force was then ordered to the break to lift an anchor, which proved too heavy; the officers threw off their jackets and assisted in lifting it to the bow, and the little adventurer entered upon her new career, throwing out to the breeze the flag of the South, and demanded a place upon that vast ocean of water without fear or favor. That flag unfolded itself gracefully to the freshening breeze and declared the majesty of the country it represented, saluted by the cheers of a handful of brave hearted men, and she dashed upon her native element as if more than equal to the contest, cheered by acclamations from the *Laurel* which was steaming away.[10]

Corbett and the others sailed to Tenerife in the Canary Islands, a province of Spain, where Lieutenant Ramsay spun a yarn about the *Sea King* having been wrecked, the survivors picked up by the *Laurel*. Ramsay then unloaded his "survivors," who were to catch the next ship for Liverpool, and steamed off.

British Consul Henry C. Grattan was puzzled by the non-appearance of Captain Corbett to request assistance. He sent for him and demanded the *Sea King*'s certificate of registry, only to be astonished when told that the *Sea King* had actually been sold and delivered on the high seas. The consul contacted other "survivors" who, when questioned, told the full story. Corbett found himself returned to England "in safe custody" for a violation of the Foreign Enlistment Act.

Eleven days after the *Sea King*'s departure from London, *The Index*, a weekly London Confederate publication edited by Swiss-born Henry Hotze, reported *A New Confederate Cruiser* on the high seas. The article went on to describe the vessel receiving arms, "far beyond any neutral jurisdiction, there can fortunately be no pretence of accusing her of any violation of municipal laws or international operations ... long live the *Shenandoah*!" Needless to say Hotze's sentiments were not echoed in the United States when the same news hit the American news stands a few weeks later.

The *Shenandoah*'s new commander, James Iredell Waddell, was described by one of his Annapolis students as "a handsome, well-proportioned man, slightly over six feet tall, and weighing about two hundred pounds," and of "noble bearing ... gracious ... courtly ... radiant with kindness."[11]

Born in Pittsboro, North Carolina, to Francis and Elizabeth Waddell on July 13, 1824, Waddell was one of eight surviving children. He came from a distinguished family that had included two generals and a Justice of the U.S. Supreme Court.

He entered the U.S. Navy as a midshipman in 1841 at the age of seventeen, and was soon assigned to the *Pennsylvania,* the navy's only three-decker, carrying 120 guns. Having been brought up in a gentle home, harsh naval discipline came as something of a shock. Despite his gentle ways, or possibly because of them, he found himself in conflict with another Midshipman, Archibald Waring,[12] and the resulting duel saw him receive a hip wound which put him out of action for eleven months, causing a slight limp thereafter. The conflict was caused by his affection for a young lady, a prelude to future problems in his life. Waring, who had entered the navy only one month after Waddell, survived the encounter, but would resign from the service in 1848.

Waddell saw naval service in the Mexican War of 1846, and was promoted to passed midshipman the following year. In November of 1848 he married Anne Sellman Iglehart of Annapolis who would own at least one slave, Violetta Jacob, usually called Lethe. She would be given her freedom five days before slavery was outlawed in Maryland on November 1, 1864.[13]

After serving on various ships Waddell was promoted to lieutenant in 1855, and in 1857 received an honorable mention for taking command of the supply ship *Release.* He brought her safely home when the crew, himself included, were stricken with yellow fever.

The year 1858 saw Waddell's appointment as an instructor in seamanship, gunnery, naval tactics and navigation at the United States Naval Academy, Annapolis. The following year on February 9, his wife gave birth to a child, Anne Harwood Waddell.[14] The treasured daughter, however, would die of scarlet fever on February 16, 1863, aged four.

In 1859 Waddell left the Naval Academy and joined the East India Squadron in San Francisco, serving aboard the USS *Saginaw,* visiting China and

5. Never Return to Europe 35

Japan. He transferred to the *John Adams* and, following news of hostilities breaking out, mailed his resignation at St. Helena while en route to the United States.

Following a disagreement with the navy over back pay, he covertly traveled south, and in March 1862 was commissioned a lieutenant in the Confederate States Navy. Assigned to the ironclad ram *Mississippi*, under construction in New Orleans, he had the disheartening duty of destroying her when that city fell to the Yankees. He served with distinction at the battle of Drewry's Bluff, earning a promotion, and then did garrison duty in Charleston Harbor.

Waddell ran the blockade the following month, bound ultimately for Liverpool, England, via France, for assignment to one of the ironclad rams under construction. He was offered a blockade runner to sail between Bermuda and any port of the Confederacy for a fee of one thousand pounds per round trip. His commanding officer gave this lucrative opportunity his blessing, but Waddell declined the offer. He wished to stay with the regular navy.

After the Laird rams were seized by British authorities, Waddell was given his first command, the CSS *Shenandoah*. The legendary Raphael Semmes had been in his mid-fifties when captain of the *Alabama*, and John Maffitt and Charles Morris, in turn skippers of the *Florida*, in their mid-forties. Thus Waddell, aged forty, was a younger commander than most. He would suffer perplexing moods and make curious decisions, for reasons to be explained within this book, but overall would prove to be vigilant with the handling of his ship, captives and crew. In the final analysis results are what count, and James Bulloch would write that he carried out his duties "faithfully and with success" and "with unusual precision and effect."[15]

Anne Sellman Waddell, James Waddell's "sweet little wife," as Whittle described her; the lady left behind (Naval History and Heritage Command).

The ultimate aim of the cruise was the destruction of Yankee whaling ships in the North Pacific and Okhotsk Seas. Bulloch's orders were to sail via the Cape of Good Hope and Australia, re-coaling in either Sydney or Melbourne, where Waddell was to claim his right under the Queen's neutrality rules to take on an adequate supply to carry him to the nearest port of his own country. He was then to proceed to New Zealand waters, and northwards through the Pacific destroying all Yankee commerce along the way. Once Waddell had completed this task it was recommended that due to the "great distance between the North Pacific and Atlantic ports," he sell the craft "on the west coast of South America or to adventurous speculators in the Eastern seas." The ship "would never return to Europe, where, as Confederate States property, her presence might give rise to harassing questions and complications."[16]

Perilously short-handed, the *Shenandoah* steamed by day and ran under topsails, foresail and jib by night, all the canvas the available crew could manage. Fortunately her rolling topsail-yards, worked from the deck, made light work of shortening the upper canvas. The officers worked alongside the men. Together they cut gun ports, built magazines and stored ammunition.

The senior officers under Executive Officer William Whittle were: Second Lieutenant John Grimball; Third Lieutenant Sydney S. Lee; Fourth Lieutenant Francis T. Chew; Fifth Lieutenant Dabney M. Scales; First Surgeon Charles E. Lining; Paymaster William B. Smith; and Sailing Master Irvine S. Bulloch—James Bulloch's half-brother and uncle of a future president of the United States, Theodore Roosevelt. Charles Lining, at thirty, was the oldest officer aboard with the exception of James Waddell. The class-conscious Whittle would proudly write that the junior officers were all "to the manor born," which, unfortunately, was no qualification when it came to seamanship.

In his 1883 memoir *The Secret Service of the Confederate Service in Europe* James Bulloch commented:

> The master, Irvine S. Bulloch, the paymaster, W. B. Smith, and the chief engineer, Matthew O'Brien, had made the cruise on the *Alabama*, and had seen some rough and tumble work ... but the remainder of the wardroom sea-officers had been trained by no such experiences. They were mostly young men fresh from the United States Naval Academy at the breaking out of the war, and had seen little or no sea-service, except in the smart school-ship, which is sent out yearly for a summer cruise from Annapolis. Waddell was an officer of twenty-three years' experience in the United States Navy, and Whittle, the first-lieutenant, a smart, intelligent young officer, had seen some service. Lieutenant S. S. Lee had picked up some rough experiences in the merchant service, and was therefore more at home than most of the others.[17]

The *Shenandoah*'s armament consisted of two very formidable 32 pounder Whitworth rifled guns, four smooth bore 8-inch shell guns and the two 12 pounders from her *Sea King* days. (Ship's language spoke of guns and round shot, not cannons and cannon balls. Thus; gun port, gun deck, pivot gun, gunner's mate, gun drill, etc. The main armament were called "great guns" in dispatches when distinguishing them from small arms.)

Waddell wrote:

> The guns were on their carriages, and as the fighting bolts and gun tackles could not then be found, they were secured fore and aft the deck, close to the ship's side, and in the absence of bolts, straps were passed through the scuppers and toggled outside of the vessel, to which the guns were secured.[18]

Along with Cardiff coal which gave off a thin white vapor, hard to see at a distance, an apparatus for consuming the *Shenandoah*'s smoke helped conceal her position. Merchant ships were still mainly sailing vessels, and Union warships seeking enemy cruisers would keep a weather eye for a telltale smudge of smoke on the horizon. The *Shenandoah* was also equipped to condense seawater for drinking when running under steam.

Steam engines liberated ships from the wind, but the coal bunkers took up valuable space and the soot covered "black gang" working below would appreciate a fair wind which freed them from their toil. The *Shenandoah*'s two metal engine-room ventilators helped relieve the hot, putrid conditions below, but firemen, stokers and trimmers worked virtually naked, clad with a sweat rag around the neck, and heavy boots to divert falling red hot coals from scorching feet when the ship surged in heavy weather. The stoker would thrust the coal into the fire box, twisting the shovel to ensure an even spread. These men could be singed by exploding coal and burned when thrown by turbulent seas against scalding metal firebox doors and metal pipes; a hell hole in the tropics, but a more benign location as, later on, the *Shenandoah* steamed through icy Arctic seas.

On October 28, 1864, nine days into her voyage, the cry of "sail ho," was heard from aloft. Men scrambled into the rigging and the *Shenandoah,* with all hands on deck, extra canvas billowing, set out after her prey. The chase continued through the night and through the following morning.

Midshipman Mason recalled:

> On starting out the Captain said he would not capture anything until the news of our transfer of our ship from British to Confederate owners could have reached England; but after being out three or four days, he concluded to capture all he came across, in order to get some more men.

"We sailed much faster than the chase and rapidly gained on him," wrote William Whittle. "At 11:30 we lowered the propeller, got up steam and stood for him. Took in Royals and Topgallant sails as we approached. We hoisted the English flag, and he, to our great joy, hoisted the hateful Yankee flag."[19] The

Shenandoah had her first victim. The Confederate naval ensign was sent aloft, and the boom of a blank shot from a twelve pounder rang out. The bark *Alina,* of Searsport, Maine, shortened canvas and hove to, her voyage from Newport, Monmouthshire to Buenos Aires curtailed. A boatload of men armed with cutlasses and revolvers rowed from the *Shenandoah,* boarded her and took possession.

Her captain, Everett Staples, and his crew of eleven were taken aboard the Confederate cruiser, where a "prize court" was held in the *Shenandoah*'s wardroom, Waddell presiding. Whittle and Staples sat on his left, and the other officers sat around the table. The ship's papers were examined and Staples was questioned about his vessel's ownership, tonnage and cargo, then the first mate was brought in to confirm the same answers. The decision went against Staples, the *Alina* declared a prize of war, to be destroyed.

"This painful duty which sometimes became necessary would have been avoided had we been able to take our prizes into port for adjudication," recalled Waddell. He lamented the neutral powers decision to ban captured prize ships from their ports. But he let nothing go to waste:

> She was a valuable capture, furnishing the blocks for the gun tackles, a variety of blocks which the steamer needed, and cotton canvas so very suitable for sail making. The officers partly fitted themselves out with basins, pitchers, mess crockery, knives, forks, etc. A spring bottom mattress fell to my share, and a small supply of provisions were removed to the steamer.[20]

As the *Alina* carried heavy railroad iron, it was decided to scuttle rather than put her to the torch. Holed from inside below the waterline, she "reared up like a war horse and went down stern first" recalled Lieutenant Chew. Seven of her crew immediately signed for service in the Confederate States Navy. These recruits eased the *Shenandoah*'s burden, much to the captain's delight:

> This capture produced a marked difference in the bearing of my crew. The work pressed heavily still upon them, but we were now gathering strength in numbers from our captives, and the cry of "sail ho" was always greeted with manifestations of pleasure.

Captain Staples, described by Lining as "a black hearted rascal," was paroled, but when he thanked Whittle for his kind treatment, the executive officer replied that it was just for humanity's sake, and he felt nothing for Staples but "hatred of the most intense kind."[21] Those captured seamen who had not signed to join the Confederate service were placed in irons as an inducement to change their minds.

Standards of discipline onboard usually followed those laid down in 1850 by the United States Navy. Flogging had been abolished to be replaced with the options of being placed in irons, tattooing, branding, confining in sweatboxes, or tricing up by the wrists. This meant suspension from a grating with the toes barely touching the ground.[22] Irons and tricing were usually employed by Whittle, or in the case of drunkenness, withdrawal of grog as well. "If you do not rule them they will rule you," he recalled.

The *Shenandoah* continued southwards under the bright rays of a tropical sun, which showed itself alternately between black clouds dropping a mist of fine rain.

On November 5 the distant canvas of their second victim was sighted. They chased and captured the schooner *Charter Oak*, of Boston, with a mixed cargo including two thousand pounds of canned tomatoes. These were transferred to the *Shenandoah* and became part of the crew's staple diet. Preserved fruit and fresh lobster were also a welcome addition to the mess, and a cargo of furniture was seized upon with relish. Such basic commodities as bureaus and chairs were in demand. The crew of six along with Captain Gilman and his wife, her sister and young child, were taken on board. Midshipman John Mason recalled:

> Our women prisoners were certainly a bore, as for the men we put them all in irons except for the Captain, who we paroled and put in the mess with the engineers and the Master's Mates; but of course gallantry demanded that we should take the ladies into our mess and give them quarters in the cabin.... These women were certainly the most stupid I ever saw. They were not pretty in the least and could not talk or say a word, then they came to meals with the most remarkable looking dressing gowns on.[23]

The sister had been widowed when her husband, a Union sergeant, had been killed at Harpers Ferry. Gilman had two hundred dollars in currency, which Waddell confiscated, then gave to his wife on behalf of the Confederacy, on condition she would not return it to her husband:

> For the fact was I felt a compassion for the women, because they would be landed I did not know where, and the thought of inflicting unnecessary severity on a female made my heart shrink within.

The decision was made to burn the *Charter Oak* and she was prepared for destruction: combustibles scattered throughout the vessel, bulkheads torn down and piled in cabins and forecastle. All hatches were opened. This allowed fresh air below, and all halyards were released to allow the sails to hang loosely. Burning coals were taken from the galley and deposited in various places below and about the deck. The fire spread along her timbers, then up to the deck, and the *Charter Oak* was soon a blazing inferno, coils of smoke billowing skywards.

As the captain of a commerce raider dealing with such matters, and sometimes boarding neutral vessels suspected of flying false colors, Waddell was required to have the knowledge of a sea-going lawyer and study legal publications including Phillimore's *Laws of Nations*.[24]

Fighting was a profession that I had prepared myself for by the study of the best models; but now I was to sail and fight and to decide questions of international law that lawyers had quarreled over with all their books before them. I was in all matters to act promptly and without counsel; but my admirable instructions and the instincts of honor and patriotism that animated every Southern gentleman who bore arms in the South buoyed me up with the hope which supported the interior difficulties and the degree of responsibility bearing on me.

On November 8 the bark *D. Godfry,* bound from Boston to Valparaiso, was the next vessel to burn. More recruits enlisted for service on board the *Shenandoah,* including one African-American, John Williams, who had escaped the destroyed USS *Congress* at Hampton Roads.

A neutral Danish vessel, the *Anna Jane*, was sighted the next day. Waddell negotiated with her master to relieve him of some prisoners in exchange for a captured chronometer and barrels of beef and bread. Waddell hoped to place his female captives aboard a neutral vessel bound for America, so they and Captain Gilman stayed with the cruiser, as the *Anna Jane* was bound for Rio de Janeiro.

The cruiser continued southwards towards the Cape of Good Hope. She captured and scuttled the bark *Susan* on November 10, bound from Newport to Rio Grande. Three of her crew agreed to sign for service in the Confederate Navy. Two days later the clipper *Kate Prince,* from New Jersey, was taken with a load of Cardiff coal. Captain Sibley offered proof to Waddell that the cargo belonged to British owners, so the clipper escaped destruction. She was ransomed for $40,000, and Sibley handed the ship's registry to Waddell in exchange for a certificate. He signed a bond on behalf of himself and the owners agreeing to pay the stipulated sum to the Confederate States six months after the signing of a peace treaty. If the South lost the war, of course, no payment would ever be made.

The *Kate Prince* was bound for Brazil, but being a Yankee vessel guaranteed good treatment for prisoners and a return to the States. Waddell was happy to place Captain Gilman, the ladies and child on board.

William Whittle recalled:

> They were all exceedingly grateful for our kindness particularly the women, who I am quite certain would have preferred to have stayed. Therein we differ for I am very glad to get clear of them and I hope never to have a female prisoner on board again.[25]

Later the same day the bark *Adelaide,* sailing from Baltimore to Rio, was captured flying Buenos Aires colors. The vessel's build was American and her master could not show proof of ownership, so Waddell ordered the ship burned.

Destructive preparations were well under way when a letter was discovered in a mailbag for her consignee at Rio. The ship had been sold without the captain's knowledge. Waddell complained that the owners "had done a great wrong to her captain by not informing him of her true nationality, for the concealment exposed him to very grave suspicion. Her destruction was prevented by sheer accident."[26] She was ransomed for $24,000.

On November 13, the fast sailing schooner *Lizzie M. Stacey* was overtaken and captured. She was a nifty craft in excellent trim, and would have been armed and sent out as another raider, if Mr. Whittle had his way. "She was a fine little vessel and would make a fine cruiser, and if we had the men I would have applied for her." Whittle's journal reveals a young officer dissatisfied with the role of executive officer, a privilege in fact for a twenty-four-year-old. John Kell, formerly a skipper, was forty when executive officer on the CSS *Alabama*. Both the *Florida* and *Alabama* sent out captured vessels as commerce raiders, but not commanded by the executive officer. For Waddell, an older, experienced first lieutenant, his first duty to the *Shenandoah*, would have been a blessing. This would have bridged the generation gap that separated him from the young officers under his command.

The *Lizzie M. Stacey* was put to the torch. The flames caused "immense excitement" when a sudden change of wind sent the blazing wreck quickly towards her captor, as though bent on revenge. The yards were backed and the ship wore around, the burning danger averted.

The following day, two of the crew, including one African-American, signed for service on the cruiser, but Whittle ordered those who had not signed to help shovel coal from the birthdeck. He felt "they would prefer it to confinement":

> Two of them who were Yankees positively refused, but as I had given the order it must be obeyed, so I determined to punish them. I might not have been right in giving the order although for their good ... I triced up one fellow and the other said he would prefer going to work to being similarly dealt with. Tricing up had a most wonderful effect—in two hours the man begged to be let down, as he desired to ship.[27]

Whittle writing, "I might not have been right in giving the order" was correct; prisoners of war not supposed to receive such treatment. Once in Melbourne John Colby, not considering this for his "good" would desert the ship and allege being "triced up by the thumbs and being compelled to join the vessel in order to relieve myself of tortures and punishments."[28] Whittle did not define how exactly Colby was triced, possibly by the wrists, not the thumbs as claimed. But the United States consul in Melbourne would prove to be as flexible with the truth as the Confederates themselves. Another seaman also signed up, the fourth of the *Lizzie M. Stacey*'s seven crew. "And that I consider doing wonderfully," wrote Whittle. "We now have 43 men and 24 officers, which makes in all 67 souls."

On November 29 the American consul in Rio de Janeiro, James Monroe, was "pained to be compelled to report that a new piratical steamer" commanded by James Waddell was sinking United States vessels. The arrival of ships carrying refugees and Brazilian newspaper reports had alerted Monroe, and he listed the prizes taken to date. His report, which confirmed the Americans' worst fears, was dispatched northwards to U.S. Secretary of State William Seward by steamer on December 9.[29]

December 4 saw the New Bedford whaler *Edward* come under the cruiser's guns. Her crew did not even see the *Shenandoah*'s approach, preoccupied with butchering a victim to their harpoons. The unfortunate vessel went up in flames two days later after the transfer of crew and supplies, the portent of escalating whale oil prices before the *Shenandoah* finally finished her run.

Two days later the rebel raider dropped anchor at the island of Tristan da Cunha. Although isolated, the population of about thirty-five were well aware of the war, recalled John Mason, and "knew the flag when it was hoisted." Waddell left the prisoners there with provisions for three months.

On December 28 they were rescued by the USS *Iroquois*[30] now on the *Shenandoah*'s trail. Captain Rodgers steamed to Cape Town in pursuit, deceived by Waddell, who had sailed in that direction in full view before he changed course. Rodgers sent a report to Secretary Welles at Washington, including a detailed description of his prey furnished by the burned vessels' skippers. Despite defective boilers and being undermanned, Rodgers resolved to continue his pursuit. "I shall follow her with all dispatch, for in spite of the defective motive power of the *Iroquois*, I shall not abandon the hope that she may have the good fortune to arrest the progress of this new buccaneer."

The "*shenanigan*," as some on board were calling her, was in no fit state to take on a Yankee warship, as William Whittle wrote on December 10, Lieutenant Grimball having had his first gun drill:

> I do wish that our ports were in proper order but as yet all we can boast of is there is a round hole through which the muzzles of the guns point. If however we were to get into a fight all "ginger bread work" would come down, and we would do our best, however poor that might be—but I trust that we may have no fighting to do as we would fare badly.

But Yankee warships were not the only threat to a Confederate vessel sinking merchantmen on the high seas. On December 16 the fast cruiser passed the meridian of the Cape of Good Hope into the stormy Indian Ocean, two weeks ahead of the schedule suggested by the Navy Department. "Today it has been blowing a whole gale of wind and a very heavy sea. The ship behaves very well except that she ships an immense amount of water. At midnight she shipped a very large sea and was a long time in clearing," wrote William Whittle.

Lieutenant Francis Chew was to take the midnight watch, to be followed by the equally inexperienced Dabney Scales four hours later. Chew had a reputation for being "jinxed"[31]; bad weather and other accidents happened on his watch. "I am all theory and very little practice," he admitted.

Master's Mate John Minor, on the other hand, was a very capable *Alabama* veteran, and Waddell ordered that he take Chew's watch. But Whittle felt it was not fitting for a petty officer to replace "a First Lieutenant of the Navy, so appointed by the President of the Confederate States." Whittle, who "had seen some service," as noted by James Bulloch, seemed preoccupied with protocol to a distorted degree, while his far more experienced commander was concerned with running his ship safely through heavy seas with a short-handed crew.

Whittle proposed Waddell and Whittle should share watches with Chew and Scales, but Waddell replied, "No, you have enough to do," thus deciding against it. Other officers needed sleep too.

The ship survived the night, John Minor having taken the critical watch, but the following day Chew offered his resignation. Waddell had told him the blunt truth, "he did not consider him competent." Again Whittle confronted the captain: "And then I asked him what right he had to say that Mr. Chew was not to be trusted on the deck, when the wording of Mr. Chew's commission was identical to his own." One can only wonder at the state of Whittle's mind when he wrote these perplexing words. The captain obviously not only had every right, but was obliged to make such decisions, especially in a gale. Little wonder Waddell, at one stage, felt obliged to caution his subordinate: "Whittle, be careful, you are speaking to me."

"I was begged by Waddell to forget what has happened," Whittle claimed in his one-sided account.

The captain could hardly have his executive officer charged with insubordination, a disaster for morale; thus he allowed Chew to be restored to duty on the understanding that Whittle would share watches in rough weather.

"God knows I want peace for the good of the service," wrote the self-righteous Whittle. But he did the opposite by spreading his own biased version of events. Charles Lining wrote, "Any row between a Captain and an officer always breeds discord in a ship, and I want nothing like that during this cruise"; and of Waddell, "if he would only act rightly we would all be with him." Whittle's lack of discretion undermined Waddell, and he also contravened his own written orders: "You will report to Lieutenant-Commanding Waddell and thereafter act under his instructions."

In the course of this dispute, Waddell said to Whittle, "Well, sir, I have not a friend in the ship. You are all against me."[32]

6

She Will Thank Me Even More

The *Delphine* was the *Shenandoah*'s next catch, on December 29, and Lillias Nichols arrived on deck with her canary birds; a captivating friend for Captain Waddell.

Becoming "tamed down" the Searsport lady charmed the officers as the *Shenandoah* moved steadily eastward across the Indian Ocean towards Australia.

Midshipman Mason recalled:

> I have charge of all the chronometers captured and they are screwed down to a shelf in the starboard cabin as this is the only room vacant and suitable for the purpose it is always given to the "female prisoners" but at the same time the chronometers must be wound up, which necessitates my going into the cabin every day to wind them. Mrs. Nichols did not seem to relish this much at first, but soon found it best to make a virtue of necessity and put a smiling face on it. She is not such a tartar as I thought.[1]

Lillias Nichols was described by Mason as "a handsome woman, has a genteel look about her," and despite apparently having some problem with her Maine dialect, "she has a delightfully clean look and is always dressed neatly, even *very well* dressed and what is *still* more important, she dresses in good taste." Compared to previous women "passengers" on board the *Shenandoah*, Mason commended Mrs. Nichols' "queen like" appearance and her "spiritual" quality of conversation.

The prisoners settled into the ship's routine. The *Delphine*'s second mate was Captain Nichols' younger brother, Edward Payson Nichols. In later life Edward would gain some renown as the only person to publish a newspaper—the *Ocean Chronicle*—on sailing vessels. This occurred first onboard the bark *Clara*; named for Lilli's sister and grandmother of Charles Blanchard. The *Clara* was wrecked in 1880, but this did not sink the *Ocean Chronicle*, as publication continued on the *Frank Pendleton* until 1891. But Edward was not open to debate, apparently, as the caption beneath the title clearly showed—"This is printed for PASTIME ONLY, and sent to friends as a letter, therefore not open to criticism."[2]

When the ship dropped anchor at St. Paul, Master's Mate Cornelius Hunt, according to his account, observed Mrs. Nichols standing alongside the rail, her eyes filled with tears. When he asked what was wrong, she replied she had no wish to be a castaway in such a remote place as St. Paul. Hunt asked why she thought the captain would be so inhuman as to abandon them there. She told him that was her husband's expectation, and they had read stories "about the outrages committed upon defenseless men and women by your rebel cruisers," and she "naturally assumed they were founded on fact."

A Yankee publication might well choose to interpret future events, regardless of the truth, to be an "outrage" committed upon a "defenseless" woman, which was "founded on fact." Perhaps this is why the master's mate included this[3]; a reminder to Captain Waddell of having risked the ship's reputation, "a most scandalous romance at our expense once they got on shore." One example of the double-edged wordplay that occurs throughout Hunt's book.

As the cruiser surged through the Atlantic's crests and troughs, the ship's propeller revealed problems. On December 8 Waddell had detected a suspect noise and ordered the propeller triced up. Chief Engineer O'Brien discovered a fractured brass propeller shaft coupling, "which if it had not been seen might have proved fatal to us," recalled Whittle. "It is an old break and has been done for a long time, as we saw where the screws had been put

William Green Nichols, a man "obliged to suspect his wife, to have to keep his eyes on her to prevent her doing wrong" (courtesy Charles Nichols Blanchard).

in to repair it. As our propeller is to us our life we stopped all work to have it fixed."

To facilitate repairs, the pilot house roof was removed and the complete propeller well raised on a line suspended from the mizzenmast spanker boom, reinforced by a prop of wood and tackles from the mast head. Temporary repairs were carried out, but the problem returned to haunt them, as Whittle wrote on January 18:

> Upon tricing up our propeller we found that all the bolts which we had put on the c[o]upling strap had broken and that it was as bad as ever. Mr. O'Brien got to work at it and I hope will soon have it in fine order. We want a new strap for this has been drilled so often as to weaken it.[4]

This fault must have come of something of a shock to Waddell. He also found that rough seas sent "a fine spray through the open seams of the hull into the birth deck," the decks "leaking dreadfully." Bulloch had reported to the Navy Secretary, "Yesterday she went into the graving-dock to have her bottom examined and the screw-shaft carefully inspected, and the report on both these points is favorable."[5] And his orders to Waddell advised, "she has been docked and carefully overhauled, and every caution has been taken to insure her commencing the cruise in good and sound condition."[6] Obviously this was not the case. The ship needed recaulking and this was "evidence of the deception practiced in the London docks," recalled Waddell. In other words, the Confederacy had been duped. Certain work had not been carried out.

On January 6, 1865, the *New York Times* reported "THE PIRATE SHENANDOAH; Some of her Recent Exploits." The public had already been alerted to the cruiser's escape the preceding October, but now Captain Gilman of the *Charter Oak*, arrived in the United States, had attended the newspaper office in person. Waddell had "gravely informed him that nothing could save the schooner," Gilman said. He gave a full description of the *Shenandoah* and damage wrought to other vessels while he was on board.

By now the news was well out. The papers carried alarming stories of a new rebel raider causing havoc on the high seas, much to the delight of the Confederacy, and the horror of the North. More owners would sell their ships to foreign flags, usually British. The American mercantile marine was being driven from the seas.

Captain Gilman, however, gave no hint of the cruiser's future plans. In his *Secret Service* memoir, James Bulloch wrote in regard to the *Alabama*, "I never told any *employé* more than was necessary for him to know, and never gave any reason for an order having reference to the outfit or movement of the ship."[7] Waddell also knew that "loose lips sink ships" and was tight-lipped with all on board. This precaution negated any chance of an overheard conversation alerting prisoners who, like Gilman, would safely return to the United States long before the *Shenandoah*'s voyage was over. Without this measure, a flotilla of Yankee warships could well have been ready to strike in the North Pacific.

U.S. Secretary of War Edwin Stanton, unable to lay hands on the pirate chief himself, imprisoned Mrs. Waddell instead—a somewhat ironic action, as though mere distance between husband and wife was not enough to prevent future unseemly events on the opposite side of the world.

The USS *Suwanee*, a new, iron-hulled steam side-wheeler with ten large guns, was ordered out after the *Shenandoah*. Union Navy Secretary Gideon Welles instructed Captain Paul Shirley to pursue her "anywhere in the West Indies or the Caribbean Sea, on the coasts of South America, Europe or Africa, or to the East Indies or the Pacific."⁸

Later in the voyage, after the trials of stormy Cape Horn, Midshipman Mason would write that his experiences had "destroyed all the romance of a sailor's life." Included in his grievances was the "total deprivation of the society of females, which has so softening an influence on all men."

But James Waddell now enjoyed the "softening" influence of Lilli Nichols. He conversed with her "frequently" as the rebel cruiser continued on her easterly course towards Melbourne. He told her of the *Shenandoah*'s escape from London, the rendezvous with the *Laurel*, the arms and men taken on board, and the capture and destruction of other vessels before the *Delphine*. But he assured his charming passenger that she was "not a prisoner of war."⁹

No doubt Lilli told him of her older brother John who had disappeared in these waters along with his vessel *Solferino* only two years before. Perhaps they also talked of the Battle of Penobscot Bay during the Revolution, when an American force besieging Fort George—opposite the settlement that would become Searsport—was surprised by a British Fleet. The Americans retreated up the Penobscot River, their ships either captured or destroyed.

Britain won that battle, but still lost the war. At least *Shenandoah* captor and captive would have been on the same side in that fight.

On January 19, three days after his twenty-fifth birthday, Lieutenant Whittle recorded a revealing exchange with Mrs. Nichols; an enticing lady who liked to get her own way.

The executive officer felt the captain "was to[o] yielding and asked him to refer all prisoners to me." The ironclad Whittle would not put up with any nonsense from prisoners, apparently. In doing so, however, he was hazing a line of communication between James Waddell and Lilli Nichols. So with the new regime in place, the determined lady decided to put the ship's disciplinarian to the test:

This morning I was standing by the wardroom door and Mrs. Nichols came up and commenced talking to me. She said, ["]Well Mr. Whittle, I trust that we may soon have peace.["] I concurred in the hope. She then said, "Do you think we can ever be friends?["] Said I, "No Madam, never." "But Mr. Whittle, if after the Peace was made you were to meet me, would you speak to me?" "Certainly Madam, I would speak at any time to a female." "But would you not speak to my husband?" I simply said, "I might do as he has never served against us." She was admiring the uniform cap of one of our men, and wondered if she could ever make one. I replied, No, as it was woven. She said of all things she would like to have one. She said this in such a way I was forced to yield, and said that I thought I could get one for her. She thanked me a little, but when she gets it she will thank me even more.

1st Lieutenant William Conway Whittle. "Do you think we can ever be friends?" asked Mrs. Nichols. "No Madam, never," he replied. James Waddell and William Whittle had little in common apart from fighting for the Confederate cause (author's collection).

Said in *such a way,* and she would *thank me even more.* The flirtatious Mrs. Nichols taught Whittle that he was just as "yielding" as anybody else if she so chose. "If proper I can always say no to a man, but not so with a woman," Whittle conceded.

Lieutenant Grimball overheard this exchange and informed Waddell, who sought Whittle out:

> He says he will tell all in Annapolis of how I flirt with Yankee prisoners, and says that he would advise me to write to my sweetheart and make a clean acknowledgement as she will certainly hear of it.

The jealous Waddell warning the younger officer off, disguised as a joke. Whittle continued:

Now I contend that before one of our southern women would have done such a thing as this she would have cut her hands off. Such is the marked difference ... any woman who has so little delicacy as to place a gentleman in the fix I am, he has the perfect right to consider the promise as not made and on this principle I will let the cap alone.[10]

James Waddell and Lilli Nichols had now been together for three weeks, plenty of time for fervors to be aroused. Here we had an attractive, vibrant, young woman with unfulfilled passions, trapped forever in an arranged marriage, her husband no match for James Waddell in either looks or charm. And both commander and captive were people of the sea, knowing wild weather, the threat of shipwreck, visits to foreign ports and exotic lands. Given half a chance, Lilli Nichols could command a ship in any gale, no woman of the land like Waddell's "sweet little wife," as Whittle described her, that lady now thousands of miles away. If the fate of the *Alabama* was any indication, Waddell may never see her again. And both James Waddell and Lilli Nichols shared a bonding loss they both understood, the loss of their daughters Hannah and Anne a few years before.

"All marriage is such a lottery," wrote Queen Victoria, "the poor woman is bodily and morally the husband's slave."

A hard fact of life for both Lillias Nichols and James Waddell was the death of their young daughters. Hannah Nichols' weathered headstone, 1991. The inscription reads "Little HANNAH *Whose all of life a rosy ray blushed into dawn, then passed away*" (author's collection).

Lilli's marriage was such a lottery, but she was hardly Nichols' slave. She had little regard for her husband, and he felt "obliged to suspect his wife to have to keep his eyes on her to prevent her doing wrong." What better way to reward Nichols' distrust than to fulfill his suspicions with their captor, a man noted for his kindness and compassion, a man she could truly love.

A prolonged liaison on board a small ship would have led to

detection. Their relationship would have reached fruition as the ship neared Melbourne, their time running out, their fervor unsatisfied. A flutter of eyelids and a sensual smile were all that was required, along with a few softly spoken words, to show Lilli Nichols was ready for action; a rare chance in life to experience sexual liberation with the right man in defiance of the repressed moral codes of the time.

A series of events occurred which give a good indication of when the epithet "*shenanigan*" gained a truly relevant meaning.

On January 19, the same day that Waddell warned Whittle that his "sweetheart" would hear of his flirting "with Yankee prisoners," Grimball informed the captain that William Nichols had disparaged his running of the ship behind his back, "all the time so anxious and called so frequently during the night." The captain "got in a rage" and yelled "He is a liar" before departing in anger.[11]

William Nichols may well have felt obliged to "keep his eyes on her," but eight hours sleep, private demands and other diversions prevent observation 24 hours a day, and where there's a will, there's a way. The Great Southern Comet of 1865 first appeared over the *Shenandoah* on January 20,[12] a poetic symbol of emerging, clandestine events. The passions of the star-crossed couple were fulfilled, Waddell's port cabin convenient.

On January 21, Dr. Lining warned Waddell "that the mail left Melbourne on the 26th." Lining was concerned the mail steamer would spread word of their whereabouts, so it was best to avoid docking before then.[13] But Mason recalled "going along leisurely with 8, 9 and 10 knot breezes, the wind suddenly left us and the Captain becoming impatient ordered steam."[14] The machinery came to life on the night of January 21–22, "so this morning we are steaming along at the rate of eight knots," the doctor wrote. This surprised everyone including Midshipman Mason: "the propeller had gotten out of order twice & the Chief Engineer had told the Captain he would not like to run the engines unless absolutely necessary." But Waddell said he wished to send dispatches on the mail steamer for "the meeting of congress; that it would have such a tremendous moral effect throughout the country." This was a puzzle to the officers. Mason noted that "the country must have heard of our performances off the South American coast,"[15] as indeed the country had. "I cannot help thinking that it would have been better policy to have concealed our whereabouts from the civilized world for a month longer for his reports, so much everyone thought."

In his memoirs Waddell claimed steam was raised on January 23 because a "westerly current" and "easterly wind" had thrown the ship off course, and "working to windward was no easy task against a current."[16] But December 23 was not the correct date. Steam was raised on the night of January 21–22 after what Whittle described as a "nice breeze" had dropped away. There is no corroboration for the adverse conditions mentioned by Waddell during this leg of the voyage, including December 23.[17]

Waddell moved the date away from his assignation with Mrs. Nichols, and fabricated the prevailing sailing conditions. Perhaps his stated reason, "to communicate with a mail steamer," was a fabrication also.

The report he wished to send to Navy Secretary Stephen Mallory in Richmond would go via Commodore Samuel Barron in Paris, then into the Confederacy via blockade runner, assuming Yankee shells missed their mark. Lieutenant Grimball doubted letters from Melbourne making it through "as there is much uncertainty connected with all communications with the Confederacy."[18] If delivered, it would take well over two months to arrive from Melbourne, the news even more dated. Had the ship been running behind schedule there may have been some need to send a report, but she was, in fact, running one month *ahead* of the Navy Department's program, expected to be "leaving the coast of Australia on the 1st of March."[19] To meet this the *Shenandoah* would not be required to dock in Melbourne or Sydney until late February.

Waddell's stated reason makes little sense.

John Mason recalled, "when we came to hoist the screw after anchoring in Hobsons Bay, behold part of the coupling bond was gone entirely and we wondered that the whole stern post was not out of her."[20]

On the evening of arrival, January 25, Waddell wrote the report and covering correspondence he claimed was worth risking this damage.[21] The report, of about 800 words, implies no urgency

Chief Engineer Matthew O'Brien. James Waddell ignored his advice not to run the ship's damaged machinery, and steamed into Melbourne one month early supposedly to send a routine dispatch (Naval History and Heritage Command).

outlining "the work done by, and on the condition of this vessel, under my command." He describes events since departing Las Desertas, the vessels captured and their fate. He commends her "good sea quality," then mentions some "objectionable points"—the result of having not been constructed as a warship—well known prior to purchase.

He requested that Barron please forward the report "at your convenience."

If feeling this report would provide a "tremendous moral effect throughout the country," one would think "at your *earliest* convenience" would have been requested, at the very least.

Conspicuous by its absence in regard to "the condition of this vessel" is "part of the coupling bond was gone entirely and we wondered that the whole stern post was not out of her." This damage received no mention whatsoever. "I shall be detained here a few days, making some repairs," is the only hint given.

He informed Barron the next mail would leave Melbourne "on the 10th of February,"[22] when he would write once more. By then the ship was high on a dockyard slipway, the full damage revealed, and expensive repairs were under way. An update would oblige him to reveal this information.

But no further report exists.

It would appear the cause of so much damage was something Waddell did not wish to delve into or explain. "our propeller is to us our life," Whittle wrote. It is impossible to believe Waddell would ignore his engineer's advice to mail a routine report carrying dated news, one month early, with no guarantee of delivery.

The small ship becalmed, Waddell now had the prospect of seeing Lillias day after day on a flat, breezeless sea, the ship going nowhere; a situation rife with sexual tension. It would take only one emotional outburst from the volatile lady for his officers to learn the compromising truth, and a violent encounter with her jealous husband also a possible result. "The Captain becoming impatient ordered steam," wrote Mason.

Waddell ignored his engineer's advice to curtail a steamy situation which should never have begun, the mail ship providing a convenient, but inadequate excuse.

On January 22, shortly after Waddell ordered steam, this event took place, as recalled by John Mason:

> making all haste under steam and sail when we sighted a large ship, American rigged; but the captain would not go out of his course to overhaul her, being of the opinion that she was the English ship *Nimrod*, which we had spoken a few days before. Most of the officers were of a different opinion, which was justified by the sequel; for when we got to port we learned beyond doubt that the ship in question was the *David Brown*, an American vessel owned by the father of Mrs. Nicholls [*sic*]. Captain and Mrs. Nicholls had recognized the ship at once, and trembled for her safety.[23]

On January 22 Waddell saw the *David Brown*, but identified her as the *Nimrod*. The same vessel was seen again the following morning. The cruiser had "stopped the engine for half an hour in order to repair valves and set all fore and aft sails," recalled Whittle. He took the ship "to be a Yankee," but Waddell repeated his belief she was the *Nimrod* and again declined to give chase.[24]

The *David Brown* was on her maiden voyage carrying a cargo of lumber to be sold in Adelaide, South Australia. Her skipper was Lilli's brother, Phineas Pendleton 3rd.[25] Whittle wrote that Captain Nichols, once in Melbourne, "said she was the ship we passed at this time, was certain of it at the time, and was very uneasy for fear we would give chase."[26] Thus Nichols spoke first, not his wife. Had Mrs. Nichols been seen in a quiet tête-à-tête with Waddell just before the misidentification, suspicions would have been aroused. She kept quiet until after her husband spoke. Nichols talked freely because he had no idea of what

Phineas Pendleton 3rd with family, circa 1890. Lillias Nichols' brother had his ship the *David Brown* spared two days before the *Shenandoah* docked in Melbourne (courtesy Charles Nichols Blanchard).

had taken place. Waddell had deliberately misidentified the *David Brown* as the *Nimrod*, her family spared further financial strife. "The thought of inflicting unnecessary severity on a female made my heart shrink within"; especially so with the handsome lady who had become his lover.

"The Captain said he was running for the mail," wrote Lining, "and would not turn out of his way for anything."[27] Other ships did come into view, however, and a "large sail on the lee beam" was chased in the early hours of January 25.[28] Their quarry turned out to be British, but had she been Yankee the delay in burning her would have lost critical time, the mail probably missed.

Yet the *David Brown,* seen over two days, had escaped investigation.

Waddell was in an awkward situation. To avoid inflicting further hardship he had spared the *David Brown*, but was duty bound to chase suspect ships. Amidst this he also wanted the lady ashore, especially since January 23 when she had flown into a rage. Paymaster Smith had summonsed her to sign a parole not to do anything to the detriment of the Confederate Cause. But the queen of the *Shenandoah*, the captain's mistress, had been relegated to a common prisoner. "I was not a prisoner of war and Captain Waddell had frequently told me so," she cried.[29]

Lining recalled the altercation:

> The Capt. signed it very willingly, but when it came to Mrs. N's turn she let loose with her tongue, pitching directly into her husband for telling her to sign it and say nothing, by telling him that she did not intend to hold her tongue, nor did she consider herself bound but what she was going to sign, that she would talk, for at least they could not stop her tongue. After signing it she turned sarcastically to "smith" and said, "Is there anything you want Phinny to sign?" "Smith" answered very coolly, "No Madame, we are much more afraid of you than we are of him." She went out in a towering rage. Not to get the vials of her wrath poured in on me, I kept quiet.[30]

"Heaven has no rage, like love to Hatred turned / Nor Hell a Fury, like a Woman scorned" (William Congreve, *The Morning Bride*, 1697).

7

A Most Scandalous Romance

"First and foremost I can not see what induced our Captain to go into Melbourne so early.... A great many people in Melbourne said to me they wondered the Captain did not wait till the mail left before coming in," recalled Midshipman Mason.

The afternoon of January 25 saw the *Shenandoah* steaming towards Melbourne, Victoria, across the vast expanse of Port Phillip Bay, one month ahead of schedule.[1] "A splendid harbor," wrote Lining, "thirty miles long, quite wide and of great depth; all the fleets of the world could anchor there and maneuver in it without inaccommodating each other."

Lining had hoped the Great Comet in the southern skies had been "a harbinger of good news," but the report they received from the pilot brought on board at Port Phillip Heads bode ill for rebel cruisers.[2] On the very day Bulloch had written Whittle's orders it was ironic that another Confederate raider had met her end. The *Florida* had destroyed over thirty Federal merchantmen since her escape onto the high seas from Mobile. On October 4, 1864, she anchored in Bahia Harbor and was rammed two days later by the USS *Wachusset* in violation of Brazilian neutrality. The Yankee crew fired from their battery, discharged a volley of small arms and demanded her surrender. Despite fire from the harbor fort and pursuit by a Brazilian sloop-of-war, the *Wachusset* towed the *Florida* out to sea and sent her to Hampton Roads as a prize, much to the fury and indignation of the Brazilian government.

The *Shenandoah* entered the smaller Hobsons Bay and dropped anchor at 6:45 p.m. amidst other ships at their moorings. To the south-west lay the dockyard and township of Williamstown, and to the north the port of Sandridge (now Port Melbourne), both connected by rail to Melbourne, a few miles inland on the banks of the Yarra River.

The arrival of a Confederate cruiser had been telegraphed from the Queenscliff pilot station at Port Philip Heads. The news spread like wildfire which caused "an immense sensation" recalled Dr. Lining. Sailboats, rowboats, yachts and steamers milled about, but Waddell refused requests to come on board as he required permission to stay in port. Lieutenant John Grimball was promptly dispatched to Government House, Toorak:

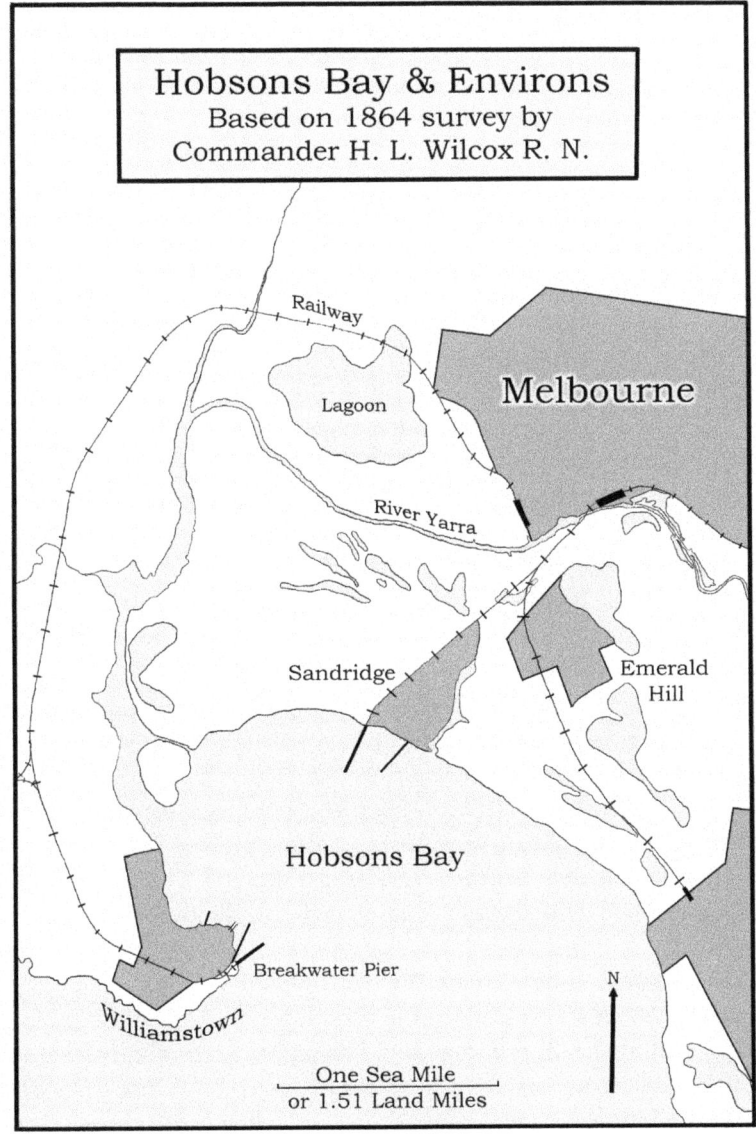

His Excellency Sir Charles H. Darling, K.C.B.
Captain General and Governor-in-Chief and Vice-Admiral,
Melbourne.

Sir,

I have the honor to announce to Your Excellency the arrival of the Confederate States Steamer *Shenandoah*, under my command, in Port Phillip, this afternoon, and also to communicate that the steamer's machinery requires repairs, and that I am in want of coals.

I desire Your Excellency to grant permission that I may make the necessary repairs, to take in a supply of coals, to enable me to get to sea as quickly as possible.

I desire also Your Excellency's permission to land my prisoners. I shall observe the neutrality.

I have the honor to be, very respectfully, your
obedient Servant,
Jas. I. Waddell
Lieutenant, Commanding.[3]

Grimball was informed that this letter would receive the governor's "early attention," and a reply could be expected the following day.

That evening Waddell wrote his report to Navy Secretary Stephen Mallory which made no mention of the propeller problems. "I shall get all the men I want,"[4] the captain assured Commodore Barron, and "My love to all the ladies." Waddell did not realize, however, that Barron would not read his report. The commodore resigned his post on February 25, deserting the sinking rebel ship, so to speak.

There would be no more official letters until Waddell surrendered the *Shenandoah* to the British authorities in Liverpool nine months later.

Next morning—Waddell's word broken, his control "by a quiet courtesy" gone—Lilli Nichols decided to take her leave. Her relationship with him was obliged to end in any case. It was easier to part in anger than a sad farewell. "The early morning rising was preparatory to desertion," Waddell recalled. Mrs. Nichols woke her husband, child and stewardess, packed some belongings and prepared to depart, with or without the governor's permission. Her husband's nautical instruments were amongst those gracing their cabin wall. "If those sextants and chronometers were mine," she said, "I guess I'd make him give them to me."[5] This she said loud enough for Waddell to be "aroused" by her words.

The prisoners went on deck and demanded that they be allowed ashore. Lillias informed the officer sarcastically that she was very much obliged for "their kindness," adding she "hoped they would sink at sea in six months." She said she liked all the officers except Dr. Lining and Lieutenant Whittle.[6] The executive officer seemed somewhat surprised by this. He claimed to have been "very kind to her." But "No, madame, never," he had replied when asked if they "could ever be friends," and upon departure took satisfaction in throwing overboard her copy of *Uncle Tom's Cabin*; the book which denigrated slavery and helped start the war.

The *Delphine* people were allowed aboard shore boats brought alongside, without the permission of the local authorities. As they pulled away Mrs. Nichols cried, "I wish that steamer may be burned!" They rowed towards the nearest vessel with the Stars and Stripes fluttering in the breeze, the *Jeannie W. Paine*— Captain Burke—a three-master of 661 tons built in Phippsburg, Maine. (She would end her days as the coal hulk *Kadina* in Adelaide.)[7]

"Our prisoners were taken on board.... This vessel kept its guidon flying every day; her Captain made many boasts about resisting us should we overhaul him at sea," recalled Lieutenant Chew.

> The men went ashore, but the ladies were taken to the *Jeannie Payne* [sic], an American ship lying in the bay, and it is said that their fervently expressed wishes were not for the welfare of their captors [*The Argus* newspaper].

Sir Charles Darling was astonished to have a Confederate cruiser arrive, but had been informed of the terms of British neutrality from Foreign Secretary Earl Russell, set out in January of 1862. British nationals were banned from serving in the armed forces of either side and, amongst other conditions, warships entering a British port were required to put to sea again within twenty-four hours of arrival, except in the case of "stress of weather, or her requiring provisions or things necessary for the subsistence of her crew, or repairs." In this case the warship must "put to sea as soon as possible."

Despite twenty-four hours being stipulated, forty-eight hours generally became the expectation,[8] and this would have been the case in Melbourne had the *Shenandoah* not required more time for repairs.

Extended time in port while repairs took place would not only provide opportunity to recruit "all the men" Waddell wanted, however, but also for earthly temptations to again override gentlemanly obligations, as is so often the case.

United States Consul William Blanchard learned from the morning newspaper that the rumors were true; a rebel steamer was anchored in Hobsons Bay. News had already been received in mid–January of the *Sea King*'s conversion to a Confederate cruiser at Madeira,[9] but *The Times* had claimed the vessel's loss on a rock, the subterfuge spread by Lieutenant Ramsay of the *Laurel*. The same story said that the famous Captain Raphael Semmes of the *Alabama* was in command, and this added to the excitement in Melbourne.

Blanchard had held the post of consul since early 1862 when the former incumbent, James Maguire, noted for his Confederate sympathies, had been removed from office. Blanchard would state that Maguire acted as a Confederate contact while the *Shenandoah* was in Melbourne.[10]

When Blanchard entered the consulate at 91 Chancery Lane[11] (Little Collins Street West) he found William Nichols and seven members of his crew already there. Lillias, Phineas and Mary Lingo had remained on board the *Jeannie W. Paine* until contact with the consulate was established.

The U.S. consul was fervent in his support for the Union; a man of energy and determination. He questioned the *Delphine* men, and took testimony from William Nichols. This described his encounter with a steamer showing "English colors":

> She fired a blank shot, upon which I immediately hove to, she hoisting the Confederate flag after firing her gun.
>
> That immediately after the gun was fired the Confederate flag was hoisted on said steamer, and on my ship *Delphine* being boarded, I was taken with my mate and ship's papers on board said steamer called *Shenandoah*.[12]

This testimony was to have some significance nine days later, when his wife made a detailed statement of her own.

Upon arrival at the consulate Mrs. Nichols, despite false claims to the contrary,[13] put nothing in writing this day, and there is no record of what she said. But she asked William Blanchard about his relatives, no doubt. Captain William H. Blanchard had married her sister Clara two years before, the future grandparents of Charles Nichols Blanchard. (Charles knew of no family connection with the consul.)

That afternoon Blanchard received a letter from Customs Commissioner James Francis, and replied to Governor Sir Charles Darling stating that he had made provision for the master, crew and passengers from the *Delphine*:

> I avail myself of this opportunity to call upon Your Excellency to cause the said *Shenandoah* alias *Sea King* to be seized for piratical acts, she not coming within Her Majesty's neutrality proclamation, never having entered a port of the so-called Confederate States of America, for the purpose of naturalization, and consequently not entitled to belligerent rights.
>
> Table service, plate etc. on board said vessel bear the mark *Sea King*, and the captain should bring evidence to entitle him to belligerent rights.
>
> I therefore protest against any aid or comfort being extended said piratical vessel in any of the ports of this Colony.
>
>   I have the honor to be Your Excellency's most obedient servant,
>   Wm Blanchard
>   Consul of the United States of America.

Thus opened a legal battle between the United States and British governments which would not be resolved until seven years after the battlefields had fallen silent.

Waddell's dispatch was to go on the mail steamer *Bombay,* and Blanchard managed to get two reports aboard the same vessel. One was to American Minister Charles Adams in London, and a copy to the U.S. consul in Hong Kong:

> Some prisoners on board, who are now being liberated, give the following details respecting her: She was the original Sea King; sailed from London on the 8th of October, 1864, and received ammunition from a ship named Laurel at sea. Part of the name Sea King is still visible, and I shall obtain of these particular letters a photograph. She is presented to have been built at Glasgow, and water-buckets, spoons, forks &c. are marked Sea King.... She has the appearance of an ordinary merchant ship with long poop, a large bright wheel-house, oval skylights on the poop; she has one telescope funnel; the mizzen top-mast and topgallant staysail both hoist from the mainmast head. She is wire-rigged.... The crew consists of 79 all told.[14]

A report from Governor Darling to London was also on board the *Bombay.* This made mention of the cruiser having "been formerly the *Sea King*," so less than twenty-four hours after the ship's arrival the government, Blanchard, and the local newspapers were all well aware of the ship's background.

While the hardworking Blanchard was impassioned in his support for the Union, his faults worked against him in his role as consul. He was of dubious moral reputation, described as a loud-voiced and aggressive American who lacked skill in tact and diplomacy, which led to his being shunned by others in diplomatic circles.[15]

Although James Waddell was not yet permitting visitors, he realized there was no more valuable ally than the press, as recounted by one newspaper correspondent:

> I, however, succeeded in getting on board, and was much struck with the general appearance of the crew, a finer looking set of fellows never trod a deck. Captain Waddell, before showing me around his vessel, invited me into his cabin. He is a fine, gentlemanly looking man, about thirty-five years of age, frank and polished in his bearing and evidently very determined ...
>
> "Any difficulty in obtaining a crew," I asked. "Certainly not. More than half the men in vessels captured by me," he replied, "have volunteered to fight under the Confederate flag; and, if we had a dozen of steamers to-morrow, man every one of them in no time."
>
> "Is this not the Sea King, or what was the Sea King?" said I. A smile crossed the captain's face, and he replied, "This is the Shenandoah, and I am happy to welcome you on board."[16]

The reporter saw, no doubt, that Waddell "had the chronometers of nine captured vessels hanging in his cabin, much as a Red Indian carried the scalps of his enemies in his belt," as recounted in the *Brisbane Courier* when recalling the *Shenandoah*'s visit over thirty years later.[17]

"Orders were given to admit all visitors," wrote Lining. Waddell yielded to demand despite still awaiting permission to remain in port, "and during that evening we were flocked and they went everywhere, poked into everything, and even while at dinner we had difficulty keeping them out of the wardroom."[18]

Lieutenant Chew recalled:

> Upon every steamer's approaching the ship we would look out for pretty faces and if found we stood near the gangway so as to take them in charge. If they were particularly agreeable we took them aft to the cabin and requested the pleasure of a glass of wine with them.... If we were asked once where was Semmes we were asked five hundred times, and it was difficult to make them believe he was not on board.

Some visitors, *The Herald* newspaper recorded,

> cruised around the vessel and endeavored by personal observation to ascertain whether she was not identical with the *Sea King*, of which information had already been received. These observers were rewarded for their pains in ascertaining some clue to the apparent mystery by the partial obliteration of the three remaining letters of the last word of the former name on the trail board ... a small whale boat when rounding to at the stern of the vessel was caught by the wind and capsized. A lady and two gentlemen who were in the boat were thrown into the water. Some alarm was created by this unlooked-for catastrophe.

Master's Mate Hunt also witnessed the event:

> The gentlemen, not withstanding their saturated garments, came on board, but the lady would not make the venture in her drooping crinoline, and returned to the shore, in a decided pet at the accident which had prevented her from inspecting the cruiser.[19]

Despite Blanchard's protests, Waddell was informed on the evening of January 26 that Governor Darling and his Executive Council had decided in favor of the *Shenandoah* being allowed to stay in port. This was subject to a board of inspectors carrying out an assessment of the vessel's damaged machinery.

Waddell called on Sir Charles Darling at Government House, Toorak, the following day. Accompanied by Dr. Lining and Lieutenants Grimball and Scales, he arrived but found his Excellency not at home. Waddell, feeling it was beneath his dignity to, "kick one's heels in his waiting room," as Lining recalled, decided not to wait. Leaving Waddell's card, the officers departed. Their carriage passed that of the governor as he belatedly arrived.[20]

The officers then went to Scott's Hotel, an opulent establishment in Collins Street where some officers had taken rooms. They laid aside their ceremonial swords, and went on a tour of inspection. This included, "the parliament buildings, which are quite handsome for such a new colony, and will be very fine when finished."

For a city which only thirty years before had been a few tents pitched along the banks of the Yarra River, the 1865 capital was impressive. It had a population of about 140,000, and was fueled by rich goldfields a little further inland. Substantial structures adorned with Greek columns and majestic porticos made it obvious Melbourne was here to stay. Attractive parks, gardens and a zoo were already established, and the installation of gas street lighting had commenced in 1857.

Lieutenant Chew recorded:

> For myself I was surprised to see Melbourne such a flourishing city. I knew of its size, its commerce and expected to see much yet looking upon it I could not but wonder and admire. In this remote quarter of the globe one almost forgets where he is and thinks he is in England. Fine, large houses, spacious streets, carriages of fine finish speak for the wealth of the city.

Both Yankee and Confederate agreed. The *Delphine*'s second mate, Edward Nichols, recalled:

> They have many things to be proud of. They boast their fine harbor, cleanliness of their city, their broad streets, their modern conveniences and their general hospitality. I think Melbourne is one of the finest cities I ever visited.[21]

But the *Melbourne Punch*, a humorous and satirical magazine, based on its London counterpart, made fun of some recent additions like the Victoria Fountain, described as "something between a washingtub and a lamp post."[22] *Punch* also had a comment some may consider relevant to recent events which had occurred beneath the Great Southern Comet: "From our Astronomer we learn that its tail is ever so many degrees long, but some yarns on board the *Shenandoah* are considered to be several degrees longer."[23]

Steamers exhibited "1 shilling to the *Shenandoah* and back." The crush of visitors inhibited the work of workmen taken on board to carry out various tasks which included recaulking the deck. "I had to tell the Captains that if they did not take off one party as they brought another I would have to stop them," recalled Lieutenant Whittle. On Sunday special trains were put on. These brought visitors from Melbourne to Sandridge on what, eleven years before, had been the first of the spreading network of steam railways in Australia. The Confederate officers were all given complimentary rail passes and Dr. Lining spent the day ashore, but returned at sundown to hear:

> *Immense* crowds had visited the ship today the railroad having brought down over 7,000 persons, besides these many came by buggies etc. from Sandridge etc. At one

time there was scarcely standing room on the decks, people were on the rails, in the tops, and two steamboats loaded with passengers were alongside, but were obliged to be sent off for want of room to stand.[24]

The crowds created inconvenience, but the officers were showered with invitations to dinners and parties. Dr. Lining found one young lady visitor most attractive, "but this lump of a fellow kept tagging after her, like a school boy, and gave very few others a chance."

Melbourne socialite Annie Dawbin recorded in her diary on Wednesday, February 1:

> Mrs Barker came here in the morning and asked me to go to her house for lunch, as some of the officers of the *Shenandoah* were to be there: accordingly I went at 1 o'clock, and met Messrs Lee (nephew of the Confederate Commander-in-Chief Robert E. Lee) and Mason, Captn Brewer, Police magistrate of Ginchen Bay, and Captain Murchison—the two former officers were very gentlemanly "southerners," nice-looking, and quiet in their manners.
>
> Dr Barker drove them to the Yarra Bend asylum after lunch, but before doing so, he drove round from the next street a Miss Clarke, who, when she got off the dogcart, never said a word of thanks to Mr Lee who had politely got down to help her from the vehicle. What must foreigners think of us English when we behave so rudely?[25]

The young officers vied for the attention of attractive young ladies amid the throng who visited the *Shenandoah* (*Illustrated Melbourne Post*, February 18, 1865).

Waddell was supposed to attend that lunch, but did not arrive. His only known social appearances were at the Melbourne Club, and a private dinner after which Police Commissioner Standish wrote: "a very clever, smart and amusing fellow—rather Yankee-ish, I beg his pardon!"

Lilli Nichols' anger subsiding, and no longer Waddell's prisoner, contact was re-established. Waddell was possibly influenced by news of the *Florida*'s demise. "We all recollect the tale of treachery," he recalled, "The *Florida* was discovered, and in a few hours, in the dead of night, her crew were butchered and the vessel towed out of port and taken to Hampton Roads."[26] Waddell's own ship may well be rammed and boarded in a neutral harbor, and he too "butchered" in the "dead of night." Best to live life to the hilt while he could. A "most scandalous romance" took place "on the shore." The couple met at some discreet location, Lilli's family and maid sidelined. The diary would have revealed Nichols' inability to "prevent her doing wrong," a big incentive for the cousins to have those "under the thumb" references removed from Waddell's memoirs nearly a century later. "She wears the breeches," wrote Midshipman Mason.

How often and where they met may never be known, but amidst the flurry of ship to shore communications, a substantial hint of what was going on emerged—the "List of Prisoners" episode.[27]

JANUARY 26

Waddell receives a letter from Commissioner for Trade and Customs, James Francis. This gives permission for the ship to stay in port and "his excellency desires to be furnished with a list of the prisoners in question, and any other information affecting them which you may be able to afford."

JANUARY 28

Captain Waddell totally ignores the request for a list in his written reply.

JANUARY 29

"The Captain is out of the ship and has been all day. Everything falls on me and the officers whose duty keeps them here,"[28] complained William Whittle.

JANUARY 30

James Francis again requests a list of prisoners "as I suggested in my previous communication should be sent in for the guidance of his excellency before 4:00 p.m. on the 31st instant." Francis, irritated by being ignored, has set a precise time limit. But Waddell makes the puzzling reply that the prisoners 'left the ship without my knowledge in shore boats shortly after my arrival in this port." Again he provides no list. One would have thought illegal arrivals on shore would have exacerbated the need for a list, not negate it. He is deliberately thwarting the governor's requirements.

JANUARY 31

James Francis renews his request for a list "with respect to the prisoners who were brought to this port." The commissioner, running out of patience, goes on to explain in some detail the need for a list; precedent, etc. stating that a failure to provide the list could lead to a future "violation of municipal or other laws or regulations in force in this colony."

That same night Waddell and other officers attend a dinner at the exclusive Melbourne Club. Afterwards, they walk to the railway station to find the last night train to Sandridge has gone. "So all of us," wrote Lining, "except the capt. went off to the *Alhambra* where we remained for some time, and then withdrew to bed."[29] Where Waddell spent the night is unknown.

FEBRUARY 1

Some officers meet at Scott's Hotel. The night before they had accepted a luncheon invitation, but "The Captain was not there," recalled Midshipman Mason. "I was sorry that he disappointed the worthy Dr. Barker."[30]

Once back at the ship, Waddell writes to James Francis. He mentions having missed "the commission of officers" who came aboard the previous day. This was due to being "absent from the ship." He makes reference to an enclosed list of prisoners, but claims to have already given one to customs official, Mr. MacFarlane, "as far back as the 25th or 26th ultimo." For some strange reason Waddell has not mentioned this before.

But the elusive list is still not forthcoming—the list is *missing*.

Francis does not waste time. He immediately writes back: "By inadvertence you have omitted to enclose the list of prisoners." By this time Francis must have really thought "inadvertence" was anything but the real reason.

Waddell's final desperate ruse has failed. He had hoped Francis would be satisfied that MacFarlane had a list somewhere in the bureaucracy and not pursue the matter. But Waddell now sends the list with eleven people named; "Mrs. L. L. Nichols" the very last.[31] Perhaps he considered leaving that last name off?

So why avoid supplying the list? The *Shenandoah* was big news. The newspapers published anything they could get their hands on—a list of officers' names, a list of ships destroyed, a list of armaments. Waddell would have supplied the list had he not resumed seeing her, and would rather risk the wrath of James Francis than that of Lilli Nichols a second time. "She went out in a towering rage," wrote Lining. This episode is unique in that it was the only routine information Waddell attempted to withhold from the authorities whose goodwill was required to allow the repairs.

Anyone doubting the possibility of such goings on need only look to the well-known precedent of Justice Redmond Barry who sat on the bench of the Supreme Court of Victoria at this time. Barry emigrated from Ireland to Australia in 1839 on board the *Calcutta*. The young lawyer became intimately involved with one Mrs. Scott, whose husband was also on board. But Barry was none too discreet with his amorous adventures. This led to protestations from the husband and others, but all to no avail. And when the ship docked in Sydney the affair continued on land. The scandal forced Barry to move to the fledgling colony of Melbourne to become a pillar of the community, despite yet another married woman—Louisa Barrow—giving birth to his children. Barry's "Day Book," would also reveal, after death, affairs with other married women such as "Mrs. M" and "Mrs. A,"[32] as both Lilli Nichols' and Mary Astor's diaries would reveal their affairs years later.

But the *Shenandoah* couple had more in common with Redmond Barry and Mrs. Scott than a romantic interlude and diary revelations. Despite greater discretion, they were also caught out, a fact which would have profound consequences for the ship's ultimate voyage.

8

A Piratical Vessel

One of the *Shenandoah*'s visitors was Captain Charles Payne of the Williamstown Naval Brigade, formerly a Royal naval officer. His report to the government on the ship's capabilities as a man-of-war highlighted some of her deficiencies should she fall in with a Federal cruiser:

> There is nothing to protect her machines from shot and shell; in fact, her boilers and the principle parts of her machinery are above the water-line. Her bunkers certainly are between the machinery and the ship's side, but from their small dimensions they would offer but small resistance to shot. The most vulnerable part, viz, the boilers, is left quite unprotected.[1]

Payne deduced that her gunpowder was kept in the forward hold and that she had no larger guns stowed below than those on her decks. He was not impressed with the discipline of the crew or the ship's cleanliness; the short-handed Confederate service obviously not that of the Royal Navy. Or perhaps this was a prejudice revealed? The finicky Whittle had commented on painting and sprucing the ship before arrival.[2]

Commander Henry King, the British naval agent on board the mail steamer, took a different view. He was shown over the *Shenandoah* before the *Bombay* sailed:

> She is strongly built, of iron coated with wood, and copper-bottomed. Her lower masts are of steel, and she is a roomy, well-regulated vessel, ship rigged.... The ship appears to be in good order; her officers a gentlemanly set of men, in a uniform of grey and gold; but from the paucity of her crew at present, she cannot be very efficient for fighting purposes.[3]

A legal battle was not the only one to take place in Melbourne during the stay of the "piratical vessel." The colony's newspapers gave a good indication of how Melbournians felt in regard to the warlike visitors. Editorials and countless readers' letters appeared which both castigated and praised the rebels. *The Age*, a popular and radical morning paper, edited by David Syme, showed no sympathy for the Confederate Cause as made clear on January 27:

> We cannot regard the *Shenandoah* as other than a marauding craft, and her officers and crew than as a gang of respectable pirates. The vessel cannot claim to rank as a ship of war, nor ought the commissions of her officers entitle them to a place with gentlemen holding similar rank in the navies of recognised powers. A ship of war carries credentials from the nation to which she belongs. She does not sail either under a false name or colours. Nor does the commander resort to the shabby subterfuge of denying his identity. This ship comes into port as the *Shenandoah*, but there is the strongest possible reason for believing she is the notorious *Sea King*.... Her vocation is not to fight, but to plunder: not to vanquish enemies in a fair struggle, but to destroy unarmed antagonists: not to shed the blood of her crew in their country's defence, but to fill their pockets with prize money. The *Shenandoah* brings prisoners, unfortunate skippers and their wives, whose livelihoods and homes are sunk beneath the ocean, and who are landed here, thousands of miles from their destination.

The editor did not know that one unfortunate wife, Mrs. Nichols, had decided to forgive the pirate chief. And this despite her livelihood and home having been "sunk beneath the ocean."

The Argus, a morning paper which reflected the conservative attitudes of the London *Times* saw things differently to *The Age*:

> It would hardly be fair to the community if Captain Waddell and his officers were allowed to carry away the impression that the bunkum that has been written and talked about him is a genuine reflection of its sentiments on this occasion. He probably will not have been surprised that the admirers of Yankee character and the partisans of Yankee institutions should naturally fall into the habits and mode of thinking of the vulgar tyranny from which they derive their inspiration.
>
> And the United States had a Government which has kept no faith with her enemies and wherever it has been possible to do so with safety, has broken every promise to its friends—A Government which under the pretext of a Crusade against slavery, has committed crimes against civilisation more detestable than any slavery.

The Herald contended:

> Peace is what the Southerners ask for. Peace meaning recognition and a new empire. The Federals declare there should be no peace without submission and their dictatorship. As far as Australia is concerned, we need not trouble ourselves either way; but we think, and we have a way of expressing our thoughts in tolerably plain language. Europe has long since acknowledged the Confederate States as belligerents, and by this time, ought to have declared the South an Empire. Australia, the Child-Giant of the English press, and a Continent that may ere long sway many destinies, can at any rate do no less than welcome the gallant outcasts of a distracted country. While

The Argus newspaper, Waddell's vocal advocate, occupied the three-story building and central white building alongside in Collins Street, Melbourne (State Library of Victoria).

deploring the enormous misery caused by the principle which actuates those in command of cruisers like the *Shenandoah*, we cannot but recognise and fraternise with the brave men who uphold their country's flag at the risk of being hanged from the yard-arm or shot after a short shrift, unrecognised by the Great Powers of Europe, and fighting against one of the mightiest in the Universe.

The Age was to be the only Melbourne paper with nothing good to say about the Confederates, and was to wage a war of words against them. The others were impressed with the new arrivals: "They are dashing fellows," said the *Illustrated Australian News*, "and seem to take great pride in their flag and in their fine ship." Waddell was described as a six-foot North Carolinian with a face the color of deep mahogany, and black hair. He was quick tempered and aloof, according to one report, and limped slightly from a dueling wound he never discussed.

The *Illustrated Melbourne Post* published a wood engraving of Waddell taken from a photograph by Batchelder and Co. and below that a picture of the *Shenandoah* surrounded with small craft in Hobsons Bay. Waddell was described as "a gentleman of most prepossessing appearance, and bears about him the frank expression of a sailor." And, "On board he is in great favour with both his officers and crew."[4]

But another article appeared immediately below. This described the new gun raft designed by Captain Elder of the Williamstown Naval Brigade, which was "eminently adapted to the purpose for which it was designed." A picture of the gunraft flanked that of the *Shenandoah*. The raft had been put into commission in December 1864 when George Verdon, State Treasurer and War Minister, had fired the first practice shot. The shell "made a capital line, though he went far beyond the mark."[5] Perhaps the editor felt ill at ease with the cruiser's presence and ran the story as a subtle warning that the colony was not entirely undefended.

Australians mirrored the population of Great Britain in their attitude towards the Confederacy. Some likened the "Johnny Rebs" to the miners who had rebelled at the Eureka Stockade in 1854. Now another oppressive government was being fought. The miner's leader, Peter Lalor, who had lost an arm as a result of the fight, was now a member of the Victorian Parliament. He did not want the *Shenandoah* matter debated by politicians in the chamber, saying it was a matter to be considered by the governor and his legal advisors.

These events were followed with interest via the overland telegraph in the other Australian colonies, and "heroic miners fighting for their rights" was not the only comparison made. The distant *Sydney Morning Herald* saw fit to compare the *Shenandoah* to outlaws like Ben Hall who were rampant in New South Wales at the time. The writer stated that the ship was:

> in a position somewhat similar to the bushrangers in this colony. Armed to the teeth, they can take their own time and place for surprising the traveller. Thus they can avoid for months together all chance of pursuit, while they have always an opportunity for catching some victim. When this is the case there can be no ground for an outburst of admiration.[6]

Outbursts of admiration continued, however. While many Australian residents may not have believed in slavery, they saw the war waged by the United States against the South as the greater crime, despite slavery having been outlawed by Lincoln's Emancipation Proclamation of January 1863. The vast majority of fighting was done on Confederate soil, thus it was usually Southern towns and homes put to the torch. The outnumbered rebel forces fought without the resources of the North, as seen with the *Shenandoah*, a converted merchantman. They appeared to many as a downtrodden underdog. Others saw slavery as an abhorrent evil, and the means justified the end. Nothing could shake their belief that the Union, scourged of slavery, must remain intact.

Australian papers carried stories from both sides, including the *Richmond Daily Whig*. The news was a few months old, as it would not be until 1872 that Australia would be connected to the Northern hemisphere by telegraph.

The Confederate officers were an attraction and Melbournians were delighted to catch a glimpse at every opportunity. The *Creswick and Clunes Advertiser* reported:

> The officers are fine strapping gentlemanly young fellows, clothed in a most abominably ugly uniform. They are at present sincerely to be pitied, for they never have an hour to themselves—they are besieged day and night on board their vessel, and mercilessly lionised on shore. I do not believe if a couple of tame tigers were to walk up Bourke Street in the middle of the day that they would be followed by so many ragged youngsters as these Southerners are by a lot of well-dressed snobs, who seem to have the worst of all country vices, the vice of flunkeyism.

One evening a large crowd stood outside the Theatre Royal. The bill proclaimed, "Under the distinguished patronage of the officers of the Confederate Steamship, *Shenandoah*." To avoid attracting too much attention the officers arrived separately, and watched from the Royal Box. "The performance was miserable I thought," reported Midshipman Mason, "but the theater was crowded. In the *eutre-acte* the band played 'Dixie' and the crowd commenced cheering and the opposition put in hisses and boos all of which was excessively annoying to ourselves." The name of the play? *The Wonder, or, A Woman Keeps a Secret*—and one Searsport woman did until 1933.

If dissatisfied, Mr. Mason may have become aware of the cafe attached. This offered other entertainments, as there were "two mysterious closed doors," recalled one senior police officer, "the far-famed 'saddling paddock' of the Royal. It is a small bar presided over by a man. The proceedings here are too unpleasant for a barmaid to witness. Here the most notorious women in Melbourne nightly throng, and run in the companions they have caught ... Poor Devils!"[7]

On another occasion a special performance of Shakespeare's *Othello* was put on for the officers at the Haymarket Theatre, located in Bourke Street. This vibrant hub was the center of Melbourne's nightlife. Albert Cars, omnibuses and fine carriages rattled to and fro, bathed in gaslight from all-night hotels and dancing halls. Street-singers competed with barrel organ music as people bustled about patronizing fine restaurants or one of the many coffee stalls. Others might watch vivacious dancing girls at The Bull and Bush, the Casino, or the Alhambra. Turkish baths, street stalls and the Waxworks were popular. Sailors seeking more intimate pleasures could find comfort in elegant bordellos, boarding houses, or small cottages where discretion was assured. One reporter wrote: "From ten o'clock at night it may be said that the public thoroughfares are taken possession of by abandoned women, all elaborately and expensively attired."[8]

The officers' journals only mentioned entertainments acceptable in polite society, of course, and they could not possibly gratify every invitation.

On a more somber note, Waddell recalled:

Apparently as a kind of protest against the recognition of the stranger, those American houses whose sympathies were known to be strongly Federal hoisted the Stars and Stripes, but there was no similar demonstration on the part of the firms whose affections were believed to be the other way. This, I believe, was owing to an impression that the exhibition of the Confederate flag would be protested against by the American consul. A very strong feeling was more than once manifested by some of the citizens, and in one instance a knock-down between partisans was with difficulty prevented.[9]

Perhaps Waddell had this incident in mind, as reported on February 1 in the *Creswick and Clunes Advertiser*:

> It appears that on Thursday the officers of the *Shenandoah* were taking some refreshments at Scott's Hotel, surrounded by a large company of their admirers, when an American merchant, who is very stout and largely interested in the kerosene trade, took occasion to remark in their hearing that they were a "d____d set of piratical scoundrels," when one of the Southerners quietly left his seat, took the Federalist gently by the nose, and led him to the door, where he turned him round in the most artistic manner, so as to present his rear to the company, to which portion of his person he administered several hearty kicks, which sent him down the stairs at a pace which Volunteers call the "double."[10]

Which sounds remarkably like another incident. It was probably the same one in fact, but embellished by Master's Mate Cornelius Hunt, who rewrote Scott's Hotel as a saloon of the Wild West:

> We were just sitting down to a sumptuous repast when an individual entered, invited himself to join us, and forthwith commenced a tirade upon rebels and the Southern Confederacy, making use of such language that gentlemen seldom submit to in silence.
>
> He had not proceeded in this manner many minutes ere our Assistant Surgeon sprang to his feet, and dealt him a blow between the eyes that sent him sprawling. In another instant the fight was general; glasses and decanters were diverted from their legitimate use and turned into missiles of offence; knives were drawn and one or two shots were fired, but fortunately without any serious results.[11]

Waddell procured the services of the Langlands Brothers and Company of King Street Melbourne, engineers and iron founders, to carry out the repairs to the *Shenandoah*'s damaged machinery. On January 28 a diver was sent down to examine the propeller sternpost bearing. Apart from providing recruitment and recreational opportunities, the news was not good. Mason recalled that the diver "reported the bearings all torn to pieces and a large crack, long and wide, in the stern cleeve, this of course necessitated our going on the slip which otherwise would not have been necessary."

Two days after the diver's report, Langlands estimated that as she could not be placed on the patent slip at Williamstown for three days, "we will not be able to accomplish the repairs within ten days from date."

Waddell forwarded Langlands' assessment to Governor Darling, and received a reply from James Francis. This requested a list of supplies required, and informed him that a marine board would, "examine and report whether the vessel is now in a fit state to proceed to sea, or what repairs are necessary."

Waddell replied that every facility would be extended to the marine board, and he required light material for summer uniforms, fresh meat, vegetables and bread daily, and some liquid "sea supplies" which, no doubt, necessitated the *Shenandoah*'s cruising plans being kept to himself: "Brandy, rum, champagne, port, sherry, beer, porter." Molasses was also required, and to keep scurvy at bay, good healthy lime juice.

The punctilious James Francis was a partner in the firm of Francis and McPherson—merchants—and also a director of the Bank of New South Wales. No doubt he needed a healthy income to support his growing family, ultimately with fifteen children. His temper was not sweetened by recurring pain from a hatchet wound to the head received from a burglar many years before in Tasmania.[12] Francis would become Victoria's ninth premier, serving from 1872 to 1874.

The commissioner appeared to have little sympathy for the Confederate cause, and would lock horns with Waddell who claimed Francis was a business partner of the American consul.[13]

Francis had customs official James MacFarlane, who held the curious title of "Tide Inspector," keep the vessel under surveillance. Not happy at a distance, MacFarlane often came aboard and befriended some of the officers. But Waddell was not enamored with this situation:

> There was a Mr. MacFarlin [*sic*], a customs official, who did not have the intelligence to recognize the distinction between a national and private vessel, who for many days, with his assistants, kept watch over the *Shenandoah*. His visits to the ship were daily, and always very friendly towards us, but that was to cover the indelicacy of his visits.
>
> I took occasion to inform him of the character of those visits, and explained to him the difference between a merchant, privateer, and national vessel, which distinction he accepted, and we were not troubled by such visits as much as we had before.[14]

William Blanchard, meanwhile, continued to question the crew of the *Delphine*. Seamen informed him that most of the *Shenandoah*'s crew had been pressed into service, he claimed, and would desert the ship if the American consulate could protect them from arrest. Blanchard said he would give that guarantee, and urged the *Delphine*'s men to direct any such seamen to him should they be seen on shore.

He also followed up two requests to Governor Darling for the *Shenandoah*'s seizure with another, more detailed, plea on January 28. This stated, in essence, that the ship was British built and cannot change her registry on the high seas; the Neutrality Proclamation prohibits British subjects giving assistance; the ship's registry can only be transferred in a so-called Confederate port; being legally an English merchant ship cannot be considered a man-of-war; she is a lawless pirate dishonoring the flag used to decoy her victims; she uses British weapons cleared under British seal, or if without it, in violation of established law; she is liable to seizure, and the crew guilty of piracy.

Blanchard received a reply on January 30. The governor had consulted with the Crown law-officers and "his Excellency has come to the decision that, whatever may be the previous history of the *Shenandoah*, the government of this colony is bound to treat her as a ship-of-war belonging to a belligerent power."[15]

A "solemn protest" was immediately dispatched by Blanchard. This warned the governor that the United States would claim compensation for all damage done by the *Shenandoah* before and after her stay in Melbourne if she were allowed to proceed. As the vessel was legally a pirate, he claimed the right of the United States to pursue, capture or destroy her in any port or harbor in the world.

On January 28 Blanchard wired the U.S. consul in Sydney, E. Leavenworth. This requested that the governor of New South Wales intervene. Blanchard was unsure, but believed him to be the governor-general of all the Australian colonies. Victoria, however, had been a separate colony since 1851, and Blanchard was informed that Darling was governor in his own right.[16]

Governor Sir Charles Darling was a British aristocrat of the old school and nephew of former New South Wales governor, Sir Ralph Darling, for whom he had acted as aide-de-camp. Prior to his appointment to Victoria, he had been governor of Jamaica. Sir Charles was to have his mettle tested over the next few

Governor Sir Charles Darling was pestered by the American consul for the *Shenandoah*'s seizure, while rebel officers were wined and dined by the social elite (State Library of Victoria).

weeks, but would be advised by his two Crown law-officers, Minister for Justice Archibald Mitchie and Attorney-General George Higinbotham.

Mitchie, a London born lawyer, was also the Melbourne correspondent of the London *Times*. A great believer in Free Trade, he allowed publicans to keep open-house all night with unfortunate results, according to Police Superintendant Sadleir: "the streets were never free from drunken men and women ... the experiment was a very disastrous one. Fortunately it lasted but a short time."[17]

Dublin-born lawyer George Higinbotham had replaced Mitchie as attorney-general in 1863.[18] "Mr. Higinbotham was a most determined man," wrote solicitor John Gurner, "but he had many endearing and attractive qualities. He was possessed of a beautiful voice, of choice diction, of great courtesy."

On the evening of January 31, sixty members of the exclusive Melbourne Club rose as one and drank to the health of Waddell and five of his fellow officers. Then, to the surprise of many, three cheers were proposed, which received a hearty response, and "two more to make them good." This was normally against club rules and had no precedent. The officers of the *Shenandoah* had been given honorary membership, and found themselves being entertained with the elite of Melbourne's male society; judges, politicians, military officers and wealthy businessmen. They had already enjoyed a sumptuous meal served by stewards in fine livery; blue coat with red collar and gilt buttons, scarlet waistcoat and black plush breaches. Captain Waddell sat on the right side of the president and Lieutenant Lee on the left. Paymaster Smith, Dr. Lining, Lieutenant Scales and Midshipman Mason were "badly arranged at table," complained Lining, "Too many of us being put up towards the head."

To the right of Midshipman John Mason sat Dr. Edward Barker, who entertained him with a talk about hanging:

> He contended that instead of placing the knot behind the ear as is usually the custom, it should be just behind the neck immediately upon the neckbone where the fall would snap the neck off and thus produce instantaneous death, whereas with the old custom of placing the knot behind the ear always five or sometimes ten minutes was required to produce death ... the sum total of it all is that if ever I am to be hung, I will beg the executioner to put the knot behind my neck.

Dr. Barker officiated at the hanging of the notorious Ned Kelly fifteen years later. He was fond of talking about hanging, apparently, which leads to some confusion regarding the doctor's methods. Sydney *Sun* reporter Brian William Cookson recalled in a newspaper reminiscence thirty-one years after the hanging:

> He extolled in eloquent tones the ability and science shown by Upjohn, the "yeoman of the rope," on the present occasion, which contrasted favorably with other events

which had been bungled by the artist placing the knot in the wrong place, such as the back of the neck.

Such as the *back* of the neck? It seems Dr. Barker had reversed his theories. Perhaps this was because of the *Memorandum upon the Execution of Prisoners by Hanging with a Long Drop* as approved by the British Prime Minister five months before Ned's hanging. The knot was to be placed "just in front of the angle of the jaw bone, on the left side, so as to run up behind the left ear when the man falls and receives the jerk."[19]

The Melbourne Club had no peer in the colonial capital and was favorably compared with similar establishments in Paris and London. The Comte de Beauvoir, a French visitor and honorary member, noted, "They drank champagne as if it were water."[20]

The exclusive dinner caused an outcry from those opposed to the *Shenandoah*. Letters from both factions appeared in newspapers and editorials were written. The following day, February 1, *The Age* wrote under "sympathy with Buccaneers":

> That the soft-headed flunkeys who are recognised as leaders of the Melbourne Club are capable of any misdemeanour against common sense and good taste, there can be no doubt. Many of them, however, are government officials, and it cannot be permitted that they should commit a breach of the neutrality enjoined by Her Majesty, without being called to account.... Success to the Confederate cause will, of course, be drunk in gin cocktails which the gentlemanly pirates are said to be skilled in brewing.... The soldier who captures a city is said to be rewarded for his bravery in the assault, not for his zeal in spoliation. Captain Waddell and his officers might as well be lionised for their ability to brew spiders and cocktails. It is a prostitution of terms to classify these gentlemen as naval officers.... If these men have a country to struggle for, why do they not fight instead of plunder? ... How unfortunate for Captain Waddell that he missed the *John [David] Brown* just arrived at South Australia. The price of his refit might have been defrayed from the proceeds of a prize captured within easy reach of an Admiralty Court.... The Club is already sunk so low as to be beneath contempt.

No doubt Captain Waddell and Mrs. Nichols were displeased to see the *David Brown* affair in the newspapers. Should their relationship ever be exposed, the connection could well be made.

Waddell saw his dinner with the "soft-headed flunkeys" this way:

> The entertainment was a courtesy which the club always extends to strangers, and the presence of the company was an expression of sympathy for a gallant people in resisting a wicked aggression. Although there was a general sympathy in the community for the Confederate cause as kindly exhibited in many ways in the hospitalities shown to the officers of the *Shenandoah*, it was equally true there were sympathies warmly disposed towards the Federals.

The reception and shelter granted to the *Shenandoah* had given serious offence to this party, and the abortive efforts to discredit the character and officers of the ship in connection with the cause for which they were in arms had, as was openly asserted, been followed by the still more unworthy cause of tampering with the allegiance of the crew.

A number of the *Shenandoah*'s crew deserted while in Melbourne, "under a promise of $100 cash from the American consul,"[21] recalled Waddell. Rumors about the city supported this claim. But desertions were not his only problem. Melbourne was a hotbed of rumors of plans to scuttle or blow up the *Shenandoah*. Waddell recalled that a carpenter had overheard Americans discussing the feasibility of smuggling themselves aboard and capturing the ship at sea. "If it is attempted they will fail, and I will hang every mother's son of them," Waddell replied.

And an article in the *Brisbane Courier* of March 7 revealed a planned attempt to seize the ship and "carry her off to California." There were various meetings, claimed the story, and:

> boats were engaged to convey 150 armed men to her sides in the night, and all risks short of actual collision with the colonial authorities were to be encountered in affecting the object. Money to any extent was forthcoming to aid the scheme, which, but for the care exhibited by the authorities arising out of the suspicions engendered by the discovery of stow-aways, would probably have been put into execution.

The writer had seen a photograph of Waddell and was not impressed with this modern day Drake of the Spanish Main. Had Mrs. Nichols ever read this article, she would have been mortified to learn that her "kind" and "handsome," lover had:

> A down, scowling look; no whiskers; a heavy hanging moustache on the upper lip; falling over the mouth; dull, sly, cruel eyes; cheeks rather flabby, and a swelling or puffing of the flesh under the eyes, such is more frequently seen than admired.[22]

One story claimed an explosive device failed to detonate after being placed alongside the ship's hull by the crew of the American bark *Mustang* and, in 1872, during a debate in the Victorian Parliament, Mr. John Woods made reference to a plot "concocted by the American residents in Melbourne, having Northern sympathies, to burst up the *Shenandoah* with gunpowder." He claimed the plot was foiled by the arrival of police in the dockyard.[23]

It seems but for the intervention of the police various Yankee groups may well have gone to battle with each other for the honor of destroying the *Shenandoah*, the ship's crew merely spectators. Little wonder Waddell wrote to Superintendent Thomas Lyttleton on January 31 requesting the co-operation of the water police in the protection of the *Shenandoah*. It took over one week for him

"Boats were engaged to convey 150 armed men to her sides in the night." One of many perceived plots to destroy the *Shenandoah* at anchor in Hobsons Bay (*Illustrated Melbourne Post*, February 18, 1865).

to receive Lyttleton's reply: "I beg to inform you that I have instructed the Williamstown and water police to give particular attention to the vessel. I should have replied to your letter before, but that from some cause which I shall enquire into, it only reached me on the morning of the fourth instant." Waddell did not receive this reply until February 8. Other official communications were often exchanged by messenger the same day.

Thomas Hamilton Lyttleton, Superintendent of the Metropolitan Police District, was a friend of socialite Annie Dawbin, who described him thus: "Just the same fidgety manner, the same admiration for beauty, and the same dear little spoilt manner his father had. Col. Haddon says Tom Lyttleton is one of the two wildest most dissipated men he ever met."[24] And Superintendent Sadleir later described Lyttleton as the "bumptious and pretentious sort" and his appointment was not a great success as "although by birth and education he was a gentleman he was wanting in some of the qualities requisite for so important a position. He was not careful in his conduct in private life."

Not the best character reference for a superintendent of police perhaps, and Lyttleton managed to take enough time off to attend the theater regularly, and dabble in the arts. He become known for his paintings of racehorses, but his level of talent posed no threat to Renoir or Manet.

Lyttleton soon emerged as one of those whose sympathies were, "warmly disposed towards the Federals." His tardiness in following up Waddell's request could well have been influenced by this.

The Marine Board made their inspection and reported:

> 1st. That the *Shenandoah* is not in a fit state to proceed to sea as a steamship.
> 2nd. That repairs are necessary.
> 3rd. That the part or parts requiring repair being the inner stern-post bearing of the screw-shaft, the extent of damage cannot be ascertained without the vessel being slipped.

James Francis advised Waddell to proceed with the repairs, making arrangements with Mr. Enoch Chambers, the lessee. The slipway, although built by the government, was now run as a private concern.

Governor Charles Darling, however, wanted the *Shenandoah* kept under observation. He wrote to Francis from Government House, Toorak, on February 3:

> I am sure that the honourable commissioner of trade and customs will take every precaution in his power against the possibility of the commander of that vessel in any degree extending its armament or rendering the present armament more effective.[25]

9

I Was Not a Prisoner of War

William Blanchard probably had little sleep during the *Shenandoah*'s stay, determined as he was to see the "pirate vessel" never leave Melbourne.

Midshipman Mason recalled:

> Although most of the people were apparently in sympathy with us, there were a number of American shipping merchants, and they, with the American Consul, tried in every way to involve us in a dispute of some sort with the authorities, in the hope that the ship might thus be detained and seized.... They induced a large number of our crew to desert, men shipped from Yankee prizes, no doubt the men were well bribed, for they were induced to swear all sorts of atrocious things; that they had been triced up by the thumbs and big toes, bucked, gagged and all sorts of cruelties practiced upon them to compel them to ship and finally they were compelled to do so in order to save their lives.[1]

Seaman William Temple, however, despite a grudge against the Confederacy for being underpaid, gave this evidence in Liverpool following the ship's surrender:

> The only inducement held out for men from vessels captured to join our ship, were these. After they were put in irons, the officers would approach them and say, now, you are in irons and will probably be kept there a month, you are earning nothing now if you will join us you will be set at liberty, treated well and earn good wages. You had therefore better consent and do it. Many agreed to this.[2]

Temple's statement reveals the normal routine. But William Whittle had triced up John Colby from the *Lizzie M. Stacey* who had refused to either enlist or work. Colby was one of Whittle's "hated Yankee race." Perhaps this had influenced this extreme, as most other captives were of other nationalities.

Prominent Melbourne solicitor Joseph G. Duffett had arrived in Melbourne on board the *Great Britain* on her first voyage to Australia in 1852,[3] and founded the legal firm of Duffett, Grant and Woolcott. Duffett was approached by William Blanchard "with sundry affidavits and witnesses at my command."[4] He wished to have the rebel steamer indicted in the Admiralty Court.

Parliamentarian Graham Berry, the Member for Collingwood, was a one-time grocer who would later become Premier of Victoria and receive a knighthood. He was an ally of William Blanchard and had no time for the Confederates anchored in Hobsons Bay. On February 1 the consul introduced Berry to Lillias Nichols, who then furnished him with an affidavit, the first of two in Melbourne. It was brief and stated, in essence, that *Sea King* and *Shenandoah* were one and the same, and armaments were brought aboard from the *Laurel*.[5] This was no news to anyone who read the newspapers. Her cooperation with Blanchard did not undermine James Waddell in any way.

That same evening there was a sitting of the Legislative Assembly in the Victorian Parliament. Graham Berry raised the issue of the *Shenandoah,* and launched into one of his long-winded, forceful monologues. "His oratory might not be polished: it certainly was not—but it was passionate, and it told," reported *The Argus* following Berry's death in 1904.

Berry echoed Blanchard's arguments. He pointed out that the *Shenandoah,* before dropping anchor in Hobsons Bay, had been engaged in the capture and destruction of American vessels on the high seas. The ship had sailed from an English port as the *Sea King,* cleared for Bombay, and was therefore not a legitimate ship of war, liable to seizure as a pirate vessel in whatever British port she might enter.

Premier James McCulloch responded on behalf of the government. He stated that there was no real evidence that the *Shenandoah* and *Sea King* were one and the same. All the evidence they had was a newspaper report and a letter in a Manchester paper, he said. The honorable member had not brought forward any other evidence except that there were the letters "*ing*" on her side, which led to the belief that she was the *Sea King.* But was that proof? Cheers were heard.

By way of proof Berry then offered to read "the deposition given in his presence that day by one of the passengers, a lady, taken by this vessel." Cries of "Order," and "No! No!" rose from the gallery. It was a short deposition, he said, and would not take long to read.

Attorney-General Higinbotham objected to the course now taken. "This was not the proper place or time (cheers) for the honorable member to read a document which might perhaps provoke discussion as to its value and effect," he said. And "If it was considered at all, it should be considered by the government in private."[6]

This debate was reported in *The Argus* on February 2. William Blanchard was aghast that the Premier could claim there was no proof that the two vessels were the same. Joseph Duffett agreed, and they wasted no time in the collection of fresh affidavits. These not only confirmed that *Sea King* and *Shenandoah* were one and the same, but alleged the use of torture as an inducement for captives to enlist.

The following day, February 3, Lillias Nichols signed a second, longer affidavit. This was an extraordinary document which gave much away in regard to her feelings for James Waddell.[7]

Her husband's testimony stated, "she hoisting the Confederate flag after firing the gun. That immediately after the gun was fired the Confederate flag was hoisted on said steamer ..."

By contrast, Mrs. Nichols stated that her vessel "was hove to in consequence of a blank shot fired towards her by a steam ship called the '*Shenandoah*' flying the flag of the so called Confederate States of America." An obvious rift between husband and wife.

Ships of war were required under the Rules of Engagement to show their true colors before opening fire, not afterwards as Nichols claimed. And crew members Edward Nichols,[8] William Scott, William Bruce, Frederick Lindborg and Edward Lingo all signed affidavits which claimed the rebel flag was hoisted after the shot was fired.

What pressure was placed on Mrs. Nichols not to say those seemingly innocuous words? What dramas went on behind the scenes?

A description of the *Delphine*'s capture followed. She then went on to say: "Waddell, the Captain of the said steamer said to me, 'Welcome on board the *Shenandoah*'! and while I was on board the said steamer I was treated with kindness and consideration by the said Captain Waddell."

Here we have a great character reference for the man who destroyed her family's uninsured livelihood, not to mention personal belongings. To put this in perspective, would a landlubber give such testimony on behalf of someone who had burned their uninsured home and business down while the police were gathering evidence for a conviction? Not likely, unless they were in love with the arsonist. Note the apparently superfluous "while I was on board the said steamer." This avoided any idea she was treated with "kindness and consideration" when *not* on board the said steamer.

She goes on to say that the guns and ammunition "were brought out by the said steamer *Laurel* packed in boxes"—common knowledge, and she makes no mention of the two British twelve pounders which were, in fact, on deck when the *Sea King* left London and used in the capture of her own ship. U.S. officials would correctly claim that these "were the principal guns used during the whole of her cruise."[9]

She follows with: "The said Waddell told me while I was on board the said steamer that he left his wife in England ... and that she would most likely hear a great many things to his detriment but not to believe them."

One could get the very definite impression she was saying that not only William Blanchard but also seamen George Bracket and John Colby, fellow natives of Maine, were telling a pack of lies. The same day, Brackett testified that Whittle said, "I will put you in double irons, and put you in the fire-room before the furnace on the coals every night, and I will keep you four months if you don't sign, and make you work every day."

And the day before, Colby had alleged being triced up by the thumbs and being compelled to join the vessel in order to "relieve myself of tortures and punishments."[10] Seaman John Ford of New York testified that "four to six born or naturalized Americans were captured prisoners, and in preference to torture, enlisted."

Mrs. Nichols went on to state that Waddell told her "he picked up his officers, some in Paris, some in Liverpool, and some in London." While rebel officers had been residing in France prior to England, they were in fact "picked up" from Liverpool and London only, thus by adding "Paris" she was eroding Blanchard's claim that the ship was wholly an "English pirate," liable to seizure in a port of the British Empire.

This testimony concludes with her own lively account of the heated exchange when asked to sign a parole:

> the paymaster one Smith called me to read a paper document which I did and found it was a parole not to bear arms or to do anything to the detriment of the Confederate cause and I then said to the said Smith that I was not a prisoner of war and that Captain Waddell had frequently told me so and the said Smith told me I must sign it to get released and in reply I told the said Smith that I did not consider it binding and that if any questions were asked of me I would answer them and he then said "It is a mere matter of form" and was the only way for me obtaining my release and on the said presentation that it was the only way for me to obtain my release I signed the said paper document protesting that I was then under duress.

"I was not a prisoner of war and that Captain Waddell had frequently told me so." Here she is saying Waddell's heart was in the right, place but the SOB had broken his word. She displays an emotional connection with Waddell, on one hand defending him as we have seen, but even now still furious for this travesty being allowed to occur. Thus we have Waddell in the preceding days avoiding providing a list of prisoners which could aggravate her once more, having gone out in a "towering rage" after signing the parole.

Delphine seamen had been put in irons, troublesome seamen had been triced up, and the *Shenandoah* had initially showed English colors. She makes

> 6 That the said Steamer "Shenandoah" arrived in Hobson Bay on the twenty fifth day of January One thousand eight hundred and sixty five and two days previous to her arrival the paymaster one Smith called me to read a paper document which I did and found it was a parole not to bear arms or to do anything to the detriment of the Confederate Cause and I then told the said Smith that I was not a prisoner of War and that Captain Waddell had frequently told me so and the said Smith told me I must sign it to get released and in reply I told the said Smith that I did not consider it binding and that if any questions were asked of me I would answer them and he then said "It is a mere matter of form and was the only way for me to obtain my release and on the said representation that it was the only way for me to obtain my release I signed the said paper document protesting as I was then under duress.
>
> 7 That I am a Native of Searsport, Maine, United States America.
>
> Lillias Lewene Nichols

The final section of the original affidavit signed by Lillias Nichols, February 3, 1865, where she describes her altercation with Paymaster William Smith. "She went out in a towering rage," wrote Charles Lining (Public Record Office Victoria).

no mention of these facts, or anything else harmful to Waddell. Her general information about the ship's background had already been covered in the press.

Mrs. Nichols had certainly "tamed down" since leaving the ship in anger nine days before. Rather than burning the steamer, this affidavit helped keep her afloat. And this, apparently, is what she felt should "be considered by the government in private."

Lillias Nichols was an intelligent and educated woman who knew the law—"I did not consider it binding ... I signed the said paper document protesting that I was then under duress." A document signed under duress is not valid or binding. She knew exactly what she was saying, each word carefully chosen.

William Blanchard must have been displeased to say the least. Who knows what he discovered between February 3 and his "forgetting" this affidavit's existence in a reminder letter to Governor Darling on February 9. He only listed her original affidavit, despite the fact it had been withdrawn.[11]

The relationship between Lilli Nichols and James Waddell was what is now known as the "Stockholm syndrome." Captive and captor had become intimately involved.

10

How Dramatic!

William Blanchard continued to entice men to desert from the *Shenandoah*. But not all those absent were due to desertion, as Dr. Lining recalled:

> Yesterday Mr. Guy, our Gunner, having been refused permission to go on shore, stole one of our boats and so went off. This morning he came alongside, and was told as he had left the ship without permission, he would not be allowed on board, but be considered a deserter. As he would not go when ordered to be put off, Bulloch shoved him down the side ladder, tore his shoulder straps off, and kicked him into the boat. Such is experience![1]

But on February 15 *The Age* published an interesting continuation of this story. The gunner's harsh comments about his former shipmates reached Waddell's ears. He was invited back on board and promptly placed under arrest. "Such is experience!" But Gunner Guy was eventually returned to active duty. He stayed with the *Shenandoah* to see the Civil War's last shot fired, and the last flag lowered.

The throng of visitors to the ship was halted to allow the workmen to proceed uninhibited, and February 4 saw the *Shenandoah* being towed by steam tug towards the Williamstown dockyard.

Midshipman Mason was not impressed. "The old blockhead of a pilot was running about the ship, bawling and giving orders and did not seem to know wheather [*sic*] he was on his head or his heels."

Williamstown had grown from its obscure origins as a fishing village to a place of relative importance. It was a seaport, arsenal and railway terminus combined. The town's business establishments fronted Hobsons Bay, and nestled behind these were numerous bluestone, brick and timber cottages. The railway from Melbourne branched in a rail yard, one line running onto the timber railway pier, and another along a timber wharf over the rocky breakwater pier. It was between these that the tug's towline was cast off and the *Shenandoah* moored.[2]

To affect repairs to the propeller shaft bearings it was necessary for the vessel to be taken into a cradle, then pulled stern first up the metal slipway by chains running to the dockyard engine house. But the *Shenandoah* drew far too much water to be placed on the cradle without considerable lightening. She became the center of much activity as a stevedore's gang came on board and lifted her stores into lighters alongside. These flat-bottomed barges rowed back and forth between ship and shore.

Two days later, as the unloading continued, William Blanchard and solicitor Joseph Duffett met with Minister for Justice Mitchie and Attorney-General Higinbotham at the Crown law-office in Collins Street. They delivered nine affidavits from persons previously on board the *Shenandoah,* and Duffett withdrew Lillias Nichols' original affidavit. This he replaced with the second, longer document.[3] It comes as no surprise that the lawyer did not read aloud her new testimony, but that of George Silvester who had been recruited from the *Laurel* and "deserted" the *Shenandoah* in Melbourne. Perhaps his desertion came as no surprise, as Whittle had written on December 3, "Mr. Minor today reported Silvester for insolence to him, upon examination I found the report correct and I triced the offender up, and kept him there until he swore that he would never be guilty of the offence again."

Silvester went into some detail describing the ship's transition from *Sea King,* flying the British flag, to Confederate *Shenandoah*. The smaller guns already on deck from London were used in the capture of other ships, he claimed, and those crew members who joined the Confederate service "did so in order to avoid punishment."[4]

After much discussion Mitchie and Higinbotham "seemed to admit," reported Blanchard:

> that the *Sea King/Shenandoah* would be liable to seizure and condemnation if found in British waters; but would not admit that she was liable to seizure here, unless she violated the neutrality proclamation while in this port, and if she did they would take immediate action against her.[5]

Without the support of the Crown law-officers, Blanchard decided to abandon his approach to the admiralty court. But it looked as though Mother Nature was going to achieve what the American consul could not. As he attended the Crown law-office, a strong, hot wind blew up from the north. On the opposite side of Hobsons Bay, the *Shenandoah* rocked and strained at her moorings, the dangerous rocks of the breakwater pier only a short distance to leeward, as recalled by Charles Lining:

It had been blowing a stiff gale from the northward all day, so much so, as to make us send out extra hawsers to the body to which we were moored ... I don't think I ever saw the wind blow harder than it did about midnight, it nearly took me from the forecastle.

The wind hit with such a violent fury that the stern lines parted at about 10 o'clock that night. The stern, driven by wind and water, veered towards the breakwater pier, but was saved from striking by a lighter which lay alongside. But then the remaining hawsers also parted, the bow now driven towards the breakwater. All hands were on deck helping to fend the ship off with coils of rope, bales of hay and anything else they could lay their hands on, "the stevedores helping manfully."[6] A pilot and steamer were sent for, but the gale was so fierce they could do nothing, and the cruiser remained stranded.

By next morning the harsh winds had given way to a gentle breeze. The *Shenandoah* was pulled away by a steam tug and anchored in Hobsons Bay midway between Williamstown and Sandridge where she would not be so vulnerable again. Lightermen brought their craft alongside, and the discharging of the stores continued.

Two days later a steamer was used to tow the *Shenandoah* to the slip entrance. An attempt was made to haul her onto the cradle by lines, but after working until the tide fell, it was apparent she was still too low in the water. The heavy propeller was hoisted and removed into a lighter, the stern floating higher "by several inches," according to Lining.

At high tide next day the ship was successfully maneuvered into the cradle, and by 3:00 p.m. "much to our delight," was drawn stern first up the patent slip, her bow pointing out into Hobsons Bay. She was raised to a sufficient level to allow repairs, though water still flanked her sides. The diver's report was found to have been accurate, the lignum vitae bearings to be entirely displaced, and the inner sternpost bracket cracked. It was estimated five working days would be required for repairs to be completed, and Waddell ordered work to commence straight away.

Visitors flocked to see the *Shenandoah* as men worked inside and out, the Confederate naval ensign flapping overhead in the breeze.

This announcement appeared in *The Argus*:

> SHENANDOAH—All parties visiting the Patent Slip, Williamstown, for the purpose of VIEWING the CONFEDERATE SHIP of WAR will be charged 6d. each; the proceeds of which will be distributed among the benevolent institutions of Melbourne.
> E. CHAMBERS and Co., lessees.[7]

With the *Shenandoah* safely on the patent slip, Lieutenant Grimball, Paymaster Smith, Sailing Master Bulloch and Dr. Lining set off, that same evening,

Recaulking the *Shenandoah* as she lay stern-first on the Williamstown patent slip. This only known photograph of the ship was taken from inside the dockyard (Naval History and Heritage Command).

for the gold-boom city of Ballarat.[8] The four officers arrived at 11:00 p.m. to be greeted, like conquering heroes, by a brass band and a crowd of some 2,000 people. A huge arch of flowers crossed the main street. Two wealthy Ballarat citizens—Americans William Eves and C. J. Brayton—had invited Confederate officers there for a "Buccaneer ball" to take place on the evening of February 10, at Craig's Royal Hotel.

Master's Mate Cornelius Hunt claimed to have been with the Ballarat party. But *The Argus* stated: "Four of the *Shenandoah*'s officers arrived in Ballarat by the train which came in at eleven o'clock last evening."[9] Lining's journal lists himself, Smith, Bulloch and Grimball, and this is corroborated by Lieutenant Chew. It seems highly unlikely that a petty officer with Hunt's track record would be a candidate for such a privilege with senior officers. The previous December Whittle had been obliged to report him for "neglect of duty. He has given me an immense amount of trouble in this way: he is either very careless or utterly worthless."[10] Also very careless with the truth, Hunt states the excursion took place several days after it actually occurred. Unable to recall the basic facts, it was a fabrication by a petty officer with delusions of grandeur, "to the manor born," so he claimed.

Ballarat was a prosperous, large and bustling town. Three hundred mines brought gold to the surface from veins deep below. Alluvial deposits had first been discovered in 1851, and by 1865 60,000 people were in residence. No doubt the rebel officers heard the story of Ballarat's Eureka uprising eleven years before. Mounted California Rangers armed with Colt revolvers and Mexican knives had been involved, although not in the stockade when it was stormed.

But if some saw an affinity between the rebellious miners and the Confederacy, at least one evening newspaper did not. It published an editorial castigating the Confederates whose business was "to repeat the worst deeds of the worst days of buccaneering in the Spanish Main, with all the reckless daring and wild uncalculating bravery of that epoch carefully eliminated!" And news of the coming ball with the cream of Ballarat society prompted:

> There are ladies we doubt not who would dance to the music of the groans of sinking seamen, and exhibit their graceful attitudes in the mazy waltz or dashing polka by the light of blazing ships. We shall not quarrel with the taste of such ladies; but we shall reserve our right to form a free opinion of their womanly feelings. They are not such ladies as we should choose for wives for ourselves and our children, nor as

"Bulloch had his flame, a young lady from Geelong, & Smith got his hand squeezed in a most tender way by some fair admirer," Charles Lining wrote. The Ballarat "Buccaneer Ball" was a great success (*Illustrated Melbourne Post*, February 18, 1865).

companions for our daughters. We love genuine womanhood in our heart of hearts. We can all but worship the glorious womanly qualities of such an angel upon earth as FLORENCE NIGHTINGALE. But we would turn away with inexpressible and immeasurable pity from women capable of sentimentally sympathising with piracy (although 'legalised') and smiling lovingly in the faces of 'chartered' buccaneering.[11]

Comments like "chartered buccaneering" and "privateer" indicate many did not understand what the *Shenandoah* actually was—a government owned warship, not a "privateer," as such.

It is not known if this article prompted any ladies to stay away from the Buccaneer Ball, but there were plenty who sentimentally sympathized with "piracy" apparently, as Lining recalled:

The sweetest looking girl in the room, to my idea, was Miss Wallace, the daughter of the Major, although several were rather good looking. Bulloch had his flame, a young lady from Geelong, and Smith had his hand squeezed in a most tender way by some fair admirer—Mrs. Sherrard was another very sweet looking lady and the two handsomest women in the room were two married ladies, one of whom was a splendid looking woman, fair, fat and thirty.[12]

The *Ballarat Star* commented:

The warfare in which this particular ship is engaged, if not the most heroic that can be imagined, is nevertheless perfectly legitimate, inasmuch as it is incident to all warfare that one belligerent should injure and weaken the other by every means in its power to employ, and to represent our visitors of today as pirates and buccaneers is simply to misstate the case. Our part is to treat the *Shenandoah* officers with every attention which hospitality and courtesy can suggest, and reserve a similar reception for the commander and officers of a Federal cruiser, if ever such a ship should visit us while the present struggle endures.

The officers visited some of Ballarat's impressive gold mines. They were taken down, by elevator, four hundred and twenty feet into the very bowels of the earth, "a horrid sensation," wrote Lining, for men accustomed to fresh air and salt water, and "certain death if any accident had happened, for if the fall had not killed us, the chain falling on us certainly would." But their efforts were rewarded with the sight of gold specks that sparkled in the gloom.

Before departure from the gold-boom city they visited the Zoological gardens and Lake Wendouree. Bulloch "got a kiss from the young lady from Geelong," surely the most pleasant way to end an exemplary visit. One of the other ladies who saw them off at the railway station had literary ambitions, recalled Lining. She was "writing a novel and intends to introduce into it the *Shenandoah* and some of its officers. How dramatic!"[13]

Little did Lining realize as he wrote these words that events had been unfolding that could well provide great drama for a novel.

11

I Will Fight for My Ship

A newspaper ad appeared in *The Argus*:

> TRADESMEN.
> Wanted, two or three respectable young men to be generally useful to travel up country, apply personally to Mr Powell, No. 125 Flinders Lane, east, between 9 and 10 or 12 and 1 today.[1]

Mr. George Kennedy, of Drummond Street, Carlton, answered. He was shown to a room where he met Mr. Powell, and he was asked if he knew anything about the working of big guns. Kennedy was a sergeant of Volunteers, and replied that he did. Powell then revealed what "up country" really meant; the North Pacific on board the *Shenandoah*. Over the next few hours Powell and another man kept Kennedy talking and plying him with drinks. At the same time others present agreed to sign up. Taken to the docks, Kennedy finally rejected their offer. He intended to report them to the authorities, he said. This brought an abrupt end to the interview.

For reasons best known to himself, Kennedy did not make his report until shortly after the ship's departure. Warrants were issued for the offenders, but never served.

In the dockyard, meanwhile, repairs and renovations continued beneath the Confederate flag. A new galley was installed below the main deck, as was normal for a warship, and the deckhouse galley would be removed shortly after departure from Melbourne.

John Mason noted the "Mechanics working day and night on the machinery and propeller," and:

> I thought certainly under those circumstances I would be able to write some letters home, but everything was in such confusion, quarters torn to pieces, carpenters and joiners at work everywhere and caulkers banging over one's head all day long and the

consequence was that I could neither read, write letters nor even write up my journal.

Mason and Scales attended St. Peter's, "A very nice little Chapel just behind the Parliament House," and after being shown into a pew by two young ladies:

> The "honest" Melbournites stared at us with gaping mouths and staring eyes, as if they were astonished most amazingly to see two of the "Piratical gentlemen" from the *Shenandoah* in a house of God—perhaps they thought we came there by mistake, thinking it was a billiard saloon or something of that sort.

Others went on shore leave to enjoy "a billiard saloon or something of that sort," but Mr. Blanchard made sure not all returned. Captain Waddell wrote to Police Commissioner Frederick C. Standish with a request to help round up deserters, but the request was denied.[2] Standish, like Superintendent Lyttleton, was "too much a man of pleasure to devote himself seriously to the work of his office," claimed Superintendant Sadleir. Standish was of dubious reputation, rumored to give dinner parties with ladies who dined perfectly nude, "their white skin contrasting with black velvet chairs." Despite Standish's own behavior, he was supplied with the names of those who attended the city's brothels, the patrons vulnerable to blackmail.[3] But it seems unlikely that he would have blackmailed Queen Victoria's son Prince Alfred. The young Royal visited Melbourne as commander of the HMS *Galatea* in 1867. Standish introduced him to "Mother Fraser," when the young man visited her elegant bordello, the best in town. The story goes that Sarah Fraser requested permission to decorate the entrance with the Royal Coat of Arms, thus denoting royal patronage.[4]

In 1880, in the wake of many police failures to capture the notorious Kelly gang, a Royal Commission would find the conduct of Standish "was not characterized either by good judgment or by that zeal for the interests of the public service which should have distinguished an officer in his position."

The police commissioner's reluctance to cooperate with Waddell on this occasion, however, was good judgment as it transpired. The Victorian government and police were to receive enough criticism in future years for their management of upcoming events without rounding up suspected deserters at Waddell's request.[5]

Standish was also well aware of the affidavit of seaman John Williams, who had absconded from the *Shenandoah*:

> I, John Williams, of Boston, Massachusetts, do make oath and say, that I was taken from the barque D. Godfrey, on the seventh day of November, 1864, as a prisoner, and put on board the steamship *Shenandoah*, now in Hobsons Bay; that I served as a cook under compulsion and punishment on board said *Shenandoah*, from the day of my capture until Monday, the sixth day of February, 1865; that on Monday last I

swam ashore to obtain the protection of the United States consul; that when I left the said *Shenandoah*, on Monday last, there were fifteen or twenty men concealed in different parts of said ship, who came on board since said *Shenandoah* arrived in Hobsons Bay, and said men told me they came on board said *Shenandoah* to join ship; that I cooked for said concealed men for several days before I left; that three other men, in the uniform of the crew of the *Shenandoah*, are at work on board said *Shenandoah* in this port; that I can point out all the men who have joined said *Shenandoah* in this port.

JOHN WILLIAMS.[6]

Governor Darling must have wondered why Waddell would conceal fifteen or twenty men on board when the ship was about to be unloaded and placed on the slip. Standish would later state that he believed "there were but very few men stowed away in her," at this time.[7] But Darling minuted the affidavit: "Refer to the Honourable the Attorney-General to take whatever steps are requisite to ensure a strict adherence to her Majesty's Proclamation of Neutrality."

Attorney-General Higinbotham sent a dispatch inviting John Williams to an interview at the Crown law-office on Monday February 13. He assured William Blanchard that if Williams could "give evidence sufficient to support a charge of misdemeanor against any of the persons concealed on board the *Shenandoah*, or against any of the officers of that ship, action would be taken."

Higinbotham also instigated a police inquiry into Williams' allegations, undertaken by First-Class detective D. S. Kennedy. A few days later Kennedy reported that Captain Waddell intended to ship forty hands while in port, preferably foreigners, and Englishmen would have to use assumed names. Boarding house keepers, McGrath, Finlay and O'Brien, were said to be recruiting men who were to receive six pounds per month wages and eight pounds bounty.[8] Superintendent of Detectives, Charles C. Nicolson, forwarded the report marked *urgent* to Police Commissioner Standish. He added a note to the effect that, based on an overheard conversation, sixty men were to be shipped on board the *Eli Whitney*, along with munitions, two or three days before the *Shenandoah*'s departure from Melbourne. The two vessels were to meet outside Port Phillip Heads to affect a transfer of men and stores.[9]

On February 13 Blanchard sent John Williams and another "deserter," Walter Madden, to the office of Crown Solicitor Henry Gurner. Madden would corroborate William's testimony of illegal recruits on board the *Shenandoah*. With them went Samuel Lord, "a loyal American merchant" to see the testimony "was properly taken."[10] But missing from their evidence were the actual names of any of the alleged recruits.

No sooner had they departed than two more seamen arrived at the consulate, Charles Behnck and Herman Whicker, Germans taken from the Searsport vessel *Alina,* the Confederate cruiser's first catch. They had left the *Shenandoah* the day before and now wished to cooperate with the American consul. The $100 cash the consul was rumored to be offering could well have been the inducement.

Blanchard questioned them closely. Not only did they claim four recruits were working in the engine room and galley, but were able to supply the first name of one of them, a cook called "Charley." Blanchard immediately sent the two Germans to the Crown solicitor's office with his clerk, Simeon Gage, then sent a dispatch to Governor Darling. This included affidavits from John Williams, Walter Madden and Thomas Jackson.

At about 5:30 that evening Superintendent Thomas Lyttleton and Inspector Beaver arrived at the dockyard, accompanied by Walter Madden. The seaman had the task of pointing out recruits illegally shipped since the *Shenandoah*'s arrival. Initially Blanchard had objected to Madden's involvement, fearing the rebels would seize him as a deserter, but the police had assured him of their protection.

Captain Waddell was not on board and Lieutenant Grimball, the officer of the deck, met them. Lyttleton told Grimball that he had a warrant for the arrest of a recruit named Charley, and asked for permission to search the ship. Grimball told them he did not have the authority to allow a search, but offered to show them their shipping articles, which they accepted. Charley, of course, was not listed as a member of the crew. Lyttleton then showed the actual warrant to Grimball, which read:

WARRANT IN THE FIRST INSTANCE
To the constable of Williamstown, in the colony of Victoria, and to all other peace officers in the said colony:

Whereas information hath this day been laid before the undersigned one of Her Majesty's justices of the peace in and for the said colony, for that Charley being a natural-born subject of the Queen, did unlawfully, knowingly, and without the leave or license of Her said Majesty for that purpose, and obtained under the sign-manual of Her said Majesty, or signified by order in council or by proclamation of Her said Majesty, enter himself and agree to enlist and enter himself, to serve as a sailor, and to be employed and serve in and on board a certain vessel of war, fitted out, used, equipped, and intended to be used for warlike purposes in the service of a certain foreign power, province, or people, or part of a foreign power or people, exercising and assuming to exercise the powers of government, to wit, the Confederate States of America; and oath being now made before me, substantiating the matter of such information: These are, therefore, to command you, in Her Majesty's name, forthwith to apprehend the said Charley, and bring him before some one or more of Her Majesty's justices of the peace in and for the said colony, to answer to the said information, and to be further dealt with according to law.

Given under my hand and seal this 13th day of February, in the year of out Lord 1865, at Williamstown, in the colony aforesaid.
JOHN WILKINS, J.P.[11]

Grimball told Lyttleton that he should return when the captain was on board. The following morning, February 14, the superintendent returned alone with the warrant. Waddell recalled, "I received him kindly, and he cautiously introduced the subject of his visit." Not "wild and dissipated" today, apparently, Lyttleton said that he had been informed on oath that fifteen to twenty British subjects had joined the ship in Melbourne, and were serving in contravention of the Foreign Enlistment Act. One such person went by the name of Charley, and he had a warrant for his arrest. Waddell denied the existence of Charley, and said, "I pledge you my word of honor as a gentleman that I have not anyone on board, nor have I engaged anyone, nor will I while I am here." Lyttleton replied that he understood the men were actually wearing the Confederate uniform, and asked Waddell if he would allow a search, which was refused. Lyttleton replied that he must try to execute his warrant even if it meant using force. Waddell replied that he would use force to resist, and if overcome would "throw up his ship to the government here and go home and report the matter to his government." It would be more than his commission was worth, Waddell said, to allow a search, and "It is only by courtesy that I have allowed you on board, as I consider a great slight has been put on me by sending you with a warrant." His word should be taken over deserters who had been induced to "annoy" him by the American consul. If he allowed Lyttleton to take one man he may well come back wanting to take fifteen or twenty, and he had been badly treated by the police for refusing to assist in the arrest of deserters.

Just before departure, Lyttleton again asked Waddell if he refused to allow him to look for the man named on the warrant. "Yes, I do refuse," replied Waddell, "and I will fight for my ship rather than allow it."[12]

This was promptly reported back to Governor Darling who was taken aback by Waddell's "very strange language."

At that day's Executive Council Meeting the Crown law-officers expressed doubt regarding the government's right to force the issue. Darling still felt he was bound to make every effort to "prevent a serious violation of the law." He regarded Waddell's refusal as "little according with the principles by which the conduct of a belligerent obtaining aid and assistance in the port of a neutral power should be governed."

At 3:15 p.m. he wrote the following minute:

GOVERNOR'S PROCLAMATION
I hereby direct that, upon receipt of an instruction from the Chief Commissioner of

Police, none of Her Majesty's subjects in this colony will render any aid and assistance to, or perform any work in respect to, the so-called Confederate ship *Shenandoah*, or in launching the same.

C. H. Darling
Governor of Victoria

A delighted William Blanchard must have been very happy to see the governor use the words, "so-called" Confederate ship. At last things seemed to be going his way.

Inspector Beaver, at Williamstown, received a telegram from Police Commissioner Standish. It instructed him to communicate to Mr. Chambers, the lessee of the slip, that British subjects were forbidden from working on the *Shenandoah,* and:

> You will at once proceed with the whole of the police at your disposal to the patent slip, and prevent, at all risks, the launch of said ship. Superintendent Lyttleton and fifty men, also fifty of the military, proceed at once to Williamstown, telegraphing anything that may occur direct to me.[13]

The new Elder gun raft, with her 68-pounder, was moved into position near the slip entrance. Her Majesty's Colonial Sloop *Victoria*, a twin-screw vessel of 580 tons, with three guns, was instructed to raise steam and stand off shore. This vessel was not naval, but was classified as an armed dispatch vessel, manned by the water-police. She had already been in one hostile situation with an American ship, the *General Nowell,* which had departed with writs for debts nailed to her mast. The *Victoria* steamed in pursuit, fired a shot across her bows, and escorted her back to Hobsons Bay.[14]

"A large force of policemen, armed with loaded carbines, took possession of the engine house, thus rendering it impossible to have the vessel let down from the cradle, and the remainder were told off as sentries," reported *The Age* newspaper, February 15, 1865 (Victoria Police Museum).

That evening Lyttleton's force, armed with loaded carbines, arrived in Williamstown by train. They quickly occupied the dockyard and engine house. Workers were cleared from long timber platforms flanking the ship, and a cordon of police took their place.

> I saw policemen on each side of the ship, with guns in their hands, keeping guard over us, while we lay perfectly helpless on the slip, unable to move, or make the slightest resistance in fact helpless. Everybody seemed to share this feeling, even the men, & a general wish to resist was expressed, if possible.
> Charles Lining[15]

Fifty men of the Royal Artillery had also been ordered to Williamstown, but the order was countermanded before their train pulled out. Captain Stewart, however, took command of soldiers already at the Williamstown battery, presumably to open fire if the *Shenandoah* moved into Port Phillip Bay, as high ground prevented the cannon from posing a threat to the slip. A pier battery commanding the slip was not manned, possibly because a shot sent crashing through the ship's rigging could well do more damage to Williamstown than the *Shenandoah*.

> All the militia at Melbourne were turned out under arms, and the artillery companies were sent to the beach to threaten the *Shenandoah*, which was a display of intellectual military weakness I was not prepared to witness.
> James Waddell[16]

In Melbourne, news of the dockyard drama spread like wildfire. People gathered and talked of nothing else. Blanchard immediately traveled to Sandridge and crossed Hobsons Bay to Williamstown by steam ferry.[17]

The Argus of February 15 reported that there had been a collision between Confederate and British arms, and that the *Shenandoah* had been set on fire. But a contrary story also appeared. This stated that the military demonstration was to frustrate a supposed Yankee conspiracy to blow up the ship.

The siege, amid a warlike atmosphere, settled down to a stalemate. The antagonists stared at each other across the bulwarks of the stranded vessel. Colonel Anderson, Major Hall and other military men stayed on duty at the slip during the evening, but from the incessant clanging of hammers on board it was obvious that the repairs were going ahead, governor's proclamation or not.

At 6:00 p.m. Waddell received a communication from Customs Commissioner James Francis. This informed him that in consequence of his refusal to allow the execution of a legal warrant, the facilities hitherto afforded would be suspended. He urged Waddell to withdraw his refusal and allow the search to take place.

It comes as a surprise that the authorities sent the police first and this communication second. The arrival of armed police without explanation could have led to an exchange of gunfire, given Waddell's fighting words and the *Shenandoah*'s status as a man-of-war.

At about 9 o'clock that night four shadowy figures appeared on the deck of the *Shenandoah* in company with a uniformed officer. The tide was in and a small rowboat moved quietly from the darkness of Hobsons Bay into position alongside the ship. At the oars were waterman George Nickle and another man named Clark. Nickle climbed a companion ladder onto the ship. The four men on deck scrambled down into the boat, but at that moment a police craft under the charge of Senior Constable Alexander Minto moved in from the night. Minto asked the men who they were and what had they been doing on board. One replied they had been doing day work. Suddenly a cry of "George" was heard from the officer on deck as Nickle, in a panic, scrambled down into the boat. Both he and Clark pulled strongly on the oars and their boat rounded the *Shenandoah*'s bow out into Hobsons Bay. The police boat gave chase but they lost their prey in the darkness.[18]

Senior Constable Minto, however, a shrewd Scot of 11 years exemplary service, was not about to give up easily.[19] He ordered his craft beached and, in anticipation of the escapees next move, led his men to the railway station. Here he found two on the platform, then the others in the "water-closet." He asked them why they hurried away so quickly and one, James Davidson, said, "Oh, the *Shenandoah* you mean?" and asked Minto what he wanted. Minto replied that there was a gentleman who wanted to see them. The police took the escapees into custody and marched them off to

Superintendent Thomas Lyttleton, described as sometimes "wild and dissipated," was in charge of the police surrounding the *Shenandoah* (Victoria Police Museum).

Superintendent Lyttleton. "You are the very Charley I have been looking for," he said, having recognized James Davidson from descriptions given.[20]

Waddell, meanwhile, had called a council of war in the wardroom; Whittle, Lee, Grimball, Smith and Lining in attendance. They discussed Francis' letter and drafted a reply which was dispatched at about 10:00 p.m.

> I have to inform His Excellency the governor that the execution of the warrant was not refused, as no such person as the one therein specified was on board, but permission to search the vessel was refused. According to all the laws of nations the deck of a vessel of war is considered to represent the majesty of the country whose Flag she flies, and she is free from all executions, except for crimes actually committed on shore, when a demand must be made for the delivery of such person, and the execution of the warrant performed by the police of the ship.

The letter went on to say that a thorough search had been made, and there was no one on board except those who were part of the vessel's original complement. In conclusion, Waddell protested in the name of the Confederate States Government against any action that would detain the *Shenandoah* in port.

At 3:00 a.m. the clangor from below ceased and Waddell was informed that the repairs were complete. He immediately dispatched a message to the slip manager, Enoch Chambers, saying that he wished to launch his ship, and also sent word for a tug to assist. An hour later the steamer *Black Eagle* moved towards the slipway, her towlines ready for use. But her skipper was hailed from a pier by the police, who told him to sheer off. As the *Black Eagle* turned away, Waddell received word from Chambers that the government would not permit his vessel to be launched.

Dawn's first light saw the *Shenandoah* still under siege, as recalled by Charles Lining:

> Got up this morning and still found the "Bobbies" on each side of us, keeping watch and ward over us. Saw by the papers that one of the men, whom we sent out of the ship was the identical "Charlie" whom they were looking for, and that he had been arrested and will be tried for breaking the foreign enlistment act.

The papers were brimming with stories about the night's activities. "Seizure by the Government of the *Shenandoah*," read *The Age*. The story commented on the intense excitement caused by the siege, and then defended the action:

> The steps taken by the government thus far have been in strict accordance with international law. It is entirely a matter of grace on the part of a neutral power to allow a vessel belonging to a belligerent power to enter a port for repairs, or to take in stores. This international privilege is conceded on one hand, and accepted on the other, on the distinct understanding that all the conditions of strict neutrality will

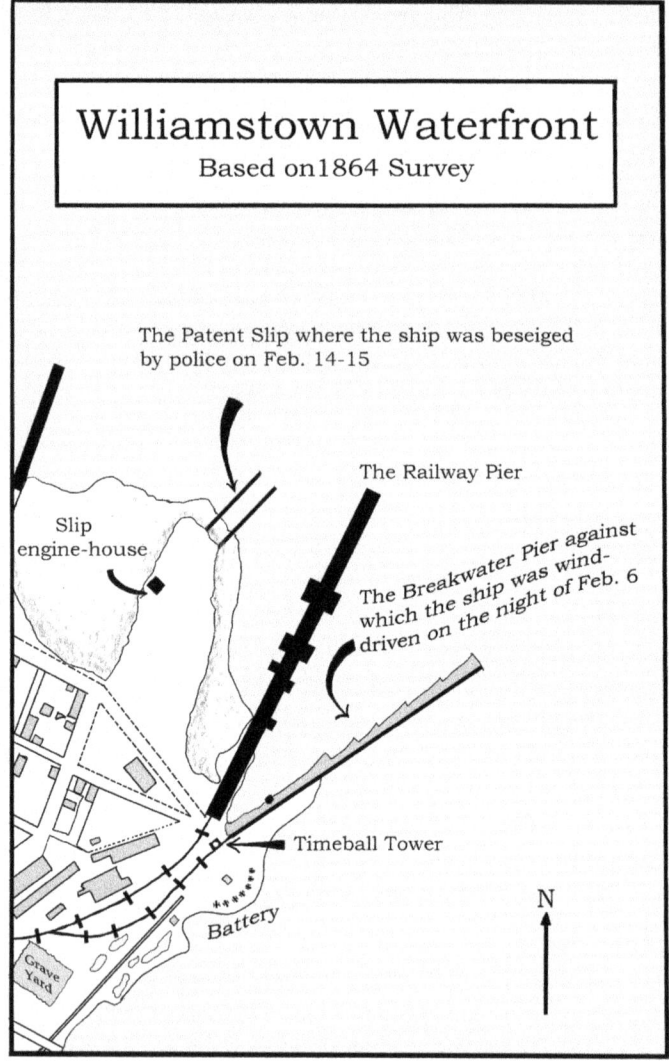

be honourably observed on the part of the belligerent; and that, if anything is done by him which is either a violation of international or municipal law, the privilege that had been granted may be suspended or absolutely withdrawn.

Another article, "Exploits of the *Shenandoah*," gave details of alleged tortures inflicted on captured seamen. Many of these could not be verified as the people concerned had been put ashore on Tristan da Cunha.

The Argus, of course, defended Waddell, but also gave an account of the arrest of the four escapees. This included the notorious Charley.

Confederate States Str. "Shenandoah"
February 14th 1865

Sir,

I am in the receipt of your letter of this date, in which you inform me that you have been directed by His Excellency the Governor to state "that it has been reported to the Government that I have refused to allow the execution on board the "Shenandoah" of a warrant issued upon sworn information according to Law alleging that a British Subject is on board this vessel, who has entered the service of the Confederate States in violation of the British Statute known as the "Foreign Enlistment Act" that it is not consistent with British Law to accept any contrary declaration of facts, whatever respect be due to the person from whom it proceeds as sufficient to justify the non-execution of such warrant; I am then "appealed to to reconsider my determination", and concludes by informing me that "pending a further intimation from me" the permission granted to repair and take supplies is suspended.

Page one of the letter to James Francis in the handwriting of James Waddell denying the existence of a British recruit on board the *Shenandoah* (Public Record Office Victoria).

When William Blanchard read of Charley's arrest, he did not rest on his laurels, but sat down to write an argument of over fifteen hundred words to Governor Darling. This refuted the Crown law-officers assertion that the *Shenandoah* could be liable to seizure in British home waters, but not Australian waters. He evoked numerous persuasive legal arguments: "If a vessel be fitted out against the law in Sydney, must the authorities in Melbourne refuse to move when the offender comes to this port? Are criminals escaping from England not liable to arrest here?"

Shortly after sending this to Governor Darling, Blanchard received a note from Superintendent Lyttleton:

Sir:
I have the honor to inform you that I arrested four men last night, who were making their escape from the ship, *Shenandoah*. They are now in the watchhouse at Williamstown, and I shall feel obliged by your sending Madden or some other person who may possibly be able to identify them.

Blanchard immediately arranged for Madden, Williams, Behnck and Whicker to travel to Williamstown. They returned to the consulate later the same day and informed him that Charley was among the prisoners, and they had been able to put names to the others upon seeing them. The prisoners had been remanded to appear in the Williamstown police court next day.[21]

Blanchard may well have been pleased with this result, but many Melbourne citizens were not. People sent protests to the government and gathered to hear the latest news.

The Herald reported:

Melbourne was in a complete fever of excitement. The business streets of the city were crowded with persons anxious to hear what has been done with the *Shenandoah* and groups of the species gobemouche were to be met at every turn, exchanging their stock of information and occasionally fabricating news on their own account.

Even Superintendent Lyttleton found himself under fire from friends. Annie Dawbin recorded in her diary: "I met Tom and he was telling me all about the *Shenandoah* affair, and seemed quite astonished at my not admiring his proceedings. I think the Victorian government should feel very crest-fallen at the manner in which they have treated that ship."[22]

Posters appeared on walls and fences. A meeting was to be held at the luxurious Criterion Hotel, in Collins Street, at 3:00 p.m. February 15 to protest against the *Shenandoah*'s seizure.

The Herald commented:

The public are already aware of the obstructive and almost menacing attitude which Mr. McCulloch (the Premier) caused the police and a few military to take up in reference to the *Shenandoah* as she lay helpless and out of trim upon the slip at Williamstown. It is really a monstrous scandal that with law officers of the Crown so handsomely remunerated in this colony, our local government should be at the mercy of two such wigblocks as Messrs Mitchie and Higinbotham have shown themselves to be.

The morning after the dockyard's occupation, the two "wigblocks" sat with Governor Darling at an Executive Council meeting along with James Francis. They discussed the inconsistencies between Waddell's statement that Charley was not on board and the recruit's subsequent arrest. Then a letter arrived from Waddell addressed to James Francis:

> Sir:
> I am informed by the manager of the slip upon which the Confederate States steamer *Shenandoah* now rests, that the slip has been seized by authority of His Excellency the Governor, to prevent the launching of the C. S. str. *Shenandoah*, which is of necessity is a seizure of the vessel under my command. I therefore respectfully beg to be informed if this seizure is known to His Excellency, the Governor, and if it meets his approval?[23]

And *The Argus* of February 16, under the heading "The *Shenandoah* Affair," stated:

> The course which Captain Waddell proposed to pursue, in case of a reply to the effect that His Excellency was aware of the seizure, was to regard himself, his officers, and crew as prisoners of the British Government, and if the launch were not permitted before noon on Thursday, to irrevocably haul down his flag, and proceed with his entire company to London by the next mail boat. In truth this gentleman spoke to his friends on shore in somewhat bitter terms. He had thought, he said, that the bleeding condition of his country was an appeal to the generosity of the English.

Governor Darling disagreed with Waddell's interpretation of events. The ship had not been seized, he said, and perhaps Francis should write to Waddell clarifying the precise instructions to the police. But the question was, what do they do now? It was obvious the Foreign Enlistment Act had, in fact, been violated. It was pointed out, however, that as Charley had been arrested, the warrant had been served.

Then another communication arrived, this time from slip manager Enoch Chambers. He informed the meeting that the *Shenandoah* was in an unsafe position on the cradle and should she be damaged by a gale, the "government (having prohibited me from launching the so-called Confederate steamer) must now take that risk, and also be responsible for all expenses etc."

Governor Darling then dispatched this minute:

"One of the four men is the person named in the warrant," protested James Francis. This cartoon depicts the customs commissioner venting his fury against James Waddell (*Melbourne Punch*, **February 20, 1865**).

> The direction issued yesterday, under my hand, suspending the permission to aid and assist the Confederate States vessel *Shenandoah*, in effecting necessary repairs and taking supplies, is hereby cancelled, and the said permission revives and is again in force.
> C. H. Darling, Governor.[24]

The news was received with elation on board the *Shenandoah*. Preparations were made to launch. The propeller had already been hoisted back in position, and the boiler room became a scene of intense activity as preparations were made for flashing up the furnaces. Lines were run out to tugs in Hobsons Bay, and the slip gates were opened.

> The cradle was started, the tugs steamed away and the *Shenandoah* glided into her element, amidst the cheers of a large crowd of friends and the curious assembled on either wharf. We returned the cheers with a good will, at the same time dipping our flag to a few vessels which had extended this salute. How proud we felt as soon as clear of the slip! We were masters of the situation, they were at the mercy of our guns.
> Francis Chew

Tugs towed the vessel to a point midway between Williamstown and Sandridge, and the lines were cast off. Water was drawn into the condensers and the furnaces lit, the boilers slowly heated to avoid distorting cold metal.

Waddell ordered the ship to ride at single anchor only, and steam to be kept up in preparation for a speedy departure should the need arise. The *Shenandoah* bustled with activity as lighters moved to and fro, and vital coal was taken aboard from the recently arrived collier *John Fraser*.

Earlier that afternoon people had begun arriving at the Criterion for the 3:00 p.m. protest meeting. Established by Stuart Moss, an American, at the height of the gold boom, the Criterion was a favorite with the large number of Americans living in the colony. It was favorably compared with luxurious establishments in Europe, featuring a lofty Grecian hall, a hair dressing saloon, a 500 seat theatre, a bath-house with vapor, hot shower-baths, and luxurious rooms. A huge American flag was raised every July 4 and the marble bar was crowded with Americans celebrating Independence Day, which ended with a superb banquet.

The mixed crowd gathering on the sidewalk were greeted with a sign which informed them that, as the *Shenandoah* had been released, the meeting was cancelled. Many had come to vent their feelings, however, and moved inside. Following considerable debate, a resolution was put forward by Mr. Kuilan, barrister-at-law: "That the course adopted by the government in seizing the *Shenandoah* was ill-advised, and likely to be subversive of our friendly relations with neighboring neutral states." This was then carried amid loud cheers.[25]

That night, at about 11 o'clock, a lengthy letter for Waddell arrived on board from James Francis. The customs commissioner rejected Waddell's assertion that the government had seized the *Shenandoah*. The police, he wrote, had been instructed to see that no British subjects rendered aid pending Waddell's reply, and:

> it has been reported by the police that at about ten o'clock last night four men, who had been in concealment on board the *Shenandoah* left the ship, and were arrested immediately after so leaving by the water police ... I am also able to observe that, while at the moment of the despatch of your letter it may be true that these men were not on board the *Shenandoah*, it is beyond question that they were on board at the time it was indicted, your letter having been despatched at five minutes before ten o'clock.
>
> It thus appears plain, as a matter of fact, that the Foreign Enlistment Act was in the course of being evaded.

In his reply Waddell claimed the four men were not part of the ship's complement. They were ordered out of the vessel by the ship's police immediately on their discovery, "which was after my letter had been dispatched informing His Excellency the governor that there were no such persons on board." They were stowaways, Waddell claimed, and he could in no way be accused of an evasion of the Foreign Enlistment Act. He concluded with, "I consider the tone of your letter remarkably disrespectful and insulting to the Government I have the honor to represent, and that I shall take an early opportunity of forwarding it to the Richmond Government."

It is interesting to note Francis and Waddell quibbling over the timing of the letter's departure and Charley leaving the ship. Neither Francis nor Waddell are correct in their assertions. Senior Constable Minto's report gives the time of seeing Nickle's boat alongside at "about 9:00 p.m.," approximately one hour before Waddell dispatched his letter. Minto's report was corroborated by the watchhouse keeper who received the prisoners at 10:00 p.m.[26] This allowed approximately sixty minutes for Charley's departure, capture and internment, which is realistic. Lyttleton erroneously reported the escape time as "about 10 o'clock," thus Francis was misled.

It was impossible for the Victorian authorities to keep on the right side of either party. The ship being surrounded had unnerved Waddell and his supporters, and those who wanted to end her career were now furious because she was riding free on Hobsons Bay.

That evening, during a parliamentary debate, the chief secretary pointed out that as no actual *search* warrant had been issued, Waddell was correct in refusing to allow a search. Only a warrant for the arrest of a British subject had been issued, and this warrant had been served. The law thus satisfied, "they ought not proceed to extremities in this matter."

Blanchard's parliamentary ally, Graham Berry, however, urged the government to take stringent steps to ensure compliance with the neutrality proclamation:

> It is the duty of the government to see that this vessel strictly observes the neutrality proclamation, even though they should have to go on board against the will of the captain or any of his officers. For anything that can be known to the government, unless an examination is allowed, it might be that this vessel is now being fitted up both so as to increase her speed and render her more efficient for war purposes. Now, I again ask, can that be ascertained without an examination? It may be that at the very last minute it may be the duty of the government to stop the vessel.

No doubt, however, the authorities were well aware that the two Whitworth guns at Waddell's command, with an accurate range of three miles, were capable of shelling the very center of Melbourne itself.

The next day, February 16, Police Magistrate Call took testimony from Williams, Behnck, Madden, Whicker and Senior Constable Minto. The policeman stated: "I asked him (Charley) how long he had been on the *Shenandoah*, and (he) said only a few days, and was sorry he could not go in the ship, I would have liked to go in her."²⁷

The Argus said:

> The *Shenandoah* is again afloat on the broad waters of Hobsons Bay, and though not absolutely secure against the possibility of annoyance from the Hon. Commissioner of Customs, it may be presumed that his ingenious spite having exhausted all the expedients at its command, will attempt nothing further against the peace and dignity of Captain Waddell and his officers, and let us add, against the honour of the Queen, deeply compromised as we deem it to have been by the conduct of the McCulloch ministry.

In Hobart, Tasmania, *The Mercury* would soon join the fray:

> Anything more contemptibly crawling and mean could never have been perpetrated by any government. As holding first rank in these colonies, Victoria has degraded the whole of us by this act of hers. The government are craven to the very core ... what do they say to SHERIDAN'S devastation of the Shenandoah valley? There, that worthy Federal general swore that a blade of grass should never more grow, and he commenced his fiendish work by leveling the widow's houses, and turning the orphan children out of doors ... if Captain WADDELL should fit to visit Hobart Town, he will, we can assure him, meet with a hearty welcome.

Waddell, no doubt, agreed with these sentiments. He accused Commissioner James Francis of being "part owner of a shop which dealt with Yankee notions. He fraternized with the Yankee consul in business and politics."²⁸

Francis' supposed business partner, Blanchard, received a communication from the governor's private secretary. This was in response to his latest argument refuting the Crown law-officers' assertions that the *Shenandoah* was not liable to seizure in Australian waters:

> Sir:
> I am directed by His Excellency the Governor to acknowledge your letter of the 15th, and to inform you that His Excellency is advised that it furnished no ground for an alteration to the views respecting the presumed character of the ship *Shenandoah* which have already been communicated to you.

"There are eyes that do not see and ears that do not hear," complained Blanchard, "instead of being assisted by the authorities I was only baffled."²⁹ Baffled or not, the restless Blanchard had to do something, and took an affidavit from Mrs. Nichols' stewardess, Mary Lingo, which added nothing new, except that she had taken a knife and fork engraved *Sea King* from the ship, "which I now produce."³⁰ Mrs. Lingo did not state which flag was flying when the *Shenandoah* opened fire.

Not all publications saw the *Shenandoah* affair in a serious light. The comic *Melbourne Punch* used the cruiser's visit to humorous effect. A full page cartoon showing Francis arresting Charley while Waddell stands nonchalantly by, was accompanied by this verse:

> NEW SONG TO AN OLD TUNE
> Wha wadna fight for Charlie?
> Wha wadna, like a bird,
> Fly to seize the foreign foeman,
> At the noble FRANCIS' word?
>
> CHARLIE took a dram o' rum-
> CHARLIE as a cook enlisted:
> CHARLIE for the *Shenandoah*
> Went to battle, single-fisted.
> Wha wadna fight for CHARLIE-
>
> Scullion midst improper grease,
> Wha wadna fight for CHARLIE
> With some fifty-strong police?[31]

Fictitious letters also appeared under the heading, "CORRESPONDENCE":

Mr. Punch,

Dear Sir

I am in a constant terror lest we should be murdered in our beds by those horrid American pirates. What can our stupid Government be thinking about to let such people come here. So nervous have I become that I have spent a small fortune in sal volatile. As we have only you to look to, do pray do something to protect our hearths and homes.

Yours distractedly,
Tabitha Singlelife

Dearest Mr. Punch,

Oh how very romantic to have a nice dear Pirate come to see us. Do tell me, is he like Lord Byron's Corsair, or Captain CLEMENT CLEVELAND in Scott's novel? Oh! Mr. Punch, I should so much like to go on board, and even be captured, if the Captain is at all good looking. Has that duck of a TENNYSON written anything about Pirates? If so, do please let me know. I have been in such a flutter ever since that darling *Shenandoah* has been here, and though I have been a dozen times to Melbourne on purpose, I cannot catch a glimpse of any of the officers.

Yours devotedly,
Angelina Gushington[32]

Miss Gushington would have been jealous had she known her "captured" fantasy had already been fulfilled by another. This letter was influenced by the popular fiction of the day. In popular Victorian novelettes highwaymen and pirates had the charisma of being romantic figures. While voluptuous heroines sighed, heaved and fainted, tall, handsome piratical heroes came dashing to their rescue. Escapist fiction reveals virile males, sword in hand, thrusting and sweating. This enthralled millions of largely female readers. Daring, gentlemanly pirates captured ships, suggestively flourishing their pistols from the hip, and swooning lady captives fall into their arms. Sea-faring melodramas like *The Boy Pirate; or Life on the Ocean,* 1865, featured pictures of the hero, a dashing young man, fighting off the hordes while the helpless damsel Lilia (of all names) cowers behind him, having been saved from the clutches of the rapacious Harwolf.[33]

Perhaps James Waddell and Lilli Nichols had been well aware that they were turning popular fantasy into reality; a romantic interlude as in a novelette, the romantic connotations urging them on.

The American consul, however, saw nothing either amusing or romantic in the exploits of the *Shenandoah*. As he traveled across Hobsons Bay to Williamstown on a steam ferry to the committal hearing of James "Charley" Davidson and his three companions, he was aghast to see the ship *John Fraser* alongside the rebel cruiser, and coal being swung aboard. Tide Inspector MacFarlane, also on the ferry, told Blanchard the *Shenandoah* was taking on three hundred tons of coal. This, naturally, resulted in a protest to Governor Darling, concluding with, "The *Shenandoah* is a fully-rigged sailing vessel, steam is only auxiliary with her, and I cannot believe your Excellency is aware of the large amount of coal now being furnished said vessel."

At the Williamstown court the four men—James Davidson, Arthur Walmsley, Franklin Glover and William Mackenzie—were brought before the bench, Magistrate Mr. F. Call presiding.

James Davidson, alias Charley, was a twenty-two-year-old native of England, a protestant, and able to read and write. He had previously arrived in the colony from London in the steamer *Great Britain*. It was against him that the prosecution opened its case.

John Williams testified that Charley joined the *Shenandoah*'s crew two days after the vessel's arrival in port, and commenced wearing the uniform of the Confederate navy. Sailing Master Bulloch instructed him to stay out of sight of visitors, and when they came Charley stayed locked in the forecastle.

Davidson was undefended by legal council, and asked Williams if he ever told him his name. Williams replied that when he had once called Davidson "Bill," he had been corrected and told his name was "Charley." Davidson challenged this, asking Williams to "think again." Williams said that Charley had come on board with a beard, and the verbal exchange had taken place when he asked Williams for a razor to shave so as to disguise himself. He shaved, leaving only a mustache and chin tuft, as he appeared in court.

Other witnesses corroborated Williams' story, and Senior Constable Minto gave an account of Charley's flight and capture.[34] When the prosecution's evidence was complete Charley was asked if he had anything to say. Davidson denied having ever given the name Charley and claimed those witnesses who testified otherwise were perjurers.

Mr. Call decided there was sufficient evidence against Davidson for him to stand trial. Franklin Glover next stood before the bench, and offered proof of American citizenship. He was discharged and set free. Evidence was also heard against William Mackenzie and Arthur Walmsley, and they were committed to stand trial alongside Charley at the March sitting of the Supreme Court of Victoria.

Waddell supplied *The Argus* with copies of the complete correspondence between himself and James Francis. The paper attacked the customs commissioner for his handling of the affair and the tone adopted, and supported Waddell's explanation of stowaways having been removed from the vessel.

> The statements made before the magistrate at Williamstown tending to implicate the officers of the *Shenandoah* have met with the most distinct and emphatic denial. If these gentlemen leave our waters feeling embittered against Mr Francis, they will not make the mistake of supposing that he represents the views and feelings of this community.

The *Bendigo Advertiser* took a very different view:

> The proceedings of the Government in the matter of the *Shenandoah* have been little short of imbecile. The Government withdrew all its assistance from the vessel when they had information that there had been an offence, but have again granted it, when there is proof of it. What sort of neutrality is this? How is the imperial Government to justify such conduct to the Federal Government?

How indeed, as would come to light at the Alabama Claims Tribunal seven years later. But letters from Whittle, Grimball, Smith and Bulloch now appeared in *The Argus*. They all declared John Williams to be a liar and drunkard, and insisted Charley had never been a member of the crew.

The tenacious Blanchard did not rest. On February 17 he forwarded to Darling a dispatch which reminded the governor of testimony already in his possession. This showed that "some ten or twenty persons had been shipped on board said vessel while in this harbor." He informed Darling that he had forwarded to the attorney-general testimony regarding the sale of chronometers taken from destroyed vessels, in violation of the port's neutrality, and also the "solemn declaration of Michael Cashmore, a highly respectable citizen." This stated that Cashmore had gone on board the *Shenandoah* and had been hailed below deck by a man in the Confederate uniform, whom he recognized as a former digger from the gold mining town of Scarsdale. Cashmore said he did not know his name, but could readily identify him.[35]

12

I Want My Dinner, Lord

On the morning of February 17 frantic activity continued on board the *Shenandoah*. Carpenters were again at work on alterations not yet complete, and stores were brought onboard. Amidst the din the officers awaited mail and newspapers just arrived on the *Great Britain,* sixty-odd days out from Liverpool.[1] The giant, iron-hulled steamer, the forerunner of the modern ocean liner, traveled under both sail and steam between Britain and Australia carrying thousands of settlers from the old world to the new.

Waddell had written to the attorney-general. He wished to know if British jurisdiction ended three miles from the light houses on Port Phillip Heads, or in a straight line drawn from Point Lonsdale to Cape Schanck. Much to Waddell's irritation, Higinbotham declined to answer without an explanation. He possibly suspected a plot to transfer recruits from another vessel, or plans to attack Yankee shipping outside the Heads.

Waddell was surprised when the brother of John Nicholson (not Mr. Johnston as Waddell recalled),[2] the Scots pilot who had brought them safely into Hobsons Bay, came aboard. He explained that since Waddell's arrival his brother had been unfortunate enough to run a vessel onto a shoal. This accident did his reputation great harm. "If you will let him take your steamer out he will again be on his feet."

Waddell accepted the grateful pilot's services, who informed him that Harbor Master Captain Charles Ferguson—"a miserable apology for a man" who "lent himself" as a spy, claimed Waddell—had asked Nicholson to inform him "if the steamer received any additional force in men after she left her anchorage." Waddell blamed James Francis for this, pressed on by the "miserable wretch" of an American consul.

The "miserable wretch" knew that time was running out, the rebel cruiser due to sail early the following morning. But at about 5 o'clock that evening a last chance to thwart Waddell came his way in the form of a man named Andrew Forbes. He had seen several persons, Forbes claimed, and spoken to one of them, preparing to go aboard the ship *Maria Ross* with the intention of joining the *Shenandoah* beyond local jurisdiction. "Deeming that this information was important and no time was to be lost," Blanchard set out with Forbes and Samuel Lord, the "loyal American merchant," to the Crown law-office in Collins Street.[3]

Crown Solicitor Henry Gurner walked, with his clerk, along the pathway from his office. Upon seeing Blanchard's approach Gurner mumbled something to the clerk who "accosted" the new arrivals. He said there was no one in. Lord said they had to talk to Gurner, and introduced Blanchard to the crown-solicitor. But Gurner ignored Blanchard and, with a haughty air, said that he could not be detained as he was going to have his dinner. Blanchard then said, "I come as the representative of the United States with evidence to lay before you, the crown solicitor, of a large number of men, about violating the neutrality laws of the country."

Gurner replied with a sneer, "I don't care, I want my dinner, and I am going to have it. There are plenty of magistrates around town; go to them."

Lord could see that Blanchard was not happy. "Let us then go and see the attorney-general," he said.

Gurner walked through the gate, and when a short distance away he turned and called out, "My dinner, my dinner! Lord, that is what I want." He turned and walked off.[4]

While Gurner headed for the railway station, Blanchard, Lord and Forbes set off at speed for police headquarters in Russell Street. Finding Police Commissioner Standish not in, they hastened to parliament house in Spring Street, where they were received by the attorney-general, who "patiently" listened. Higinbotham informed them Forbes' testimony would have to be in the shape of an affidavit. Their carriage then clattered to detective headquarters where Superintendent Nicolson informed them that he could do nothing without a warrant, and the metropolitan police magistrate, Mr. Sturt, was the correct official to take Forbes' testimony. They dashed over one mile to Sturt's home in Spencer Street to be told the correct authority was the water police, so Mr. Call, the Williamstown police magistrate, would handle the matter. Mr. Call was four miles distant over Hobsons Bay.

Exasperated, they returned to the consulate. Blanchard took Forbes' testimony, then sent Lord to Higinbotham at Parliament House with the document. By the time he arrived the attorney-general had departed. Blanchard, meanwhile, had set out for Williamstown with Forbes who, upon hearing of their destination, "refused to proceed." He feared bodily harm from his acquaintances, presumably supporters of the Confederate Cause.

But Blanchard could not yet rest. During the night a stevedore named George Washington Robbins told him that boatloads of men with luggage were going directly aboard the *Shenandoah*. Blanchard told Robbins to go to the Williamstown water police, "and that he, as a good subject, was bound to inform them of any violation that came under his notice."[5]

As Robbins rowed across Hobsons Bay to Williamstown, he saw a boat pulled by Jack Riley and another man named Muir. They had about twelve men on board. On the return trip he saw Riley and Muir rowing away from the *Shenandoah*, their boat now empty. Muir and Riley pulled close to Robbins' boat and Muir took hold of it, while Riley lifted an oar as if to strike. Robbins struck back at both men in retaliation. Muir let go and Robbins pulled strongly for the pier, his assailants in pursuit. Unfortunately for Riley and Muir, the attack was witnessed by Superintendent Lyttleton, and they found themselves charged with assault.[6]

It seemed Blanchard had achieved nothing. The word had filtered through, however, and a customs boat pulled alongside the *Maria Ross* in Hobsons Bay early the following morning. But a search revealed only her normal crew on board. The ship was apparently on her way to Portland, Victoria, to pick up a cargo of sheep and six passengers bound ultimately for Camden Harbor.[7]

But the master of the *Maria Ross* seems to have something to do with the *Shenandoah*, as Lining wrote these curious remarks:

> Captain Ross and his endeavours to get us to take some men from him—story about his having his ship searched for men whom the government supposed he was going to take out all of which I firmly wished—this final bidding us adieu in disgust. Is he a true friend of ours, or is he an infernal scoundrel?[8]

Despite the *Maria Ross* being searched a second time at the Heads, Darling wrote a week later to Commodore Wiseman in New Zealand: "The bark *Maria Ross* left Hobsons Bay on the 18 instant, with a considerable number of men on board, having cleared for Camden Harbor, on the north-west coast of Australia. It is confidently believed that these men are intended to augment the crew of the *Shenandoah*."[9]

Stores were hastily placed below the cruiser's decks in great confusion. This chaos caused Whittle considerable aggravation after the *Shenandoah*'s departure. But the furnace fires were kept well stoked, and the boilers hissed steam for a hasty departure. Waddell recalled:

> The afternoon of the 17 of February found the *Shenandoah* at single anchor under steam, and ready for sea. I was visited after dark on that evening by Mr.—, with a request from the proprietors of the *Argus* for a copy of the correspondence which passed between the Government and myself and expressing their intention to publish it if I would give them copies.[10]

Next morning guns were heard booming from Hobsons Bay. Smoke billowed from the *Shenandoah*'s gun ports. But Melbourne was not being shelled as some aboard may have wished. A salute had been fired as she steamed into the broad expanse of Port Phillip Bay. "I received orders from the Captain to call all hands and get under way," recalled Lieutenant Chew. "Soon the cheering notes of the Boatswain's pipe and the clanking of the windlass was heard. About 8:00 a.m. the anchor was hove up and the ship steaming along, with her head pointed seawards." But there was a certain amount of tension on board as Dr. Lining recalled "Large bets had been offered that our ship would never pass through the heads in safety, consequently all our guns were loaded to prepare against any emergency."

Despite the bets offered, the *Shenandoah* steamed safely under the battery on Shortland's Bluff at Port Phillip Heads, then into Bass Strait. This treacherous strip of water dividing the mainland and Tasmania had seen many a fine ship come to grief, but the austere William Whittle must have been pleased being "a hater of port" who had "wished we were out of the place."

The ship's pilot slipped over the side to a waiting boat, and Waddell recalled, "No letters or words of affectionate recollections were to be conveyed through him to those we had left behind ... no regret was entertained for the separation."[11] These words dampened any suspicion of having had a liaison on shore. Lieutenant Chew, with nothing to hide, made a more honest appraisal, "I might venture to add that some of our officers might have left their hearts in the 'Golden Empire.'"

Eighteen men had "deserted" in Melbourne, "under a promise of $100 from the American consul," recalled Waddell. But next day he mysteriously discovered:

> thirty-four young American seamen and eight others of different nationalities, who had smuggled themselves on board the steamer the night before she left Hobsons Bay. The increase placed on our deck seventy-two men, equal to any emergency, all quite homeless and accustomed to a hard life, more in search of adventure and fun than anything else.

The seventy-two on deck did not include officers, and Whittle put the total crew at ninety-six.[12] Midshipman Mason recalled the following precautions prior to sailing:

> four officers and half the ship's crew were kept on watch, the officers had their side arms, loaded revolvers and muskets were at hand for the men and guns cast loose so as to be at the ready in case of any emergency.

All things considered, "smuggled themselves" seems most unlikely. The "stowaways" were actually welcomed on board, all chosen recruits for the Confederate service. According to seaman William Temple only five of the recruits were American, the rest mostly English, Scots, and Irish. And Waddell wrote that, "A sergeant, a corporal and three privates formed the nucleus for a marine guard, and their uniforms were to be made cap-a-pie" (head to foot).[13]

The marine sergeant was George P. Canning, a new recruit, who said he had been wounded at the battle of Shiloh while an aid to Confederate General Polk. Another Canning, Henry, also joined the *Shenandoah* in Melbourne, but would find himself triced up by Whittle, who wished this troublesome Canning "was out of ship."

Melbourne ran hot with rumors of recruits going on board. George Robbins revisited Blanchard saying six boatloads of men had left the wharves during the night and had been taken on deck through the propeller hoist hole.

Seen on board the *Shenandoah* as she got under way was a black boy believed to be the steward of Captain John Blacker of the steamer *Saxonia*. Senior Constable James Whitcher visited this ship and was informed by the chief officer that Captain Blacker had departed the vessel the day before the *Shenandoah* sailed. He had taken with him not only his steward but most of his effects and nautical instruments. The chief officer declined to say where the captain could be found, but commented that he was a first-class pilot for the Australian, India and China seas.[14]

The *Australasian* said, "With all the sympathy we may have had with her, as a representative of those who are gallantly fighting against long odds, she, in the fulfilment of a warlike errand, was most unwelcome in our still peaceful port, and we are unfeignedly glad of her departure." Perhaps the editor of the *Australasian* was now qualifying his enthusiasm for the *Shenandoah*'s visit as it became apparent that Waddell had flouted the Queen's Neutrality Proclamation.

The Age commented:

> Had it not been for the openly manifested sympathy of the Melbourne Club, Captain Waddell had not dared to act as he has. Judges, magistrates, and government officials set at naught the injunction of the Governor and his ministers. What does the Melbourne Club think of its precious associates now?

Higinbotham asked Police Commissioner Standish to investigate the claims of men going aboard the on the night of February 17. On February 21 Detective Kennedy reported a waterman named Riley had taken ten or twelve men out, and Senior Constable Minto had seen three or four boats set out with about twenty men aboard who had not returned. Seven Williamstown residents who had been employed coaling the cruiser had gone on board supposedly to get paid for their work, and they had not returned. A letter had been received from Harry Sutherland, a ship's carpenter, sent back with the pilot, saying he was very comfortable on board. In all, Kennedy estimated that sixty or seventy men had gone on board.

Even Waddell's most vocal supporter, *The Argus,* commented, "It is not to be denied that during Friday night a large number of men found their way on board the *Shenandoah* and did not return on shore again."

Kennedy's report to Standish confirmed the newspaper stories, and the police commissioner forwarded the information to Governor Darling on February 22:

> There can be no doubt that the men referred to in these reports were shipped on board the *Shenandoah*, but I think there would be some difficulty in getting witnesses to make a declaration in support of the statements made to the police, as they are aware they have infringed the law by conveying these men on board the Confederate ship.

Darling reported to London that the *Shenandoah*'s visit will, "probably form the subject of representations to Her Majesty's Government by the Governments of both United States and the Confederate States." We know with hindsight that representations from the Confederate States would not be a problem, the death of that administration only months away, but the United States would certainly be another matter, much to Britain's cost.

The rebel officers' memoirs unanimously insisted that they were innocent of any wrong doing. Lieutenant Chew wrote that the Yankee consul "had enough influence to have a warrant gotten out for one 'Charlie' said to have been shipped. Now this was all humbug, no one had been shipped and no encouragement given to them to come on board."

Considering Charley's arrest, the evidence presented at his subsequent trial, and the findings of the Alabama Claims Tribunal at Geneva, it seems Confederate officers were good at closing ranks and writing "humbug" when the occasion demanded it. The Tribunal president, Count Sclopis, stated he had "no doubt that Captain Waddell did actually enlist men in Melbourne, and afterwards ship them on board the *Shenandoah* for his expedition against the whalers."[15]

The Argus claimed that Waddell had been interested in purchasing the armed steam sloop *Victoria*, if possible, as another Confederate raider. If Waddell actually stated this, it must merely have been bravado on his part as the *Shenandoah*'s stay was expensive enough, her treasury depleted, without such an additional cost.

The paper asked what would have happened had the *Shenandoah* been a warship of a hostile power? Her guns were able to shell the most distant parts of Melbourne:

Fortunately, the Mother Country is at peace with every power whose flag is known upon these waters: but the little episode of the siege of the Williamstown slip brought the Colony to the very verge of hostilities with a foreign naval power.... This is the practical lesson taught us by the visit of the *Shenandoah*, and it is not to be despised.

Those in the corridors of power agreed. State Treasurer George Verdon traveled to Britain to arrange improved naval protection for Melbourne. The result was the loan of the wooden man-of-war, HMS *Nelson* and, to keep pace with the times, 100,000 pounds was allocated towards a twin-turret ironclad warship, the *Cerberus*. She was completed in Britain in September 1870 before sailing to Victoria, and eventually became one of the first vessels of the Royal Australian Navy. After many years of service she ended her days as a rusting breakwater in Half Moon Bay, Black Rock.

William Blanchard's tenure as American consul did not last beyond the following year. He resigned in October 1866 because of "ill health." Samuel Lord and other American citizens had petitioned for his removal because of his "immoral habits" and "improprieties" and considered him "a disgrace" to them and their country.[16]

13

Utterly Worthless

Once in Bass Strait, the *Shenandoah* steamed south-west, then steered south. She disappeared like a ghost ship into a heavy fog at 2:30 p.m. The rebel raider now commenced the most devastating part of a destructive cruise that, in the short term, would create even more contention between the United States and Great Britain than the damage wrought by the *Alabama*.

The fog cleared, and "The moon shone beautifully bright," recalled Waddell, "the atmosphere was clear, cool, and the sky looked more distant than I had ever observed it."

> The Stars that oversprinkle
> All the heavens seemed to twinkle
> With a crystalline delight.[1]

Waddell recalled these soft, soothing lines from Edgar Allan Poe's *The Bells*. But this poem goes further with more poignant lines:

> In a clamorous appealing to the mercy of the fire,
> In a mad expostulation with the deaf and frantic fire,
> Leaping higher, higher, higher,
> With a desperate desire,
> And a resolute endeavor
> Now—now to sit or never,
> By the side of the pale-faced moon.
> Oh, the bells, bells, bells!
> What a tale their terror tells
> Of Despair!

The bells of burning American whalers, perhaps.

And perhaps James Waddell and Lilli Nichols had talked of Poe, the writer who so influenced American literature at this time. The West Point drop-out, who had died twelve years before, was a Boston Yankee by birth, but largely brought up in Richmond, Virginia. Whether he was a Southern or Northern writer was an open question. Perhaps thoughts of Lilli Nichols, lost forever, had influenced Waddell to include *The Bells* in his memoirs, thinking she would read them and recall happy moments they had shared.

"Woe betide all Yankees going to or from the Port of Melbourne whilst she is about,"[2] said the *Hobart Mercury*. Reports appeared of the *Shenandoah* burning American vessels in Bass Strait. But the stories were false, the steamer actually heading through the Tasman Sea towards New Zealand. "Notwithstanding the delay, she was rather ahead of the time for her leaving the coast of Australia,"[3] James Bulloch recalled.

James Waddell, nearly two weeks ahead of schedule, had successfully bluffed his way out of a tight situation with forty-two new recruits on board. Apart from refurbished propeller shaft bearings, the cruiser had been recaulked inside and out, and had other improvements implemented. It would appear the *Shenandoah*'s captain had good reason to be pleased with himself.

But a perplexed William Whittle wrote[4]:

SATURDAY, 25 FEBRUARY 1865.
The cloud which yesterday I represented as hanging over the harmony of the ship still remains. The captain all day has the appearance of a man who has lost all his friends.

SUNDAY, 26 FEBRUARY 1865.
There is a dark cloud which overhangs us and she is not the happy ship she ought to be. Our C is still in the dumps.... Why what is the matter with him? Alas, I fear it is natural. I did not know him before.

MONDAY, 27 FEBRUARY 1865.
W is still in the dumps. He is the weakest man I ever saw in my life. I begin to think he is under the foolish impression that in order to retain the respect of the officers he must cease to have anything to say to them except absolutely on duty.

TUESDAY, 28 FEBRUARY 1865.
W's dumps continue. I am entirely at a loss to understand this man, who I once thought I knew. I will not put my two opinions on paper, but his conduct proves to me he is one of two things. What these things are I withhold.

FRIDAY, 3 MARCH 1865.
W's dumps continue. I do not understand them. I hope I have not been deceived in the man. I shall do all I can with proper maintenance of self-respect to bring about reconciliation. God knows I will hail it with welcome.

The captain is a man who "has the appearance of a man who has lost all his friends." Not all—just the woman he had fallen in love with and, more to the point, Master's Mate Cornelius Hunt had cast a malevolent aura over the cruise. Rated by Lieutenant Whittle as "very careless or utterly worthless," the petty officer from Northampton, Virginia, had previously served on the Confederate vessels *Georgia* and *Rappahannock*. Born circa 1842, the youngest of two boys and a girl to Thomas Hunt and Mary Nelson, he was known by his family as "Neely." His brother Thomas had been killed at Manassas.[5]

Cornelius Hunt knew of the captain's love affair with Lillias Nichols, and Cornelius Hunt was a creature of the lowest order. In his 1867 book *The Shenandoah; or the Last Confederate Cruiser,* Hunt threw out unproven accusations of theft, and Waddell being "unwarranted and ungentlemanly" unlike other officers who had "never committed an act to sully their honor while on board the *Shenandoah*."[6] This book has codes and double meanings within its words. In reference to supposedly telling lies, Hunt wrote that the Nichols "indulged in the most scandalous romance at our expense after they got on shore"[7]—code for "Mrs. Nichols indulged in the most scandalous romance after she got on shore"; a warning to Waddell not to refute the allegations.

One of the puzzles of the Civil War is why James Waddell risked his ship and crew to sail thousands of miles back to Liverpool following the war's conclusion. He needlessly circumnavigated the globe when Yankee cruisers were searching for him. It verged on disobedience of orders and caused "proper horror" amongst his officers. The ship could have been safely and correctly surrendered in Sydney, Australia, on the opposite side of the world. Also baffling are Hunt's theft charges, usually ignored, as they are not understood.

These two quandaries are interwoven.

Master's Mate Hunt became aware of Captain Waddell and Mrs. Nichols seeing each other in Melbourne. Where they met and how often is not known, but being seen together in a secluded grove, or leaving the same quarters in close proximity would have been enough; a most scandalous romance after they got on shore.

Hunt approached Waddell with the accusation. What was in it for him to hold his tongue? On the spur of the moment Waddell fabricated a fund worth thousands awaiting the ship's return to Liverpool in the care of Commander James Bulloch. Mr. Hunt would get more than his fair share, Waddell would see to it. Having no knowledge of the captain's written orders, Hunt believed him, and he looked forward to the promised payout.

How do we know this occurred? Combine "the most scandalous romance" with Waddell returning for "a considerable sum of money which he knew to be lodged in the hands of one of our secret agents at Liverpool,"[8] and we have Cornelius Hunt revealing all. Hunt identified the agent as Mr. J. D. B.—James Dunwoody Bulloch. Waddell's orders recommended the sale of the ship in distant seas with no mention of funds waiting in Liverpool, but Hunt would support the ship's return because in all probability "some provision had been made for us." As will be seen, Hunt was the only crew member under this impression, and this could only have come from the captain.

But what would be the ramifications of an exposé by Cornelius Hunt? Neither side had rules regarding the treatment of female prisoners. The closest was Article 83 of the Confederate Articles of War which called for the dismissal of officers found guilty of "Conduct unbecoming of an officer and a gentleman." And this was open to interpretation. If the Confederacy had kicked out every officer who had an affair, the war would have been lost earlier, and the womanizing General Earl Van Dorn would never have been shot through the head by an irate husband.

But there were other problems to consider. The "piratical" Waddell was now a prominent figure, his name known across the world. Any scandalous revelations would be seized on by the newspapers. Officers like the astute and critical Mr. Whittle, puzzled by Waddell misidentifying the *David Brown,* would make the connection, and with newspapers having reported Waddell's "mistake," others may realize what had transpired. Back home, his wife would be distraught with such revelations.

Master's Mate Cornelius Hunt, the real instigator of the *Shenandoah* circling the globe (Naval History and Heritage Command).

But the one most grievously affected would be Lillias Nichols. Her name would be dragged through the mud by a hypocritical nineteenth-century society which tolerated womanizing men but made outcasts of "fallen" married women. In 1859 Dan Sickles, a philandering politician who had presented his mistress to Queen Victoria, was acquitted after murdering his wife's lover right outside the White House. Sickles went on to become a major-general in the Union army while his wife Teresa was shunned and banned from public life. Her love affair had been spread across the press including her leaked, written confession: "There was a bed in the second story. I did what is usual for a wicked woman to do ... I undressed myself. Mr. Key undressed also."

A picture of the assignation house appeared, and even verse:

What though the world may say,
   "with hands all red
Yon bridegroom steals to a dishonored bed."
And friends, estranged, exclaim on
   every side:
"Behold! Adultery couched with
   Homicide!"

In a letter to the *New York Herald* Sickles lamented his wife's "hopeless future, with its dark possibilities of danger, to which she is prescribed as an outcast."⁹

And it would be especially so for a married woman who had slept with the enemy. Such would be the future of Lilli Nichols.

Teresa Sickles' treatment in the press after her love affair gave a hint of what awaited Lillias Nichols if her liaison with a notorious enemy officer ever came to light (*Harper's Weekly*, March 12, 1859).

14

Fiery Sparks

The *Shenandoah* cleared Bass Strait and moved towards New Zealand in a search for Yankee whalers. But Waddell bypassed the normal chain of command, much to Whittle's fury and frustration:

> Of all the men I ever saw, Waddell has the most provoking way of meddling. I do not know half the time what is being done in the ship, as he gives orders which should either emanate from or pass threw me. His way of doing business does not suit me and it must be stopped.... Nothing but my remembrance of his sweet little wife's last request has prevented me from having an open rupture with him.[1]

Waddell's "sweet little wife's last request" was not to argue with her husband. It seems Anne Waddell knew something of Whittle's innate disposition. "I regret simply on account of his wife whom I regard with the affection of a brother," wrote William Whittle. "The Captain now not only does not *speak* to me privately but does not *even* speak to me officially. I am fearful that the efficiency of the ship will suffer. For my country's sake I trust not."

Waddell was now confronted with having to ignore Bulloch's request that the ship "never return to Europe." And there was little chance of funds waiting for a vessel supposedly sold in the Pacific. Distraught with thoughts of inevitable censure, Waddell attempted to occupy his mind by managing every detail himself, bypassing the normal chain of command; Whittle in particular. The executive officer would be the first approached should the blackmailer realize the promised hush money was a sham. Every day Waddell would wonder if he was about to be confronted by the religious, self-righteous Whittle with charges of infidelity, and also having allowed the *David Brown* to escape. These were allegations he could not deny, and had no excuse for.

But what better way to revive the spirits of a veteran seaman than the challenge of a tempest at sea, an ocean lashed by high winds and cutting rain, as recalled by Waddell:

> I had never in twenty-three years of service seen such a succession of violent squalls; she was enveloped in salt mist and tossed about by an angry sea like a plaything. The machinery operated so well and the ship's preparations in port for contesting with adverse weather were so complete in character that wind and wave seemed bent on testing her strength.[2]

The gales passed, the sea calmed. "We are all in good spirits, and as happy as can be," noted William Whittle on March 11. The contest with the elements had lifted Waddell from his dark thoughts and concerns—for the moment. But the *Shenandoah*'s crew was still relatively sparse for the task at hand. Despite this, Whittle's desire for his own command was ever present: "All hands in fine spirits, but I longing for my little bark."

On March 1 he wrote:

> Oh how I would glory in such a chance. I think I would either call her the Dixie, the Norfolk or the Tudor. God grant me this blessing. Lee, Scales and Bulloch are all applicants for any vessel that I am placed in command of—in fact I could take any of them as all would want to go.[3]

"All would want to go." But what of Whittle's obligation to the *Shenandoah*? He made no secret of his wish to depart, and encouraged others to follow. This included *Alabama* veteran Sailing Master Irvine Bulloch, the ship's best navigator. Whittle justified himself with, "I care not for distinction or anything except as is to be won by doing my duty in my country's call." Despite his duty in his "country's call" being the executive officer of the *Shenandoah*, he extracted from the captain a promise to release him should the opportunity arise.[4]

Nearly three weeks following the *Shenandoah*'s departure, the Nichols family departed Australia. Having joined Lilli's brother on board the *David Brown* in Adelaide, they sailed on March 8, bound for Calleo, Peru. From there they took the steamer *Chile* to Panama where they debarked on May 5, 1865, to continue their journey north to the United States.[5]

Back in Melbourne, on March 17, echoes of the *Shenandoah* reverberated around the austere walls of the Supreme Court of Victoria. James "Charley" Davidson, William Mackenzie and Arthur Walmsley appeared on a charge of attempting to enlist in the Confederate States Navy, the proceedings eagerly followed in the newspapers.

Judge Robert Molesworth, presiding, had just been the center of considerable attention himself. His scandal was another example of what was in store for James Waddell and Lilli Nichols should their liaison be revealed. Justice Molesworth had been on the other side of the Supreme Court bench with a "judicial separation," an actual divorce being rare at the time, with only eight granted in Victoria during 1864. Molesworth's wife, Henrietta, seventeen years his junior, had petitioned for separation with his financial support on the grounds of cruelty. He had countered this with an accusation of adultery which resulted in the birth of an illegitimate child. In November 1864 the jury had rejected the wife's allegation of cruelty, but the separation was granted on the grounds of her adultery. *The Argus* was not impressed with the "un-English" odor of "this filthy tale of an ill marriage" and felt Justice Molesworth was "flinty hearted" wishing to deprive his wife of an income and see her "on the streets.... His name will be a by-word and a reproach, and people, instead of venerating him as a judge, will loathe him as a man. He should resign." As with Teresa Sickles, however, Henrietta would be marginalized while Molesworth would remain a pillar of society. But perhaps Henrietta did not help her own cause, as Annie Dawbin noted in her diary on June 17, five months before the case had been decided:

> Mrs Molesworth, the judge's unfortunate wife: she is a tall, stout, rather brazen-faced woman, with fair hair, and prominent pale blue eyes: she considers herself handsome, tells of innumerable conquests, and talks, oh! so incessantly! Poor thing; she is to be pitied if only on account of her children not even speaking to her.[6]

The eminent lawyer Mr. Butler Coles Aspinall appeared before Justice Molesworth to defend James Davidson, alias Charley. Aspinall, also a politician and journalist, was noted for his humorous wit and "His deep gruff voice set people laughing before his jokes were uttered."

On another occasion Aspinall appeared before Judge Redmond Barry (of the Mrs. Scott scandal). He made a point of annoying his prosecuting opponent by calling him "Mr. Smith," who objected, pointing out that his name was "Smyth." Judge Barry, when addressing the jury, had cause to use the word "myth," when Aspinall, in "his deepest and gravest voice, begged His Honor's pardon, but would he, out of respect for his learned friend," be pleased to pronounce "myth" as *myth*? "His Honor managed to maintain his gravity notwithstanding the roar of laughter that filled the court."[7]

The newspapers reported the Crown case against "Charley":

> Mr. Aspinall in addressing the jury for the defence, made a humorous speech, which excited great laughter, characterising this as the most ridiculous State prosecution ever brought before twelve men. Superintendent Lyttleton had marched up with fifty men, supported by Mr Verdon and all the artillery, for the purpose of capturing a cook; but, like the king of France, they all marched down again, for having captured the vessel on the slip, they dropped it like a hot potato. The Crown would have us believe the country was about to be plunged into war, all because this man had cooked a few chops for the officers of the ship while on the patent slip. What kind of case

was this to make a State trial of? Did the jury believe that Her Majesty was trembling upon her throne because Charley was cooking a few sausages?[8]

The man who had fried a few potatoes stood before them, continued Aspinall, "a state prisoner, awaiting his fate," having apparently subverted the British Constitution, while Mr. Langlands, who repaired the ship, thus readying her for war, was allowed to go scot-free.

The lawyer challenged the court to prove there was actually a war. Where was the Crown's proof, he wanted to know, that the Civil War was being fought? And where was the proof that the vessel was actually a Confederate ship? Evidence had been heard that she sailed under more than one flag. What right did the prosecution have to decide the Confederate flag was the correct one? Aspinall went on to say that Charley's departure from the *Shenandoah* was proof that he was *not* serving on her, yet his departure was the Crown's evidence that he was guilty. And where was the proof of the Queen's Proclamation? An authenticated copy must be produced.

Despite the spirited defense, Davidson was found guilty as charged, and Mackenzie pleaded guilty. As they had both been in custody for over one month, the Crown did not advocate severe penalties, and they received a nominal sentence of ten days imprisonment.

Then Arthur Walmsley stood before the bench. Only seventeen, he looked a few years younger, scarcely five feet tall. This caused considerable laughter, Justice Molesworth included. Wamsley had also been in custody for a month and was discharged at Higinbotham's request. "The youth, who did not seem to relish the joke, rushed quickly out of court to escape the laughter."

The *Shenandoah* surged northward through hot weather and calm seas. Whittle, who had wished to be "once more at sea" was still not happy. He complained of "the monotony which is indeed becoming terribly great."

And the lack of challenge through capturing Yankees or rough weather allowed the ever present shadow of Cornelius Hunt to darken Waddell's spirits once more. He became overly anxious about the performance of his young officers. "He takes an exaggerated view of his troubles which are far fewer than others," wrote William Whittle, in ignorance of what Waddell's real troubles were:

> He was so blue and melancholy I pitied him ... I never saw any man feel it necessary to remain on deck so much. He complains of never getting sleep enough, and it really seems to me that he gets more sleep than any man in the ship, but in his own mind he is a perfect martyr.[9]

Little did Whittle realize the torments the captain was going through, a man alone in his cabin not necessarily asleep, but tossing and turning under the threat of malicious disclosures by Cornelius Hunt.

But Whittle had worries of his own: "Surrounded as we are by rocks, islands and doubtful shoals ... if by misfortune we should run ashore and be wrecked ... we might be eaten by cannibals. This would be a terrible fate." Whittle went on to write that he may render himself "uneatable" by covering himself with black coal tar and curling his hair.

Whittle wrote that he "never saw a better set" of officers, but only three days later: "The day commenced as clear as a bell and I felt sure we were done with rain, but with the watch of Chew the unfortunate it clouded up and very soon commenced to rain in torrents as usual." "Chew the unfortunate," the man Waddell had replaced with Master's Mate John Minor that stormy December night.

The *Shenandoah* reached Drummond Island on March 23. Here they found no whalers, only a few natives in canoes. "They were very much frightened" by the ship's guns, wrote Whittle. In 1841, marines and sailors from the USS *Peacock* had gone ashore in a search for shipwreck survivors. A battle had ensued which resulted in burned villages and natives being killed. Even if the natives in canoes had not been present at the time, these events would be part of their folklore. Little wonder they were "very much frightened" by their guns.

The *Shenandoah* steamed on and a few days later encountered a Honolulu schooner trading in tortoise shell. From her skipper Waddell received valuable information regarding the movement of American whalers. Favorable trade winds sprang up, sail was hoisted, and the cruiser moved quickly to Ascension (Pohnpei) Island, part of the Caroline Group. On April 1 land was sighted and as they approached sails came into view. The prospect of action restored Waddell's morale, but the shadow of Hunt a malignant presence never far from his mind.

As the *Shenandoah* moved slowly along the coast the lookout sighted a small boat coming out to greet them. A Yorkshire man named Thomas Harrocke came aboard with an interesting tale to tell. A convict, he had escaped from Sydney and made his way to the island thirteen years before where he married a native woman. More important to Waddell, Harrocke offered his services as a pilot and interpreter, and told of four whalers anchored in Lohd Harbor; three American and one from Oahu of the Sandwich (Hawaiian) Island group, not yet a territory of the United States.

Harrocke no doubt took all due care as "Fearing some treachery on the Pilot's part we warned him that if he got us aground, death would be his instant portion," recalled William Whittle.

Once securely moored in fifteen fathoms, under British colors, Waddell dispatched four boats to take possession of the whalers, the crews oblivious to their fate. The Confederate flag was hoisted, and the boom of a gun echoed around the harbor. "This signal," recalled Waddell, "aroused all the surrounding countryside. The natives along the shore who were gazing at the vessel sought shelter in the bushes, and the American whalers hauled down their flags." The prize crews, pistols and cutlasses at the ready, came alongside the vessels, boarded, and took possession. The ship's officers were taken back to the *Shenandoah*, and "not knowing the feelings of the natives we withdrew our men," recalled Whittle. Canoes came alongside and Harrocke said the Confederates would be "heartily received" by the natives.

An invitation to the King of the Lohd Harbor tribe to visit the *Shenandoah* was sent the following morning. The natives had been frightened by the boom of his gun, so perhaps Waddell felt a party armed with firearms and cutlasses arriving on shore would be seen as a threat and not so "heartily received." One would expect a senior officer to lead an important diplomatic mission ashore, so why did the captain choose instead an "utterly worthless" master's mate to take "six good men well armed" and the pilot as interpreter?

> As we neared the beach a crowd of natives rushed down to meet us, armed with stones, which they hurl almost with the precision of a rifle-ball, and swords manufactured from shark's teeth, the edges of which are dipped in a subtle poison that leaves certain death in any wounds they inflict.

Harrocke calmed the situation, and Cornelius Hunt was taken inland to meet "His Cannibal Majesty" despite "two or three ferocious looking villains who eyed us askance, and I have no doubt considered what sort of roasts or barbecues we would probably make."[10]

Hunt was shown into the king's bamboo court:

> In it were assembled some three hundred of the most hideous looking human beings it was ever my fortune to behold. The most of them were armed like those we had met on the beach with stones, and bone swords, though a few of them had spears, and I am free to confess to feeling anything but comfortable, as I stood in the presence of that fiendish multitude, with no attendant save the demoralized Englishman who had degenerated into a worse savage than any of them. But it was too late to turn back.

"His ugly person," as Hunt described the king, accepted the invitation. They came offshore in the captain's gig accompanied by the magnificent spectacle of "a perfect cloud of canoes," recalled John Mason. Waddell and his officers greeted their visitors in full uniform, swords by their sides. With Harrocke translating, a conference was held with the natives sitting on the deck. His Majesty was presented with captured muskets and a sword. He had never worn such a weapon before, and became entangled as he descended the ship's ladder to the engine room. He unbuckled the problem and placed it in the charge of the hereditary prince. "The machinery excited his surprise and amused him, and his expression of wonder was communicated by a cluck of the tongue which his retinue echoed."

The seamen were allowed on shore in limited numbers. Amidst the palms and natives they could enjoy *gowra*, the local intoxicating beverage, and the favors of the local women. Both could be obtained with a colored handkerchief or a plug of tobacco for the men folk. "I dare say they enjoyed themselves," recalled Cornelius Hunt.

"In terms of virtue, there is none," John Mason wrote in his journal, coyly writing in French. "It is a great honor to be the mistress of a white man. The young girls since the age of eight are equally mischievous. One must say that it is this way for the entire island, it is their religion."[11]

The captain of the whaler flying the Oahu flag was unable to provide Waddell with final proof that she was not, in fact, American. As "She bore the name of *Harvest* of New Bedford," Waddell decided to burn her along with the other vessels—*Pearl*, *Edward Cary* and *Hector*—something that would have ramifications in years to come.

One hundred and thirty prisoners were put ashore. At the king's suggestion, the captured vessels were run onto shoals in the harbor, then canoes moved in as recalled by Waddell:

> Every movable plank, spar and bulkhead was soon taken on shore for flooring purposes, and the sails were removed from yards and sailroom for tents and to be converted into sails for their canoes, and as the consuming vessels floating higher, the canoes approached the sides and peeled the copper from their bottoms. The natives placed a value on that metal, and I was informed some of it would be used for pointing spears and arrows.

And as regards the natives:

> They are delicate in form, high cheek bones, flat noses, small feet and hands. The women are decidedly homely, but graceful. His Majesty made me a present of the royal princess, which gift I was rude enough to decline; I told him I was married.[12]

Even if the married captain had found the princess attractive and "queen like," there was little chance of him accepting such a gift with Cornelius Hunt watching from the shadows.

Flames and smoke billowed skywards as the vessels were put to the torch.

Waddell was elated. Besides destroying the whalers, he had captured detailed charts of the Yankee whaling grounds. He now held the key to the navigation of all the Pacific Islands, the Okhotsk and Bering Seas, the Arctic Ocean and the location of the great Arctic whaling fleet of New England.

But disturbing rumors were heard, as recalled by Midshipman Mason:

We heard from Ascension, news via California that Fort Fisher on the Cape Fear River was captured. Wilmington would soon fall, that Savannah and Charleston were taken &c. but I cannot believe all these reports for that reason I did not look at the papers, nor read any of the "official" reports. May it all be a falsehood.

But, unfortunately for the rebel seamen, the "falsehood" did not go far enough. On April 9, as the *Shenandoah* lay in tranquil waters in Lohd Harbor, General Robert E. Lee rode up to the McLean household in the village of Appomattox Courthouse. In full-dress uniform, complete with sash and jeweled sword, he waited in the living room, "dying a thousand deaths." General Ulysses S. Grant arrived shortly afterwards, straight from the field, in mud-spattered field uniform. They shook hands and proceeded to negotiate the surrender of the ragged remains of the Army of Northern Virginia.[13] The Confederates had been pursued from the trenches of Petersburg, Richmond had fallen, and an attempt to break through the Union army had failed that same morning.

Other rebel troops were still in the field with President Jefferson Davis urging them to fight on, but Northern bells chimed at news of the great victory. Washington D.C. shook to a five hundred-gun salute, the war virtually at an end.

Oblivious, the *Shenandoah*'s anchors were raised on April 13 and she steamed away with two dead chickens and a dozen coconuts on board as presents from the king for Jefferson Davis. She would not touch land again for seven months. A ten knot breeze filled the cruiser's sails that evening, the "smoke stack close-reefed" and "screw hoisted."

On April 16 Midshipman Mason wrote:

> Our ship is in beautiful trim now and runs along well with these N.E. trades at a rate of eight knots per hour with foresail, fore and main topsails and single reefed mizen topsail; for four or five days now we have not touched a brace; the breeze is magnificent and I am persuaded with royal and studdingsails set we could be making thirteen and fourteen knots with ease.

Some on board criticized Waddell for running under short canvas. This was interpreted as needless trepidation, in their minds speed the only thing that counted. But the fast *Shenandoah* continually ran ahead of schedule. Due to the lack of whalers around New Zealand, Waddell headed north in search of prey, which placed the ship even further ahead. The rebels were not required "to intercept the North Pacific whaling fleet bound for Oahu with the products of the summer cruise" until "about the 15th of September." Ultimately they would strike the northern whalers still at work in May and June, thus Waddell's lack of haste.[14]

The *Daily Alta California* of April 5 had speculated on a visit to the American west coast by the notorious *Shenandoah*. The writer had little faith in some of the protection afforded them:

> The old sloops of war, *St Mary's* and *Cyanne*, are either of them capable of taking care of themselves, so far as the *Shenandoah* is concerned, but, being unable to travel faster than a mud-waggon, are unable to pursue a steamer under any circumstances, or assist in defending our community from her attacks.

Not worried about "mud-waggons," Waddell recalled:

> In all the course of my sea life I never enjoyed more charming weather; the sun shone with splendid brilliancy, and the moon shed her particular luster from a dark-blue vaulted sky, while the vast mirror below reflected each heavenly body and flashed with sprightliness as the great ocean plow tore the waters asunder, and for ten consecutive days I would stand for hours on her deck gazing on that wonderful creation, that deep liquid world.

Waddell took advantage of the ideal conditions to train his young officers, as recalled by Midshipman Mason on April 21:

> The captain made me wear the ship this evening, which I did in rather a bungling manner but it was my first attempt & as there was little or no wind it was rather a difficult job to get the old ship around. I have now tacked "the packet" once and worn her once and the next time I hope to do better.

The Pacific winds could shift in an instant, sending men into the rigging to shorten sail, as Whittle recorded:

> At 2:00 p.m. we had a sudden shift of wind to the Nd. reduced sail to close reefed fore and main topsails and the fore staysail. Set the Main stay sail. Hauled up on the port tack. At 4 it was blowing furiously. The lee Main topsail sheet carried away and the sail blew all to pieces ... got the ship before the wind and ran before a furious gale and terrific sea ... oh how I wish old father Neptune would let us alone.

And Waddell recalled:

> Squall after squall struck her, flash after flash surrounded her, and the thunder rolled in her wake, while every timber retorted to the shaking of the heavens. It was a typhoon; the ocean was as white as the snowdrift. Such was the violence of the wind that a new maintopsail, close-reefed, was blown into shreds.

Little wonder "every timber retorted to the shaking of the heavens." As the ship ploughed through "a tremendous sea" on May 10, President Jefferson Davis was overtaken by Union forces in Georgia, the last hope of the South captured with his entourage. He was sent north to a prison cell in Fortress Monroe, Hampton, Virginia.

James Waddell may well have marveled "on that wonderful creation, that deep liquid world," but William Whittle did not seem to share such feelings. The executive officer, while astute and capable, had a fear of being "eaten by cannibals" as well as a "wholesome terror of ice." He was also a "hater of port," and despised the "terrible, terrible, monotony!" of smooth sailing.

And furthermore:

> I do detest a gale. I have seen too many not to appreciate them. Oh how much would I not give to hear from our dear ones. God protect them. I wonder if I will ever see my darling Pattie ... I am as certain that a merciful God has our holy cause in his own hands as that I am here—and I must devoutly say "Thy will, Oh Lord, not mine, be done."[15]

Unfortunately for Whittle, both "holy cause" and "darling Pattie" would soon disappear from his life. The considerable sacrifices of a cruising sailor were not tenable by some. These included an acceptance of the ocean's various moods, and being out of reach of loved ones for months, or perhaps even years at a time. Even before the voyage Whittle had penned his "great reluctance" to leave home for overseas service in time of war; strange sentiments for one whose chosen profession was the navy. Perhaps following in the footsteps of his naval officer father had not been wise. Based on his own jottings, Whittle would have been a happier man in charge of a coastal steamer, or perhaps an Episcopalian village church, his loved ones safely close by.

The tempest passed, the wind abated. The *Shenandoah*'s bow soon scattered a plume of salt spray as she moved northward into colder climes and the danger of ice.

On May 21 the cruiser moved into the Sea of Okhotsk, the great gulf on the shores of Siberia and Kamchatka. On May 27, she skirted an extensive field of flow ice and sails were seen. The master of the Yankee whaler *Abigail* mistook the cruiser for a Russian supply ship and was astonished to once more hear the boom of a rebel gun. "You are more fortunate in picking up Confederate cruisers than whales," complained one of the crew to the unfortunate skipper, Ebenezer Nye. He had lost his previous ship to the *Alabama*.

The *Shenandoah* lay alongside for two days. Her cargo was transferred including an ample supply of spirits which many crewmen imbibed to ward off the cold. They got rip-roaring drunk in the process. "Put all in irons, gagged and triced up, right and left. I never had such a time," complained Whittle. Even Lieutenant Scales found himself placed on suspension for bringing liquor on board. But a metal stove amongst the booty was a welcome addition, as the frigid cabin till now had been without heating.

The *Abigail* was put to the torch. Her second mate, Thomas Manning of Baltimore, was one of those who joined the *Shenandoah*'s crew. He offered to act as pilot in the search for American whalers, and was made a corporal of marines. Master's Mate Hunt claimed that Manning was "the most disreputable of men." But the finicky Whittle had other ideas: "I was glad to have him ... he is a fine looking fellow."[16] Hunt's opinion was no doubt influenced by the newcomer soon being promoted to his own rank of master's mate.

The next few days brought clear weather and calm seas. But then the inevitable gale struck. Waddell brought the vessel around into the wind, "head to sea."

> The wind was bitter cold, turning the rain into ice and forming a crust wherever it fell. The braces, blocks, yards, sails and all other running rigging was thoroughly coated in ice from a half to 2 inches thick, so that it was impossible to use the braces.... Icicles of great length and size hung from every portion of the vessel and her rigging.

The seamen were treated to a wondrous sight of enchantment. The *Shenandoah* appeared as an ice ship like some fantasy from a children's picture book. "When the sunlight burst upon the fairy ship she sparkled from deck to truck as if a diadem had been thrown about her, awakening exclamations of enthusiastic delight."

And nothing was wasted on board the *Shenandoah*:

> The large icicles falling from aloft rendered the deck dangerous to move upon, and it soon became covered with clear, beautiful ice. The water tanks, casks and every vessel capable of filling it were filled. A supply of several thousand gallons of drinking water was not unacceptable, for it saved the consumption of fuel in condensing.

Waddell knew how to use the ice to advantage when the weather conditions made that demand. Driven by a gale, he maneuvered the ship through an opening to where the water was "smooth as a mill pond," protected by the ice floe. "Our dreaded enemy was now become our best friend, the fury of the sea was expended on it and not against the *Shenandoah*. It was a breakwater for the ship."

Even in these freezing conditions Whittle clung to hopes of independent glory. He suggested they catch one vessel and send her into waters with dangerous ice floes abundant. "If this vessel be fitted out as I most earnestly do and will recommend, I will try and command her."

But Waddell, anxious at finding the menacing ice closing in, wisely moved southwards. He correctly believed that many whalers awaited their pleasure in the Bering Sea. "The scene was cold," he recalled, "the mercury several degrees below zero, the ice varied in thickness from 15 to 30 feet and, although not very firm, was sufficiently so to injure the *Shenandoah* if we were not very careful."

Waddell praised Dr. Lining and his assistant surgeon, McNulty, for the care they lavished on the crew. No serious illness broke out below decks despite the frigid conditions.[17]

But perhaps the lack of prizes caused some irritation amongst the crew. While the master's mates were at mess a dispute broke out between Lodge Colton and John Minor. Colton challenged Minor to a duel with swords and, to the astonishment of all, flashing blades were drawn. The two master's mates circled each other warily, neither seeming determined to draw blood. "I don't think I ever saw a more absurd spectacle in all my life," recalled Midshipman Mason. "Here were these two fellows with their naked weapons crossed. And one of them was scared and the other afraid." The exciting duel faded as the combatants withdrew, discretion the better part of valor, apparently.

No doubt Lodge Colton would have been gratified to hear of Minor's death in December, 1866. He returned to Australia following the war only to disappear on a fishing trip along with the gold watch presented by *Shenandoah* officers. Four others died with him, the remains of their shattered whale boat all that was found after a storm.[18]

Driven by a cracking southwester, the cruiser left the Sea of Okhotsk and entered the North Pacific on June 14. She made her way north until becalmed two days later in dense fog near Copper Island. Sails furled and under steam, she entered the Bering Sea. On June 17 Whittle recalled, "This morning I got up at 6:30 as usual. What with the noise of the propeller and the anxiety felt as to the true position of the ship, I slept very little and awoke feeling fatigued rather than refreshed by my last night's restlessness."

On June 21 floating blubber betrayed the presence of whalers, and over the next few days there were shouts of jubilation as sails were seen. The *William Thompson*, *Euphrates* and *Milo* came under the *Shenandoah*'s guns and hauled down their flags. On June 22 two live shells shot across the water in the capture of the fleeing *Sophia Thornton*. She was boarded and instructed to follow as the cruiser gave chase to another fleeing ship, the *Jireh Swift*. The last live shell of the Civil War was fired from the *Shenandoah*'s starboard Whitworth by Lieutenant Grimball at 5:55 p.m.[19] The *Jireh Swift*'s master, Captain Williams, wisely hove to and accepted the inevitable.

But any triumph was quickly dampened. The rebels received first word of Lincoln's assassination and General Lee's surrender. This shattering news came from Captain Smith of the *William Thompson*. The loss of Lee's command was a crushing blow barely acceptable to the rebel seamen. "I do not believe a single word," claimed Whittle. But his journal revealed the deeper truth as he once again pondered the state of his family:

> I have almost gone mad over the helpless and destitute condition in which they must be placed. In my anguish I sought consolation in reading my little prayer book which my dear Pattie gave me, when my eyes fell on these words. "I have been young, and am now old: and never yet saw the righteous forsaken, nor his seed begging their

bread." God help us I pray. Oh! God protect us.

The *Milo* was ransomed to take prisoners, but the other ships became burning infernos. A hot, red glow lit up the cold northern sky.

On June 23 the brig *Susan Abigail*, out from San Francisco, was captured. Her skipper, Moses Tucker, clad in heavy furs, had the appearance of an indignant polar bear. He begged Waddell to spare his ship, but when this failed tried bribery, with no result. His vessel traded furs, gold quartz and whale bone with the Indians for "bright articles of apparel, tobacco and whiskey." But trade goods were not all she carried. On board were San Francisco newspapers which confirmed news of Lee's surrender and Abraham Lincoln's death. "I trust that none of our people had anything to do with it," lamented Whittle. "If he had been killed in battle 'twould have been the fate of war; but not to be assassinated."[20]

Lieutenant John Grimball fired the last live shell of the American Civil War while in pursuit of the fleeing vessel *Jireh Swift*, June 22, 1865 (Archer Memorial Library, American Civil War Round Table of Australia).

But news of the removal of the Confederate capital to Danville was also reported. President Davis announced that, "The war would be carried on with renewed vigor," and exhorted the people of the South to bear up heroically under their calamities. "There's life in the old land yet," wrote Whittle. "Let us live with hope. The God of Jacob is our refuge. Oh let us trust in him." The *Susan Abigail* joined her sisters amidst cinders and flames.

Two days later Cornelius Hunt and Captain's Clerk John Blacker were placed under arrest for fighting. "Upon investigation, the former was restored to duty," wrote William Whittle.[21] Perhaps Blacker, with no liking for Hunt himself, had picked a fight, also aware of his captain's antipathy towards the master's mate.

June 26 was another bad day for the New England whaling fleet. Six more vessels came under the *Shenandoah*'s guns. Over two hundred prisoners were towed behind the cruiser in open boats to the *General Pike*, ransomed to relieve the crush. The flames consuming the other vessels were engulfed by frigid waters as they sunk to a watery grave.

On June 27 sails of several ships were sighted to windward. The *Shenandoah* followed at a safe distance so as not to arouse suspicion, and soon a whaling fleet was seen by the lookouts. Men scrambled to their posts as preparations were made to "pounce upon them." Whittle seemed to have some misgivings now about their enterprise, and started to justify the flames and misery they were creating. "They have burnt the houses over the heads of our women, stolen their clothes and all kinds of property and inflicted hardships and perpetrated outrages which makes me blush with shame for them,"[22] he wrote, as though the Yankee seamen themselves were responsible for the alleged crimes.

The following morning the Confederates captured the bark *Waverley*, put her to the torch, then steamed to East Cape Bay. Here ten whalers were anchored, one badly damaged by ice. The *Shenandoah* entered under a fine pressure of steam and "being in position to command the fleet with her guns, hoisted our flag," recalled Waddell. "The armed boats were dispatched to take possession of certain vessels with orders to send captains with their ship papers to the steamer." In the midst of this, nine whalers lowered their flags, but the *Favorite* kept hers defiantly aloft. When the boarding party approached they were confronted over the bulwark by a hostile crew armed with pikes, led by their master, Thomas Young. The captain was "between sixty and seventy years old, and belongs to the John Brown stamp of mortals who believe in fighting the devil under all circumstances, and never letting right back down to wrong, however great may be the odds against her," said the *San Francisco Evening Bulletin* of August 19. Captain Young "ordered the old blunderbuss used for shooting whales to be brought up from below, together with his revolver and ammunition."

Young threatened to fire if the rebels came any closer. For the first time, the boarding party was forced to retreat to the *Shenandoah*, and Waddell promptly ordered a Whitworth gun cleared for action. The steamer moved closer, and Young was hailed to leave the ship within five minutes or be fired upon. The crew promptly scrambled into boats and abandoned ship, but not the defiant captain. Whittle then snatched a rifle from a marine and, with the boarding party, returned to the whaler. Young almost became the Civil War's last casualty, as Whittle threatened to shoot him dead. Upon checking his guns, however, the "fighting the devil" skipper found his crew had removed the percussion caps to avoid bloodshed. Whittle's boat circled around, they boarded, and took the obstinate Young captive. Taken back to the *Shenandoah*, the old salt was placed in irons in the forecastle "at the same time telling him that if he was in any way saucy they would gag him."

James Waddell was no more impressed by these New England skippers than he had been by William Nichols: "All the Captains and masters were more or less under the influence of liquor, and some of them swore their sympathy for the South, while others spoke incoherently of cruiser fire and insurance."

The records of the Atlantic Mutual Insurance Co. reveal the panic as the *Shenandoah* approached the Bering Sea. The avalanche of policies taken out over just three days by telegraph contained the words "lost or not lost." This covered the ship owners if their vessels were already destroyed, as there was no way of knowing. Atlantic Mutual received premiums of $350,000. Her payout was $1,653,000, a disaster for the insurance industry.[23]

Lieutenant Chew had taken possession of the *James Murray* and sent her first mate to Waddell, informing him that the skipper had died some time before. A widow and two small children were still on board. The good lady had preserved his body in a barrel of whiskey for a decent burial at home.

"I sent a message to the unhappy woman to cheer up," recalled Waddell, "that no harm would come to her or the vessel; that I knew she was an owner in the vessel, and that the men of the South never made war on helpless women and children."

It also suited Waddell to ransom the *James Murray* and the *Nile* to take over three hundred prisoners off his hands. Not all prisoners went aboard, as Waddell was still recruiting and now had over one hundred and thirty men in his crew, a far cry from the forty-six who originally set sail.

The torch was set to the whalers and Waddell recalled:

> An occasional explosion on board of some one of the burning vessels informed me of the presence of gunpowder or other combustibles, and a liquid flame now and then pursued some inflammable substance which had escaped from their sides to the water, and the heavens were illuminated with the red glare, presenting a picture of indescribable grandeur, while the water was covered by black smoke commingling with fiery sparks. Discharges on board often resembled distant artillery, and while the scene of destruction was going on the steamer turned her head northward in search of additional prey.[24]

15

A Sensation of Freedom

The *Shenandoah* pressed into the Arctic Ocean on June 29. A blank shot echoed across the icy waters and a French ship hove to.[1] The Hawaiian brig *Kohola* was also overtaken, and again the rebels heard of Lee's surrender and Lincoln's assassination.

"The sun was in his highest northern inclination," Waddell recalled, "and it was with us perpetual day; when he sank below the northern pole a golden fringe marked his course until his pale and cheerless face rose again from iceberg and snow."

The sun may have been cheerless, but at least he was there. Seeing nothing but ice ahead, the ship turned south and the weather deteriorated as dense fog shut the sun from view. On July 1 a shudder was felt as the cruiser rammed a large floe of ice. Whittle ran to the bow and had protective mats thrown over the side, the machinery reversed. The ship moved astern and the rudder was put amidships just before she struck more ice at the stern. A sickening crunch was heard throughout the ship as the pressure parted one of the rudder tether chains. Panic broke out amongst some crew as they gathered their belongings to abandon ship. Even Whittle lost his cool, Mason recalling that he "has a wholesome terror of ice was very much excited and made a tremendous noise." The *Shenandoah* was in danger, but Waddell had warps and grapnels run out, and the vessel swung away from the glistening menace. Steam was gently applied, and a large block of ice was pushed along for hours opening the way until the *Shenandoah* broke free into open water.

The conditions too hazardous, Waddell continued southward through the Bering Sea. The ship was blown by a stiff northwest wind through another dense fog, and a course was plotted that should see them safely through the hazardous Aleutian Island chain which separated the Bering from the North Pacific.

July 4 saw a smooth sea and little wind. The sails were furled as steam was raised. This was not only American Independence Day, but also Lilli Nichols' twenty-seventh birthday. Now back home in Searsport, scanning newspapers for news of the *Shenandoah*, no doubt. Both captain and ship may have met their end under a broadside from a Federal man-of-war. For most, the "queen-like" lady was just a memory now; but still a vibrant presence for James Waddell due to his own memories, and the machinations of Cornelius Hunt.

On this day two years before, Robert E. Lee had commenced his retreat from Gettysburg, and Vicksburg had fallen to Ulysses S. Grant; the beginning of the end for the South. Whittle had no time for Yankees, especially on Independence Day. He felt the Confederacy had "causes ten times as strong, as those for which in 1775 they fought." He went into a long diatribe about the "wicked" Yankees:

> Who I consider a race of cruel, fanatical Scoundrels, lost alike to decency, honesty and Christianity.... Let us free and arm our slaves; let every old man, every young woman in the South be armed, let their principle, practice and cry be to shoot dead the invader, whenever and wherever he be found, putting their trust in the justice of an Almighty, all powerful and all just GOD. The God of Jacob be our refuge.

The following day the ship passed through a foggy Amukta Pass in the Aleutian Islands. The active volcano on Amukta Island was seen through the mist off the port beam. "The sight was beautiful," noted Whittle, "Smoke rushing from the crater." Waddell recalled, "It only required a little nerve. When I expected the ship to be about the center of the pass, much to my relief land was seen off either beam.... That feeling of security against a danger which is overcome is truly delightful to the senses.... The ship was safe."

The *Shenandoah* steamed into the broad, safe waters of the Pacific Ocean. Having been on his feet for three days, Waddell had to be assisted to his bunk where the boots were cut off his swollen feet. He recalled:

> I felt an unbounded sensation of freedom on that vast outstretched water before us where those who take care of ships feel at home, and when looking back in that direction where we had seen such hard and dangerous service, I voluntarily breathed away dull care; and why not? ... I felt no longer trammeled by iceberg, floe and land; no longer to hear the masthead lookout cry "Ice ahead." We had run from gloomy vapor into a bright, cheerful, sparkling ocean, and as soon as a hot sun thawed the frosty timbers and rigging of the craft, we should feel ourselves more than a match for anything we might meet under canvas.[2]

July 13 was James Waddell's forty-first birthday. By "invitation he took a nice dinner with us in the wardroom," recorded William Whittle. "As it was blowing a gale I was only present to drink his health," thus missing Lieutenant John Grimball's endeavors for the occasion, complete with white tablecloth. "We had a very fine dinner," recalled Francis Chew. "Fresh meats and vegetables, great luxuries at sea. Two or three different kinds of wine, &c."

No one could account the wind's sudden shift that brought on the gale "until it was reported the cat was overboard," wrote Whittle. Such a catastrophe was considered a cause of bad luck. "As soon as this was known there was no doubt of the cause." Mr Whittle, not superstitious, had no more time for pets than Yankees, apparently, as the cat's loss "would be agreeable to me." But "up walked the cat. No one was more surprised than I, for I thought poor pussy gone. I gave orders to let the cat live."[3]

There was uproar in San Francisco as ransomed vessels dropped anchor with news of their escape from the firestorm. Rear Admiral Pearson of the Pacific Squadron was ordered by Secretary Welles to search for the *Shenandoah* but, "Being an erratic ship, without country or destination, no definite instructions can be given you."

The *San Francisco Bulletin* thundered:

> The recent depredations of the English pirate *Shenandoah* affords another proof, if any were wanting, of the extremely fraternal nature of the feeling entertained by our English brethren for us. The frozen regions of the Arctic Seas are illuminated by the bright lights of British neutrality, and covered with the charred remains of American whalers, the unresisting victims of British perfidy. The *Shenandoah*, as is well known, is an English-built and English armed cruiser, and but for the presence of her commander and a few subordinate rebel officers, she might truly be said to be British in every point of view, and Confederate in none. As it is we claim that the English Government, by its shameful dereliction of duty in failing to observe the neutrality during the late rebellion, has placed itself in a position of a perfidious and sneaking enemy to the Government of the United States and the American people.

If the editor of the *San Francisco Bulletin* was upset by the depredations of the "English pirate" thus far, he would have been horrified had he intelligence of a plan in the head of James Waddell. Newspapers, a good source of intelligence throughout the war, had revealed the only floating defense of San Francisco lay in an ironclad monitor, the USS *Camanche*. Waddell knew her commanding officer, "an old and familiar shipmate," Charles McDougal. Waddell recalled, "McDougal was fond of his ease. I did not feel he would be in our way, any officer of the *Shenandoah* was more than a match for Mc. in activity and will."

Perhaps the captain thought of the comparisons with Raleigh and Drake in the Melbourne newspapers. Now was his chance to prove that the *Shenandoah* was not merely a destroyer of unarmed merchant vessels. The *Alabama* had proven herself in battle. She had sunk the Union gunboat *Hatteras* and delivered proof in the form of blue-clad prisoners. The *Shenandoah* would now show that she too was truly a man-of-war.

The *Daily Alta California* of March 30,[4] having heard of the ship's arrival in Melbourne, speculated on a visit from the "pirate *Shenandoah*": "There is, of course, no danger to this city. It is so thoroughly fortified that the appearance off the bar of all the ships of war that England and France could occasion her very little harm; but we have few vessels of war." The article went on to complain about the few fast warships on the Pacific coast being sent elsewhere. The *Camanche* was in port but "intended only for harbor defenses."

Waddell's plan was to steam into San Francisco Harbor under cover of darkness. The *Shenandoah* would ram the ironclad while McDougal was at "his ease." The vessel would be boarded, her deck and hatches secured and the crew taken prisoner. "No life need have been lost," speculated Waddell. The good citizens of San Francisco would wake up in the morning to find themselves under the guns of both the *Shenandoah* and the *Camanche*, and a demand for ransom enforced.[5]

Obviously the *Daily Alta California* and Waddell had different ideas about San Francisco's defenses.

James Bulloch, meanwhile, had been at work in an attempt to avoid more damage to Anglo/American relations. On June 19 he had composed a letter to Waddell for overseas circulation. Bulloch considered the war to have ended with the capture of President Davis on May 10, and he advised Waddell of the British government's withdrawal of belligerent rights. As regards the ship's disposal, Waddell was referred to his original instructions of "October 1864, for advice on that point,"[6] so the ship "never return to Europe" remained unchanged. The Maritime Powers would allow Waddell to enter their ports for the purposes of disarmament, and his crew would "enjoy the protection of the laws."

He was to pay off his crew if sufficient funds were available, but if not "pay to the extent of your funds and give each man an order on yourself, payable in Liverpool, for the balance due to him, and come here to settle your account." In other words Bulloch had now arranged for sufficient funds to cover any shortfall, but seamen would have to travel to Liverpool under their own steam to collect any outstanding pay. No doubt Bulloch realized the *Shenandoah*'s unforeseen repairs in Melbourne, covered by British newspapers, meant the "ample cruising fund"[7] provided had become inadequate.

This would have been the first news Waddell had of any money in Liverpool. But these instructions were never received, as there was "a very faint expectation" that the letters forwarded would ever reach him. Bulloch had written as a matter of principal at the war's conclusion. As the cruiser was expected to dock in the Pacific region, the directive was dispatched primarily to "the Sandwich Islands, Nagasaki and Shanghai."[8] Liverpool was the last place Bulloch expected to see the *Shenandoah*.

The last rebel cruiser moved south through warmer weather and gentle seas. Waddell, now with a full crew to handle both sails and guns, ordered his first "general quarters" drill. Having bypassed San Francisco two days before, on July 17, it seems the proposed assault had been shelved, at least for the time being, but there was still every chance of meeting a Yankee cruiser on the high seas. Two blank cartridges were fired in a practice broadside, and Whittle, all things considered, thought they had done "remarkably well."[9]

But the captain had different ideas. The following day "general quarters" was again shrilled by the boatswain's pipe. The crew scrambled and "the men did much better than on yesterday showing they only need practice to become proficient," wrote the first lieutenant.

"I suppose now that great guns drill will be the new 'hobby' for the future," speculated Francis Chew. On July 25 another "general quarters" shrilled across the deck. The seamen scrambled to their battle stations as though under attack.

Whittle, however, was depressed by the dismal war news. He had things other than gun drills on his mind, being "sad! sad! sad!!! ... when I reflect upon the helpless and perfectly destitute condition of my dear sisters, I am driven almost to madness."

16

Some Motive That Would Not Bear Explanation

By August 2 the cruiser was well south of San Francisco. Charles McDougal, Waddell's "old and familiar shipmate," would remain safe for the time being, but meet an unfortunate and premature end. He would drown while inspecting a lighthouse from a stormy beach sixteen years later.

The cry of "Sail ho," was heard from aloft. The "propeller being lowered and steam made, we furled sail and stood in chase," recalled Mason. Three hours later an iron bark under British colors was overtaken. Waddell ordered a party aboard and she proved to be the *Barracouta* of Liverpool, thirteen days out from San Francisco. Newspapers on board confirmed the rebel's worst fears, the capture of President Jefferson Davis and the cessation of hostilities, the Confederacy now just a sad memory, "all vessels still at sea under the Confederate flag declared pirates."

Waddell recalled, "My life had been checkered, and I was tutored to disappointment; the intelligence of the issue of the fearful struggle cast a deep stillness over the ship's company."

And his executive officer's worst fears had been confirmed: "The darkest day of my life. The past is gone for naught—the future as dark as the blackest night. Oh! God protect and comfort us I pray.... We now have no country, no flag, no home."[1]

Waddell ordered the ship's guns removed from the deck and all arms not privately owned discharged and returned to the master-at-arms. The *Shenandoah* was to revert to the appearance of an innocent merchant vessel, for self-preservation as much as anything. Most destruction had followed the war's conclusion, and a noose from a yardarm could well be their lot should they fall in with a Federal cruiser. Northern rage, even when Confederates sailed as a recognized belligerent, was an established fact, so now that they were pirates with no country the Yankees would give no quarter and not listen to excuses of not knowing the war was over.

A feeling of horror swept the *Shenandoah*. "If the worst comes to the worst however, I think I could hang as gracefully as any other man, though I must confess the idea is unpleasant and when I think of it, I feel a sort of choking sensation,"[2] recalled Mason. Dr. Barker's talk at the Melbourne Club in happier, bygone days may well have been on his mind.

Discussions were held on what to do next. One thought was to go ashore in the ship's small boats on foreign soil, the *Shenandoah* blown up. Others felt they were obliged to surrender both ship and crew in a Yankee port, but some including Whittle would not consider this. A return to Europe was considered too hazardous due to the presence of Yankee warships in the Atlantic. After much talk, sailing to Sydney, Australia, was considered the safest and best option for all concerned.

Waddell set course for Sydney, only a little further away than the smaller colony of Brisbane. He assumed, no doubt, that Hunt would realize the impracticality of returning to Liverpool for the promised payout, the war's end having changed their situation. Even the *San Francisco Bulletin* of August 3 considered Australia the next logical step, "the next heard of her will probably be in Australia, hobnobbing with her English friends."

"Our Captain at first decided to go to Sidney [*sic*] where he proposed to give up the ship to the Yankee consul, providing the government would not allow him to sell her," noted John Mason.[3] So Waddell was intending to follow Bulloch's instructions and sell the ship in a port of the Pacific. This was a sound and appropriate plan. The "pirates" would be safe in a short time, and if the colonial authorities permitted the sale, there would be ample funds to pay off the crew and get passage home.

Waddell retired that evening, the ship on course for Sydney. But Mason recalled:

> we all expected to fetch up in Australia, but not so, this morning the Captain changed his mind, hauled up to the Sd and Ed and intends going around the horn to Liverpool. This morning when he spoke to several of us on the poop his voice was thick and tears stood in his eyes. I was truly sorry for the poor man.[4]

Again Waddell baffled his officers with a strange decision. Only the day before, he had quashed any thought of returning to distant Britain. Now he told them he was concerned about them being abandoned in a distant port without money. "He had decided the matter on his own responsibility without calling any regular council," John Mason recalled.

Paymaster Smith and Sailing Master Bulloch approached Waddell with a request to reconsider. But "he had made up his mind to go to Liverpool," he informed them, and he would "be d—d if he did not take her there."[5] This was not just a figure of speech, Waddell would be literally damned by the disclosures of Cornelius Hunt.

The captain had been approached during the night and told to head for Liverpool, or Mr. Whittle would be the recipient of some unpleasant facts. Little wonder "his voice was thick and tears stood in his eyes." Waddell was now endangering his ship and crew by taking orders from a corrupt master's mate.

A needless three month voyage did not appeal to Charles Lining, because "carrying us to Australia and turning us loose penniless—but does he not think that the same thing must occur at Liverpool, besides the risk of getting there?"

Waddell then fudged this by saying privately he may take the ship elsewhere—a Yankee port, perhaps? But he knew officers like Whittle would back Liverpool over a surrender to the hated enemy, any time. The captain, however, now kept the precise destination vague; a ruse to get critics off his back. This would lead to bitter division amongst the officers as they disagreed about the best course to follow. It comes as no surprise that Hunt was a pro–Liverpool man. With him peering over the captain's shoulder, there was never any question of where the ship was headed. Hunt, however, feigned anger at Waddell's action in steering away from Sydney. He accused him of an "open violation of his pledge."[6]

> I speak from my own personal knowledge when I say that he promised his crew to run the *Shenandoah* into Sydney, and then without their cognizance, steered for another and more distant port, subjecting them to what they considered unnecessary peril.

Hunt has the effrontery to write this while admitting he was in favor of Liverpool himself. The master's mate would never receive the promised payout, and in retribution attacked Waddell for his own intrigues. Hunt was cunning and vicious beyond belief.

The blackmailer attributed Waddell's desire to head to Liverpool "for the sake of securing a considerable sum of money which he knew to be in the hands of one of our secret agents in Liverpool."[7] The only person who could have told Hunt of this supposed money was Waddell. It was Hunt himself securing a "considerable sum" he was talking about.

But Hunt exposed his fraud, stating that this money came into Bulloch's hands "a short time prior to the final collapse of the Confederacy," and not knowing "how else to dispose of it," decided to provide for returning Confederate naval officers—"a clue was at last furnished for our Commander's singular anxiety to take his ship to Liverpool instead of Sydney or Cape Town."⁸ The ship was in far distant waters a short time prior to the final collapse, yet Hunt asks us to believe Waddell was aware of this; obviously impossible.

Hunt also stated:

> He had his own reasons, as I have intimated, for preferring to reach Liverpool and there surrender his ship, but he should have announced this fact in the first place instead of promising what he did not intend to perform, and thus leading many to apprehend that he was actuated by some motive that would not bear explanation.⁹

The phrase "actuated by some motive that would *not bear explanation*"— Hunt's blackmail; twisting the knife in Waddell's back once again.

Bulloch's orders made no mention of money held for the ship anywhere. Waddell had supposedly been provided with an "ample cruising fund," and the sale of the ship should cover any shortfall with paying off the crew. A promise of money in Liverpool could never have been made in any case, "a voyage of fifteen months"¹⁰ having been allowed for. Bulloch was smart enough to know the Confederacy would almost certainly be history once the *Shenandoah* had completed her cruise. The fall of Atlanta, a vital hub in the deep South, took place over five weeks before the *Shenandoah* sailed. The Confederate core was now split, and the North knew the war was as good as won. This guaranteed the re-election of Abraham Lincoln who, unlike his peace seeking opponents, was pledged to crush the rebel nation.¹¹

Once the whalers were destroyed, Bulloch's instructions stated "you might proceed to Valparaiso, to get the latest news, and make arrangements to sell the ship or to bring her into the Atlantic, as her condition or the political state of affairs might render desirable." The only "desirable" reason for entering the Atlantic was a Southern victory, the heroes to be received in an open Confederate port.

Bulloch continued:

> You should at all times exercise a large discretion, and you would be perfectly justified in selling the ship and sending the crew to their homes, if they desire it, whenever her failing powers would seem to indicate that she was no longer fit for service. If you should bring her to England or France during the continuance of the war, it is extremely doubtful whether she could again be got to sea; and our ships of war have been ruled out of the continental ports of Spain, Portugal, and even Brazil. In view of these circumstances and the great distance between the North Pacific and Atlantic ports wherein you might find shelter, I am inclined to think that when you have performed the work assigned to you the best disposition you could make of the *Shenandoah* would be to sell her, either somewhere on the west coast of South America or to adventurous speculators in the Eastern seas. Thus would be realized a partial return for the cost of the cruise, and the ship would never return to Europe, where as Con-

federate States property, her presence might give rise to harassing questions and complications.[12]

Bulloch's undelivered letter, written after the South's surrender, had referred Waddell back to these "never return" instructions. Once the *Shenandoah* was sold, Bulloch had no advice whatsoever. His orders were for a captain and ship with no country let alone a "considerable sum of money" in Liverpool; a fictional ruse by Waddell to keep Hunt at bay in the short term.

17

An Evil Genius

On the afternoon of August 4 Waddell stood on the poop deck as his crew gathered on the quarterdeck below. He thanked them for their service, and said he bore no resentment to officers who had presented him with a petition requesting a clarification of their destination. He pointed out that the commissioned officers could well face long prison sentences or even hanging on piracy charges. "I shall take the ship into the nearest English port and all I have to ask of you men, is to stand by me to the last." It was an impassioned address, greeted with cries of support, and even drew tears from the eyes of some.[1] But he then said if there was a change in plans he expected the men to obey his orders "as they had always done." This paved the way for a different destination if he so chose.

It was an effective speech which drew together officers and seamen alike, and calmed any chance of mutinous threats from those who had counted on reaching safety in a short time. But questions remained unanswered. What was an "English" port? The colonial English port of Sydney was no longer their objective. Did an English port mean one on the coast of distant England herself?

John Mason wrote:

> Instead, he first squares away for Australia, then the next day heaves up again for Liverpool, then calls up all the men and tells them he is going to the nearest "English port." This shows vacillation in the first place and equivocation in the second.

This showed, in fact, the intrigues of Cornelius Hunt. The real truth had been exposed the morning after his approach to Waddell. He was going to Liverpool "or be d—d if he did not take her there."

So, with the ship headed for Liverpool and Sydney forgotten, Cape Town, South Africa, was seen as the nearest "English" port. This was a safe haven much more easily reached than distant Britain, three months and seventeen thousand miles sailing away. Waddell, however, continued to feign vagueness about the ship's destination, but behind this facade he was the most decisive man alive—bound for Liverpool.

Contrary winds seemed determined to keep the ship at sea, an easy target for Federal cruisers. On August 14 steam was raised and the propeller lowered, "but broke one of the screws of a guide rod," wrote Whittle, "and had to delay until 8:20 p.m. for repairs."[2]

"Not only the wind, but also steam seems to wish to prevent our going southward," noted Lining in despair. "Some seem to see the hand of God in it, warning us, as it were, there was danger in that direction." Prophetic words for James Waddell, who faced danger in Liverpool, unaware of any money waiting for Cornelius Hunt.

"We are all gloomy and will be so until we get to port and hear what has become of our dear ones," wrote Whittle the following day, "for the present we can only pray to get safely to some neutral port without capture."

August 24 blended with Lieutenant Chew's twenty-fourth birthday. "We are I expect the youngest set of officers who ever went to sea," wrote Whittle, "The oldest member of our mess (Lining) is but 31 and the others range from 28 to 24."

A young set of officers led on a perplexing voyage to the other side of the world by an old salt of forty-one. As the gloomy weeks passed shipboard morale began to break down. Men became slack in their duties, and disputes broke out over minor infractions. Lieutenant Scales overslept, and Whittle was no help when he reported Lee for smoking his pipe while on watch. The depressed Waddell, now obliged to discipline Lee for this infraction, removed the officer from his watch. Other officers, however, supported the offender by stating that they too had smoked on duty. Waddell reinstated Lee, but repeated the order. This dispute cast more gloom over the stateless ship which could have been avoided had the officious Whittle turned a blind eye.

And a mere master's mate felt he now had the power to defy the captain's authority. Hunt refused the captain's order that he stand watch with Captain's Clerk John Blacker, a certified skipper, "with whom he was at dagger points," recalled Lining. Hunt and Blacker had previously been arrested for fighting. But Waddell could not allow a petty officer to openly challenge his authority, and called Hunt's bluff. The master's mate was stood down and "told to consider himself a *passenger*!"[3]

But Hunt struck back. He promptly told his shipmates they would pocket only one shilling in the pound in wages; a reminder to Waddell that money was to be channeled his way, if necessary. The master's mate promptly found himself confined to quarters by Whittle. "An evil genius seemed to haunt the ship at this time,"[4] wrote Stanley Horn with apparent mystic insight in his 1947 book *Gallant Rebel*, straight after relating Hunt's rumor mongering. Horn's assurance in the book's foreword that "every statement herein made is of unimpeachable historical accuracy" was never more true than with that "evil genius" line.

"Great whispering going on all about," wrote Charles Lining, "I can't go to talk to anyone without stumbling across a private confab. and withdraw to my room."

As the unhappy *Shenandoah* ploughed towards Cape Horn, those one time supporters of the Confederacy at the intended destination had little sympathy for the fugitives. The London *Times* vented its fury on September 11:

> It is impossible not to share the indignation so loudly expressed on the other side of the Atlantic at the continued depredations of the *Shenandoah* on the northwest coast of America ... he professed to disbelieve the ruin of the Confederacy, on the ground that he had no information of it except from Northern newspapers. It remains to be seen how far this plea will avail him if he should be overhauled by a war vessel of the United States.... Justice and policy alike suggest that we should aid the United States in cutting short this lawless career, and putting down outrages so ruinous to commerce and so disgraceful to civilisation.

The *Shenandoah* rounded Cape Horn in mid–September amid freezing weather, but the ocean was still mild for this part of the world. The crew thought they had escaped the notorious, savage seas, but then the tempest struck, as recalled by Mason:

> Sometimes there would be a heavy lee roll, followed by a perfect avalanche of furniture. I would hold on like grim death in my bunk and think the ship would certainly turn over. So uncomfortable was I in bed that it was actually a relief when four o'clock came and I turned out for the morning watch.... Still, I got wet to the skin almost as soon as I got on deck and remained so for five hours ... I must say that twelve months experience at sea has destroyed all the romance of a sailor's life for me. The constant confinement within the narrow limits of the ship; this total deprivation of the society of females, which has so softening an influence on all men.

The ship, driven south, encountered massive icebergs adrift in the frigid seas. Waddell lamented, "there were moments when we would have deemed it a friendly gale which buried both our sorrowful hearts and the beautiful *Shenandoah* in those dark waters."

Waddell's heart, more sorrowful than most, continued north into calmer seas. But it soon became apparent that they were headed towards Liverpool, not the much closer South African port.

On September 28 Waddell received a petition from Chew, Bulloch, Lining, O'Brien, Smith and Midshipman Browne. This document made a most earnest plea for Cape Town: "We regard with proper horror any prospect of capture and imprisonment at this late date." This was followed by yet another petition signed by ten petty officers. This requested they be put ashore should the ship proceed north "which we infinitely prefer to the chances of capture or shipwreck." The petitions were long and detailed the declining condition of the ship and her inability "to contend with the furious weather that constantly prevails on the British coast from November to April." Over five weeks earlier, Whittle had commented, "Our ship is getting light and we have to watch her carefully. Having been out so long it stands to reason her that her weight is greatly decreased." One advantage of Cape Town, said the second petition, was its frequent use by neutral merchant vessels which could provide safe passage to England. This port was only fourteen days sailing from their current position as opposed to about forty for England.[5]

Cornelius Hunt, now restored to duty, did not sign a petition to sail for Cape Town. He felt "that some provision had been made for us in Liverpool."[6] But Hunt also wrote that the crew's "prospects for payment were not brilliant; at least none but a very credulous man would feel much confidence in the feasibility of collecting a debt due him from a defunct government"[7]; the very opposite to "some provision" having been made. Hunt was saying "some provision had been made for *me* in Liverpool," a reminder to Waddell of hush money not paid.

To taunt Waddell, Cornelius Hunt openly admits he is chasing "some provision," despite the Yankees wishing to:

> glut their vengeance with our blood, should we fall into their hands.... Every man of us knew that if the *Shenandoah* was captured before we could reach an English port that his days were numbered.... Several United States cruisers and one English man-of-war, they knew, had been dispatched in search of us, and it was like running a very gauntlet of life to hope to escape all these dangers unscathed.[8]

Yet Mr. Hunt was all for Liverpool.

To add insult to injury, Hunt wrote regarding Waddell's supposed secretive Cape Town deliberations:

> Such conduct was as injudicious as it was unjust, and gave rise to grave suspicions touching our commander's integrity of purpose, which, I am sorry to say, the event did not prove to be altogether unfounded.[9]

Hunt needling Waddell once more. He knew full well there was no "integrity" in his "purpose"; being forced to respond to blackmail. Being in favor of Liverpool himself, Hunt's flagrant hypocrisy exposes him for the fraud he was.

In response to the petitions for Cape Town, Waddell supposedly allowed a democratic decision by the five senior officers. Lieutenants Whittle, Grimball, Lee, Chew and Scales met to decide on "Europe" or Cape Town. But Lining wrote:

He *knew* before he called them into his cabin the opinion of every officer, because the thing had been loudly, and angrily discussed, time and time again, in the wardroom, where every word could be heard in his cabin. He *knew* he would have the majority of the council on his side!

Only Whittle and Chew favored Cape Town. So much for the democratic meeting.

Waddell received a petition supporting "England or France" signed by five officers; Grimball, Scales, Lee, Mason and McNulty. Another separate petition arrived signed by seventy-one of his one hundred and ten sailors, including some petty officers. This assured Waddell of "our complete reliance and trust in whatever it should please you to do under any circumstances."

But the name "Cornelius Hunt" is conspicuous by its absence.[10]

On one hand Hunt would never sign a petition for Cape Town, but on the other would never sign a petition that makes no mention of Liverpool. Hunt had no "trust in whatever it should please" Waddell to do. Hunt's missing name was a reminder to Waddell that they were going to Liverpool come what may. Most officers were opposed to Liverpool as they were the ones most likely to hang if caught on the high seas, but those seventy-one crew knew they would be relatively safe, especially those enlisted from captured vessels.

The pro–Cape Town William Whittle, despite not signing any petition, wrote in his journal, "A large majority of the officers are vehemently opposed to the unnecessary risks of going to England." He lamented the fact that not all officers were allowed to vote: "I do not think that because someone has a Lieutenant's commission he is any better able than anyone else to decide a matter of common sense."[11] Waddell's decision did defy common sense—unless you knew what was going on behind the scenes. There was no payoff in Sydney or Cape Town for Cornelius Hunt.

The following night the ship crossed the previous year's south bound passage. They had circumnavigated the globe. "The first to carry our downtrodden flag around," wrote Whittle. But he lamented being placed, "in the same category with Captain Kidd." As executive officer he now felt bound to support Waddell in anything except "any attempt to go to a Yankee port."[12] Waddell sent a bottle of Champagne to the wardroom along with a note of congratulations. A toast was proposed to the captain's health, but three of the five pro–Cape Town officers immediately walked out. Even Lining, a Cape Town man, considered this pettiness unjustified, "as I thought it was politely and kindly meant." And Mason felt the captain would have little dreamt "what unpleasant circumstances would attend the event."

One can only imagine Waddell's frustration. His stance appeared to show a lack of concern for his ship and crew. Charles Lining thought him driven by

17. An Evil Genius

Paymaster William Smith, one of those officers vehemently opposed to returning to Britain after learning the war was over (Archer Memorial Library, American Civil War Round Table of Australia).

an egotistic desire to be the only Confederate commander to circle the globe. Lieutenant Chew confronted Waddell and demanded to know where the ship was headed. The captain replied that it depended on prevailing winds "off the coat of Europe." "Still undecided!" grumbled Chew.

But Hunt now found that Waddell could fight dirty too. A few days after the wardroom farce, a rumor spread that Hunt had stolen several hundred dollars found on one of the prizes. Whittle investigated at Hunt's request, and Master's Mate John Minor, a confidant of Waddell, seemed to be the culprit. The captain had used his favored petty officer to vent his abhorrence for Cornelius Hunt.

"Another wretched scandal flying around ship," wrote Lining.[13] "A wretched scandal" as a result of a "most scandalous romance" months before.

The *Shenandoah* plowed northwards towards the North Atlantic, the lookouts keeping a weather eye for Yankee cruisers. Her hull gathered sea grass and barnacles where the northern ice had damaged her copper sheathing. Soaring temperatures, rationed drinking water, and poor food led to low morale. Despite lime juice taken aboard in Melbourne, three mild cases of scurvy were recorded. This did not become a major problem. Liverpool was now only one month away, and there is no evidence of any officer being affected.

"One year ago today I sailed in this ship from London," wrote Whittle on October 8. "It has been a year of constant anxiety and labor from then till now. And all to have such a sad, inglorious, pitiable and miserable end, is truly heartbreaking, but God ruleth." And three days later, "We are once more in the North Atlantic, and I for one never expect to get out of it again."

And if Assistant Surgeon McNulty had his way, such would have been the case. McNulty, often drunk, exchanged insults with the Captain's Clerk John Blacker. McNulty produced a pistol but Whittle intervened and took the weapon from him. Waddell confined McNulty to quarters. The following day he denied being drunk and claimed he was merely showing the pistol, not about to use it. Waddell released him from confinement. Whittle, irritated, then produced witnesses to prove his version of events. McNulty insisted he had not been drunk and Whittle's report was "an act of cruelty." The executive officer was surprised to find himself challenged to a duel. "I have but to accede to your demand for such satisfaction as you desire," wrote Whittle, but "As the ship is not a place where such things can be settled, as soon as we get ashore, full satisfaction will be given you."[14]

"Our ship is fast becoming a perfect Hell afloat," wrote Lining; a perfect hell afloat at the instigation of one master's mate.

The following day saw squalls and thundering rain. Whittle, at midnight, was woken by Lieutenant Chew yelling orders. He scrambled from his bunk and "took the deck" from Chew amidst a heavy downpour. Whittle promptly gave orders to shorten sail. "The squall was very fresh and blew our miz: royal away, and carried away the m'n royal studding sail boom. I was as wet as a drowned rat, and caught cold."[15] Chew, even after a year at sea, could not be trusted to keep watch in a gale. Whittle catching cold seems just recompense. He had undermined Waddell while supporting the inept officer earlier in the cruise.

The Great Southern Comet had appeared above the *Shenandoah* the previous year as covert events unfolded, a glowing, celestial omen of unforeseen trials; Hunt's blackmail and Waddell's forced circumnavigation of the globe. It seems appropriate that the opposite should now occur. The sun disappeared as "The moon's disk was right in the center," Whittle observed on October 19. This dark, total eclipse occurred with Liverpool only three weeks away.[16]

The captain wrote his return was "my duty as a man and an officer in whose hands was placed the honor of my country's flag and the welfare of 132 men."[17] He said it was safe to sail for Liverpool because there were "only imaginary dangers" and the ship had sailed "over 40,000 miles without accident." But the war's end meant the *Shenandoah* was even more likely to meet a Federal cruiser than had been the *Alabama* and *Florida*. The *Official Records* list no fewer than seventy-eight warships detailed as "searching for Confederate Cruisers and Blockade Runners" from 1864 to 1865. One of them, remarkably, was the USS *Shenandoah*, a screw sloop carrying ten guns and 175 men. And, amazingly, the rebel blockade runner *Lillian* had been shelled by the USS *Shenandoah* on June 30, 1864.[18] The CSS *Shenandoah* was now on a perilous cruise partly to avoid another Lilli being shelled by the newspapers, so to speak. The Yankee *Shenandoah* had been decommissioned on Lee's defeat, the name *Shenandoah* now notorious, but would take to sea once more shortly after the rebel ship's surrender. Perhaps the decommissioning was to avoid "friendly fire" until the rebel *Shenandoah* was brought to bay.

But the American warships *Wyoming, Suwanee. Iroquois,* and *Wachusett* had been dispatched to hunt the last Confederate cruiser down. These warships were far from "imaginary dangers," and British men-of-war were instructed to seize the rebels if the opportunity arose. This would appease American authorities furious about the "English pirates" still at sea.

On October 25 the cry of "Sail ho" was heard from the masthead. The crew quickly scanned the horizon, now in waters frequented by Federal cruisers. A quartermaster was sent aloft and reported a steamer; more than likely a man-of-war. Very soon sails could be seen from the *Shenandoah*'s deck, for she was on a converging course, a cause for great anxiety. The propeller was lowered to slow the *Shenandoah* down, and a drag put out, but Waddell dare not shorten canvas or change course, as this would invite inspection. As the strange vessel drew closer her identity as a warship was confirmed. The *Shenandoah*'s only hope was for night to fall before the enemy came close enough to identify her.

Waddell recalled their predicament:

> The situation was one of anxious suspense; our security, if any remained, depended on a strict adherence to the course we were pushing. Deviation would be fatal; boldness must accomplish the deception. Still she forged towards the sail, and it would be madness to stop her. Darkness finally threw her friendly folds around the anxious heart and little ship, and closed the space between the vessels. What a relief![19]

The warship was then not four miles distant. Steam was raised for the first time in thirteen thousand miles and the *Shenandoah* altered course, her sails furled, and steamed away into the night.

"If she be a Yankee she will be somewhat astonished tomorrow morning to find no vessel in sight," wrote William Whittle, "but no doubt will conclude that it was really the 'Shenanigan' but she will have a sweet time finding us as we will remain under steam until we get a good breeze."[20]

Dawn's glow on the eastern horizon revealed no sign of the enemy cruiser. The *Shenandoah*'s bow splashed once more towards the only destination ever planned, Liverpool.

Despite escaping unscathed, a few days later there was the sad ritual of a burial at sea. William Bill, from the Sandwich Islands, was committed to the deep on October 27, the victim of venereal disease. And Marine Sergeant Canning soon died from the lingering effects of his wound received at the Battle of

Shiloh early in the war. On October 31, he too slid from beneath the fabric of a Confederate flag. "It was an affecting sight," recalled Lieutenant Whittle.[21]

The closer the ship neared the captain's preferred destination, the more he seemed apprehensive and unsettled. Waddell shortened canvas on any pretext, slowing the ship down. His officers, mystified once more, assumed he was concerned the ship would capsize in a squall.

But on the horizon was the hideous prospect of facing Cornelius Hunt in Liverpool. There was no money waiting that Waddell was aware of. And James Bulloch would give a cold reception, the ship intended never to return. The bleak atmosphere permeated the ship's very timbers. Whittle picked up the ghastly ambience and wrote on November 1, "I feel somehow or other as tho' some great calamity was hanging over me—why, I can't divine—or what I can't imagine, as it really seems that our cup of grief is already full." But Whittle knew little of the ship's real grief, the real reason they were approaching Liverpool at all. The following day the mystified lieutenant wrote, "We are men with something awful hanging over us.... Why is this? I can't say."[22]

On November 2 contrary winds forced the captain to raise steam. His restive seamen were anxious to make landfall and eat decent food after months at sea. The ship now moved quickly, the winds irrelevant, the inevitable reckoning with Mr. Hunt unavoidable.

The *Shenandoah* had on board $22,000 (5,000 pounds) when she left London.[23] The Melbourne stay, including repairs, cost $18,000. This left only $4,000. These funds would be divided amongst the crew, but this covered nothing like the full money owed. Waddell assembled the crew and explained the situation. On arrival, "he would endeavor to see where the rest of our money was to come from." In other words, there was no "provision" awaiting them. Amongst Southerners in Liverpool, "there would be some who would be willing to contribute to pay us, who had done so much."[24] No doubt Waddell was praying there would also be enough money from some source to silence Hunt. But there was little hope, $30,000 being required just to pay out the crew. The captain commended the crew for their conduct thus far, "and he only hoped up to the last moment of their stopping in the ship they would behave in the same orderly manner." He added, "You have gained a name by serving in this vessel that will never be forgotten. Your acts will be talked of all over Europe." These words indicate Waddell already being aware of mutiny gossip. Some crew were bent on stripping the vessel upon arrival in lieu of lost pay, thanks to the rumors previously spread by Cornelius Hunt.

On November 3 the paymaster started dispersing money. Whittle lamented that the $4,000 available will give every man one dollar in each $7.10 he has due to him. "Upon this I got $45.90 out of $326 due me. This is probably the last money I will have for a long time."²⁵ Obviously Whittle had no knowledge of "a considerable sum" in Liverpool, and the executive officer would have known of such funds a long time before a master's mate, especially an "utterly worthless" master's mate.

On the night of November 5 the *Shenandoah* arrived off Liverpool. Waddell wisely continued the subterfuge, identifying her as the *America*, arrived from Calcutta. A flare brought a pilot on board. "The Deuce it is!" he exclaimed upon finding himself on board the notorious *Shenandoah*. She had sailed from the Arctic unscathed with Yankee cruisers in pursuit. He confirmed the South's defeat and, anxious to enter the safety of port, the ship proceeded up the River Mersey. The tide being out, she grounded harmlessly on a sandbar.

Cornelius Hunt recalled:

> During the night, the First Lieutenant came around and warned the officers to keep their revolvers about them, as he had seen enough to make him apprehensive that a plot was on foot among the crew to secure what valuables there were on board, and decamp. The fear that their wages would not be forthcoming, had suggested to them this expedient.²⁶

And it was Hunt who had first suggested "their wages would not be forthcoming." But no mutinous rush came. After three hours the ship floated free and proceeded safely up the Mersey.

The *Shenandoah* was surrendered to Captain Paynter of the first-rate ship of the line HMS *Donegal*, 101 guns, the following day—November 6, 1865. The last Confederate flag was lowered before the solemn crew. The cruiser had weathered crushing ice flows and violent storms, capturing or destroying thirty-eight vessels, without loss of life through conflict. This was ultimately a tribute to the seamanship of James Waddell. Commander Bulloch wrote that he had followed his program "with unusual precision and effect up till 28 June 1865," when the last whalers burned.²⁷

The Paymaster of the *Donegal* signed for $820.28. This was money taken from captured vessels after the war's conclusion, thus not paid out to the crew.

Hunt's machinations had caused Waddell vexing problems, to say the least, and his officers just concerns as a result. But no frank captain's journal—like those of Mason, Lining and Whittle—exists, thus we see no honest assessment of those under his command. His memoirs praised all, regardless of performance, for reasons to be explained in the following chapter. But William Whittle made a perceptive observation late in the cruise: "As to a commanding officer pleasing all hands it is impossible…. It is disgustingly true that men are bound to differ at all times."²⁸

18

Mercilessly Defrauded

A few hours after the *Shenandoah* dropped anchor, U.S. Vice-Consul Henry Wilding telegraphed American Minister Charles Adams in London. He described the astonishing event; the pirate rebel cruiser thought to be on the other side of the world had docked in Liverpool. That same afternoon Adams called on the British Foreign Secretary, Lord Clarendon, who "was utterly incredulous" at the *Shenandoah*'s arrival. Little wonder, the arrival did defy all expectations, British, Yankee and Confederate alike. No doubt James Bulloch was just as incredulous as Lord Clarendon.

Waddell sent a letter to the British authorities with an explanation of his supposed situation. Upon hearing the war was over he had disarmed the ship and shaped his "course for the Atlantic Ocean" and "sought this port as a suitable one to 'learn the news,' and if I am without a government, to surrender the ship."[1] Bulloch's instructions, however, had advised "get the latest news" at Valparaiso in the South Pacific, then sell the *Shenandoah*.

Hunt mocked Waddell by reproducing this letter with his false explanation. The blackmailer was no doubt amused by, "I was in an embarrassing situation... . History is, I believe without a parallel." The captain had indeed been placed in an embarrassing situation, history having no known parallel. A scandalous romance and subsequent blackmail had forced a warship to sail thousands of miles, thus circumnavigating the globe.

Times and attitudes had changed since the ship's joyous reception in Melbourne. The gallant rebels were now accused by British and Americans alike of being pirates who had refused to lay down their arms. The last thing the British wanted was verification of the ship's origins, the Americans already screaming about British connivance. Bulloch had requested the ship never return because "her presence might give rise to harassing questions and complications," which is exactly what occurred. Charles Adams wrote to Lord Clarendon with the assertion that as the ship had been received in Liverpool, Britain had assumed responsibility for the damage wrought.[2] Hunt goaded Waddell once more by writing that the British press asked "why we had come there to get them into trouble with the United States."[3] On November 21 *The New York Times* reported, "The pirate *Shenandoah* has at last returned home." The article described the destruction of American vessels, and "Some months ago she was outlawed, and now has the audacity to seek an asylum under the protection of the flag which aided, supported and guarded her in safety until she could place herself beyond the reach of Federal cruisers."

"The North are fighting for Empire, the South for freedom," the London *Times* had proclaimed during the war. But now the *Shenandoah*'s arrival was, "an untoward and unwelcome event." The article expressed doubts about Waddell's claim that he had no authentic news of the war's end until contact with the *Barracouta*, and commented on the sharp rise in sperm oil due to his incendiary activities.[4]

And the *Pall Mall Gazette* lamented, "It is bad enough to have let the *Alabama* get to sea, but it is worse luck that the Americans could not contrive to catch Captain Waddell for themselves, and so save us from the vexation of deciding upon his position.... Is he a pirate or not?"

Cornelius Hunt, blackmailer and liar, proved himself to be a man of no honor. To avoid piracy charges alongside his shipmates, he broke his word and bribed a British marine with a bottle of whiskey, then deserted the ship disguised as "an old salt."[5] The desertion was futile, however. The British authorities accepted Waddell's version of events. No piracy charges were laid, and Captain Paynter turned a blind eye to British seamen who claimed they were Americans. All were released from the ship on November 8. Customs checked their baggage, and Waddell felt obliged to state in his memoirs that he had "neither thoughts nor stores to conceal from anyone."[6] Stores, perhaps.

Hunt's concern for his fellow seamen, at this point, became most touching for a skulking deserter. Waddell received wage money from Bulloch in Liverpool, then cheated his officers, Hunt claimed. He only give the full amount of "two hundred pounds" to "a few of his favorites ... the balance he coolly appropriated for himself."[7] Lieutenant Grimball, however, wrote a letter to his father which revealed the receipt of "three hundred pounds" before leaving England—his full wages.[8] Thus we have a false claim by Hunt once more.

The precise facts of who got what are unknown. Bulloch's records disappeared after the war, and by the time Hunt's book appeared, those concerned had scattered to the four winds. Whittle was farming in Argentina along with former officers Browne, Mason and Smith, the proposed duel with McNulty forgotten. They would return to the United States after a general amnesty, and

Whittle, his "darling Pattie" nowhere in sight, would marry another lady, Elizabeth Page, in 1872.

Cornelius Hunt states that Waddell, once on shore, declined Paymaster Smith's offer to pay out the crew. But even before arrival, and unaware of the wages being held by Bulloch, Waddell had informed his crew that Signal Quartermaster Lewis Wiggins would act as his contact in Liverpool. The captain promised a pay certificate to each man as proof of what they were owed in the hope money could be found to pay them out.[9]

After Cape Town Lewis Wiggins had signed a petition in support of Waddell, while others verged on mutiny. Smith had confronted Waddell upon changing course from Sydney to Liverpool, and signed the pro–Cape Town "proper horror" petition. Waddell would be most reluctant to have further dealings with a mutinous officer once on land, and was not obliged to do so as they were no longer naval officers.

Hunt stated that Waddell:

"We are men with something awful hanging over us," Lieutenant William Whittle, November 2, 1865. The *Shenandoah*, a ship with a dark secret, following her surrender to the British in the River Mersey (*Illustrated London News*, November 18, 1865).

sent our old quartermaster Wiggins, as honest and straight-forward an old sailor as ever walked a deck, to get them together and pay them from one third to one half of what was actually due them, and promise the remainder at some indefinite time in the future. For weeks after, his residence at Waterloo, a little way out of Liverpool, was besieged by these poor men clamoring for the hard-earned pittance out of which he had mercilessly defrauded them.[10]

William Temple, however, "a very intelligent seaman" according to American Consul Dudley, threw different light on "mercilessly defrauded" funds in an affidavit sworn out one month after the ship's arrival.[11] Temple stated that on November 11 Lewis Wiggins and Seaman Charles Morton, acting as his clerk, paid half the crew in full at the Liverpool Sailors' Home "one by one." The following day Wiggins informed Temple "there would not be enough money to go round and pay all. The next morning he commenced paying the crew about one half their wages and retaining their certificates." Wiggins said, "we need not worry we would get the rest of it." But "That same evening Wiggins went to London in disguise. Morton took a second class ticket to Bristol."[12] And Cabin Boy Robert Rosel testified, "I received eight pounds from Wiggins at the Sailors' Home, all in English money. I think Wiggins has gone to London."[13] Thus it is Wiggins and Morton who have defrauded the crew, not James Waddell.

Cornelius Hunt, however, wrote Wiggins was "as honest and straight-forward an old sailor as ever walked a deck." So why does the blackmailer give a glowing character reference to a man who has defrauded the crew?

Hunt and Wiggins are in league, it is fair to assume.

The probable scenario: After leaving the ship on the evening of November 8 Waddell takes a room in George's Hotel, Dale Street, Liverpool.[14] Over the next few days Hunt demands his hush money, by now aware Bulloch has provided pay for the crew. Waddell, however, refuses to steal wages to satisfy Hunt. The blackmailer goes off in a fury vowing vengeance, saying he will reveal all.

On November 11 Wiggins and Morton start handing out wages in full at the Sailors' Home. That night Hunt makes contact and suggests they "mercilessly" defraud the crew. In return for a cut, he will share scandalous information about Waddell which will prevent retaliation.

They agree.

Next day Wiggins mysteriously pays no one saying there will not be enough money to go round. Bags are packed, a disguise is arranged and travel plans made. The following day, the 13, Wiggins only pays out about half the money owed to the remaining crew telling them they will receive the rest in full.[15]

That night Wiggins and Morton split the money with Hunt, thus we see his "honest and straight-forward" endorsement of Wiggins who flees to London

The Liverpool Sailors' Home. It was from here that Lewis Wiggins fled "to London in disguise" while "Morton took a second class ticket to Bristol." They took a substantial part of the crew's wages with them (Wikimedia Commons).

in disguise while Morton heads for Bristol. This divides any possible pursuit. Wiggins and Morton take the lion's share, as they are exposed as the fraudsters, the "evil genius" safe in obscurity. Hunt, however, still feels cheated as he has nothing like the money first promised by Waddell.

William Temple approaches Waddell on November 17, now moved to the Waterloo Hotel. Temple hopes the captain has more pay, but is informed that Wiggins had been given "enough money to pay all the crew all that was due them and he had no doubt but that Wiggins was acting for the best."[16] Waddell cannot believe the man he trusted has defrauded his shipmates. But Wiggins is gone, and will lie low for five months. He does not return to his home in Savannah, Georgia, until mid–April 1866.

Temple stated November 17 was the last time he saw Waddell but "several of the crew have seen him subsequently." Thus we have Hunt claiming the captain was "besieged by these poor men clamoring for their hard-earned pittance out of which he had mercilessly defrauded them." The true story is "clamoring for their hard-earned pittance out of which myself, Wiggins and Morton had mercilessly defrauded them."

This is consistent with the pattern established in Hunt's book; charging Waddell with his own intrigues.

Hunt claimed to have received only ten pounds before leaving the ship, "the sole proceeds of my thirteen months cruise in the *Shenandoah*."[17] Another lie we may assume, Hunt receiving his full pay plus "mercilessly defrauded" funds from Wiggins.

American Consul Thomas Dudley wrote to Secretary of State Seward on December 14 that seamen were "paid at the Sailors' Home with money subscribed or given by the people of Liverpool for the purpose." So the stolen shortfall may have been covered, but not by December 6 when Temple swore out his affidavit. This alleged British support for the *Shenandoah* because Temple "considers himself defrauded by the Confederate authorities of twenty-two pounds due to him for wages,"[18] testified Captain Paynter of HMS *Donegal*. But Temple exposes Wiggins and Morton as the fraudsters, thus a witness for the prosecution does, in fact, clear James Waddell.

Some aspects of Temple's anti–British affidavit were disputed and, as his testimony was taken some ten months after the Australian stay, he did make mistakes. Temple claimed the "Governor of Melbourne" was entertained on board the *Shenandoah*, when he probably meant William Bayles, the mayor.[19] His list of those who went to Ballarat includes both correct and incorrect names, but it comes as no surprise that Hunt's name is missing.

The "very intelligent" Temple included a great deal of other correct information which was not disputed, and Charles Adams wrote to Clarendon on June 7, 1866, that Temple's statements were corroborated "by much incidental testimony which has since that time come to my knowledge."[20]

The only participant to cast doubt on Temple's charges against Wiggins and Morton is the "utterly worthless" Cornelius Hunt.

Accosted by seamen in a futile search for missing pay, and Hunt's hush money not paid, it must have been a hideous time for Waddell, his heart made to "shrink within." Waddell's wife, now removed from prison to house arrest,

Waddell's late return was satirized in the press. But this all added to his fame, the last rebel commander to surrender (*Harper's Weekly*, December 9, 1865).

was about to have her husband's scandal exposed to the world. The *David Brown* connection could well be made; a captain who had not done his duty.

But what of Lilli Nichols? Papers like the *New York Times* had exposed Teresa Sickles, but at least her paramour had been Phillip Barton Key, son of the composer of *The Star Spangled Banner.* Teresa's treatment gave only a mild hint of what awaited the Yankee lover of the "rebel pirate" who had destroyed Yankee ships and "richly deserved hanging" according to the *New York Times.*

Near death, a mere twelve days after the ship's arrival, Waddell was bedridden in the Waterloo Hotel.[21] He had lung hemorrhages, coughing up large amounts of blood. This was probably due to sheer trauma, but even an attempted suicide cannot be ruled out.

Hunt, however, remained silent. No sensational exposé appeared.

The longer nothing was heard, the better for James Waddell. Over several months, he made a full recovery. The ordeal was over, he thought.

So why did Hunt not carry out his threat to expose Waddell? Because to do so nine months after the affair was far too late. He would have exposed himself as a blackmailer and informer, a man of no honor himself.

Twelve months' silence passed. Waddell must have felt secure. But then the dreaded blackmailer reemerged with his savage retribution. His poison pen had been at work, and *The Shenandoah; or the Last Confederate Cruiser* hit the stands, released in London and New York in early 1867.[22] If the blackmailer could not expose Waddell without exposing himself, a pack of vengeful lies claimed to be his "truthful narrative" was the next best thing, making money from book sales along the way. Waddell's circumnavigation, "which has made his name famous"[23] had achieved little for the scheming instigator, thus his exposé to "exhibit the man to the world in his true colors." Far from writing "hastily and inartistically" as claimed, Hunt spent considerable time concocting his revenge. He accused Waddell of his own schemes; endangering the crew by heading to Liverpool for "a considerable sum"; ignoring Sydney and Cape Town; stealing wages from the crew. The "most scandalous romance" and other double-edged remarks prevented Waddell from refuting the allegations.

Seven weeks after docking in Liverpool the recovering Waddell wrote a private letter to an associate in Mobile, Alabama. This gave his own account of events at sea. It was leaked to the press and printed right across the now re–United States:

> among some of the officers I witnessed a terror which mortified me ... the officers set a bad example to the crew. Their conduct was nothing less than mutiny. I was very decided with some of them. I had to tell one officer I would be captain or die on the deck.[24]

Hunt feigned great exception to the mutiny charges. He asserted that "nothing like" a mutinous spirit "was ever manifested by any officer from the time we left English shores till we returned to them."[25]

But William Whittle had other ideas: "There is a position approaching panic among them which I consider very disgraceful and injurious. Some look as though they have already been hung ... let us support the Captain. Even if we are caught and hung, why, are we not men?"[26] The war over, his chance for independent command gone, Whittle now supported Waddell against the mutinous mood of others, despite being a Cape Town man himself.

Hunt, however, accused Waddell of being "unwarranted and ungentlemanly," and contrasted his conduct with other officers "who certainly never committed an act to sully their honor while on board the *Shenandoah*"[27]—his liaison with Mrs. Nichols.

Hunt wrote "It is exceedingly painful for a sailor to write such things concerning a commanding officer under whom he has served"—delighted, really, and he spitefully reproduced Waddell's mutiny letter to make sure it remained fresh in the officers' minds.[28]

Lilli Nichols would have read Hunt's book, sharing Waddell's anxiety and aware of the hidden meanings. Who knows what words crossed between her and her husband, who knows what trepidation occurred?

Missing at this time is any denial from either Bulloch or Waddell to the assertions in Hunt's book. Where are Waddell's letters of denial to the same newspapers that published his leaked "mutiny" letter? Where is James Bulloch's rejection? There is none; no defense presented.

Waddell was unable to deny the accusations for fear of Hunt's revelations. One drunken binge and he may carry out his threat to reveal the "motive that would not bear explanation," regardless of consequences. It was far easier to live with the theft charges which at least left Lilli Nichols' name unscathed, and he could deny the accusations in private.

Waddell joined his wife in Paris during 1866, then returned to England the following year.[29] Hunt's book appearing in early 1867 would have provided the catalyst, returning to make private denials to old colleagues. Waddell would have informed James Bulloch, now a permanent resident, of certain unseemly events, and request he make no response for fear of exposure. Boys will be boys, when all said and done, many prone to failings where the fair sex is concerned. Bulloch concealed these events in his *Secret Service of the Confederate States in Europe*. He admits excluding parts of Waddell's orders which were "descriptive and advisory, or merely confidential as between ourselves."[30] It comes as no surprise that "confidential" included, "proceed to Valparaiso to get the latest news," and "never return to Europe." This was appreciated by Waddell, no doubt, who was residing in College Ave. Annapolis at the time of Bulloch's publication in 1883. The two old colleagues closing ranks, Bulloch also stated that Waddell, after leaving Melbourne, had followed the prescribed route with "a light heart and in hopeful spirits"[31]; the exact opposite to the truth, the captain depressed beyond measure by the blackmailing Hunt.

A review of Hunt's book appeared on the front page of the *Charleston Daily News* on April 10, 1867:

> The age is rich in puerile books, and the public has grown very lenient, but this is even below the poorest endurable standard of weakness and folly ... the attacks, too, upon Captain Waddell, whether justified by facts or not, have a sinister look, for we do not like to find a man assailing his superior officer, whatever the cause, when the

latter is placed by circumstances in a defenseless position and the hearing of his case is thus rendered an *ex parte* one. The book is substantially trivial, school-boyish, and, worse than all for this kind of book, surprisingly dull; and the dash of malevolence which, like the sting of Martial's epigrams, winds up the tail, leaves an impression as unfavorable to the author's generosity as the impression previously made is unfavorable to his taste, culture, and literary capacity. Trash of this sort, whether written by Northerners or Southerners, has been dealt with far too lightly, and it is high time a little truth were spoken of it, if only to warn publishers to be chary of the credit of their imprint, and to have some little respect for the patience, as well as the intelligence of their readers.

This was reprinted from *The Round Table*, a New York weekly literature and art publication. It would appear both the reviewer and William Whittle shared the same opinion of the "utterly worthless" Cornelius Hunt. Despite the attack on Hunt, however, the reviewer did not actually dismiss his claims, writing that they had a sinister look "whether justified by facts or not."

When Hunt's book was released in America Waddell was overseas. His lack of response to the charges, confirmed by the reviewer, did not imply that it was beneath his dignity to respond to a mere master's mate. In his memoirs, revealed after death, he explained the ship's finances "as showing how much or little of the funds of the Confederate Government accumulated in Europe towards the close of the war came into my hands ... I desire to acknowledge by this public statement my responsibility to the judgment of the people of the South"[32]—a plea for his word to be taken over Hunt's.

Waddell could have published this defense in the press in 1866, and libel laws had been in force since before the American Revolution. But no action was taken against Hunt's charges.

Cornelius Hunt became an officer in the Egyptian army and died in a horse riding accident in 1873, but to publish a defense eight years after publication could well revive old memories. Some confidant of Hunt's may speak out; best to let sleeping dogs lie. A defense could not be published even with the blackmailer dead.

Little wonder another ten years would go by before Bulloch's subtle denial of Hunt's claims appeared in his *Secret Service* memoir. Bulloch made no direct mention of Hunt's accusations, but wrote Waddell followed his program "faithfully and with success."[33]

"Hunt and his charges have to be viewed with suspicion," wrote James Horan.[34] *Totally ignored,* would be a realistic assessment.

But Waddell had little idea of who Hunt may have told, and would wonder every day if the scandal was about to be revealed. In his memoirs, even the unseaworthy, pro–Cape Town Francis Chew transformed into an "intelligent and promising young officer,"[35] and those whose "conduct was nothing less than mutiny" became "Gentlemen by family and cultivation, naval officers by preference and education":

> One word before I close to those noble men who were officers under my command ... to each and all of them I shall ever feel bound by strong ties of personal and professional attachment ... their having merited by their devotion and conduct the grateful regard and remembrance of the people whom it was their pride and happiness to serve.[36]

Waddell could have correctly surrendered his ship in Sydney or Cape Town. But his baffling decisions, his moody behavior, his obsession with Liverpool, and the unproven theft charges, are all explained by his love affair with Lillias Nichols and the subsequent blackmail by Cornelius Hunt.

19

The Crinoline Under Which Thou Hast Kindled an Incendiary Fire

In 1932 the ninety-fourth birthday party story appeared in the *Bangor Daily News*. Lilli Nichols was showered with flowers and gifts, and telegrams were received from Lillias Jnr. and John, the grandchildren who, with Lilli's passing the following April, would inherit her diaries. Only quotes from officers' journals about her *Shenandoah* adventure are included in the article. Lilli herself made no contribution. "During her long life she has seldom referred to this incident," says the story—probably never if she could help it.

It is significant to note the total silence from the Nichols family following these events. There was a black hole of information; a hole just as black as that presented by James Waddell after Hunt's claim of "mercilessly defrauded" funds.

Following the Nichols' return to the United States the *Shenandoah* continued to be big news. Federal cruisers were on the hunt for the pirates who were bent on destruction despite the war's conclusion. The *Sacramento Daily Union* of August 4, 1865, attacked Waddell for damage done not only to ships but the wives and sweethearts of the mariners as well:

> Many a new gown and yards of bright ribbon, bonnets without number, and shawls innumerable as the stars of heaven, were burned when those ships' flames lit the darkness of night.... You have despoiled virgins' wardrobes.... For think of the vast dome of crinoline under which thou hast kindled an incendiary fire.

It seems most unlikely that Mrs. Nichols would wish to remark on that last line regarding her time spent with Captain Waddell. In fact, "no comment" was all the newspapers got if any approach was made.

The only family letter to emerge about the event is written from California by a cousin, Ransom Carver, in 1958.[1] She recalled a visit in 1912 when Ransom's father remonstrated with "cousin Lill" about the fact she kept a jewelry box under her bed. He asked what could she do if accosted by a burglar. She characteristically replied "What could I *do?*" she glared. "What could I *do?* Do you think I'd let any man walk off with my jewel box? I'd grab his arm, gun or no gun, and break it across my leg like this!" And she took an imaginary man's arm and broke it over her knee as one would snap a tree-twig. The letter then went on to tell of her defiance of the rebels aboard the "Confederate gunboat." But the account is absurd, Lilli wrapped in an American flag when she came aboard by a direct line strung between *Delphine* and *Shenandoah*. Then they "had to keep her locked in a cabin or hear themselves condemned continually," said Ransom's father. It was he who provided of the distorted account, not Lilli Nichols.

Lilli's son Phineas rejected both the seafaring and marriage traditions of his family. He became a dentist and married Maud McCready, a Canadian, in 1891. The *Biographical Review* of 1896 goes into his background which includes his seafaring family "prominent in business and marine circles, being ship captains or ship builders." He moved from Searsport to Northampton, Massachusetts, where his dental practice flourished, purchasing "his elegant residence on Elm Street, which is one of the finest in the vicinity." A lengthy obituary about Phineas in *The Dental Cosmos* after his death in 1911 goes into many details about his life. These included being descended from a family "who trace their ancestry to the Mayflower's company."[2]

But a glaring omission in either article is any mention of his childhood adventure on board the *Shenandoah*. Phineas kept quiet about this, apparently, unlike his other seafaring connections. Who knows what he saw or heard as a child, or had learned since? Silence can speak louder than words.

Although Lilli Nichols never volunteered any information, others have written articles about her over the years based on the officers' accounts. One such 1990 account appeared in *MAINE Boats and Harbors,* entitled "Yankee Heroine." The author painted a romantic picture of the happy couple, William and Lillias, being abducted at sea by the rebels, and Lilli's determination not to be cowed by the dastardly "Captain Waddell ... not the most compassionate man; he relished privateering." The article says William put his arm around Lilli's waist and said, "To tell you the truth I'm very proud of you. A lost ship can be replaced, but never lost honor."[3] Perhaps that last statement was correct, if little else.

A 2002 article about Lilli in *Chatham Crossroads* entitled "Captive captivated Lt. Commanding James Waddell" moved closer to the truth, revealing her obvious allure based on the officers' accounts.[4]

Another story about the *Shenandoah* included an artist's imaginary impression of Lilli Nichols. She looks most "queen like," as she stands proud and erect with officers giving her furtive glances in the wardroom. The caption reads "Wife of *Delphine*'s master and daughter of her owner, this tall young lady flirted with her captors."

But there was much more to that story, as we now know.

Although the *Shenandoah* took on board a number female prisoners at various times, they rated very few words in the officers' writings, being "a bore" according to Midshipman Mason.[5]

But with the Enchantress of the *Shenandoah*, there was much to be said about. Waddell described Lillias as a "tall, finely proportioned woman," and as it was he who got to see the "naked truth," so to speak, he should be believed. Other comments include: "a finer looking women I've seldom seen—queen like—good taste—handsome—delightfully clean look—pretty—a brave, cultivated woman—cultured—attractive." And also, a "woman who has so little delicacy as to place a gentleman in the fix I am."

That last quote is from Lieutenant Whittle, but it should have come from James Waddell.

When reading the officers' journals it is hard to imagine all this going on in the background. Even the "most scandalous romance" comment is well cloaked, the real meaning only apparent to someone who knows of the love affair. But anyone reading without other evidence would swear black and blue that the seamen taken on in Melbourne were mere stowaways, not the selected recruits they actually were. A carefully orchestrated pack of lies occurred. The journals make no mention, not surprisingly, of intimate sexual encounters while the ship was in Melbourne. Does this mean these young men, shut off from the "softening" influence of women, remained celibate? Most unlikely.

Perhaps the most revealing and honest quote in the whole affair was from Charles Lining, Captain Nichols a "man to be obliged to suspect his wife to have to keep his eyes on her to prevent her doing wrong."

But much of what appears in the journals is an airbrushed version of events, and Waddell's memoir is another example. It has been claimed that this was written only for family reading, but "One word before I close to those noble men who were officers under my command," and his appeal through "this public statement my responsibility to the judgment of the people of the South" show quite clearly his memoir was meant to be read by both his officers and the public at large.[6]

Mention of *Shenandoah* officers "having sought to establish themselves in South America and others in Mexico"[7] reveal the work to have started in 1866. A letter written by brother Charles to their father after Waddell's return to Maryland on July 19, 1867, mentions reading his manuscript of "about 500 pages."[8]

But Charles stated, "I begged him to finish it and have it put in print, but he would not consent." On one hand Waddell wanted to defend his actions at sea, but to publish his description of the ship's finances, with an appeal to be judged by "the people of the South" would have invited retribution. On the other hand, to publish without some rebuttal of Hunt's charges would suggest guilt. Waddell had the "most scandalous romance" hanging over him like the Sword of Damocles. The memoir remained unpublished, and he wrote additional material over the years.

Charles Waddell's letter reveals his brother's arrival back in America in July 1867. With Jefferson Davis having been released the previous May, and a Presidential Amnesty coming on September 7, the former rebel captain must have known he was on safe ground. On September 11 Charles wrote that "Mr. Johnson has issued his Amnesty Proclamation which embraces him, and places him beyond annoyance."[9]

Following Waddell's death, his wife gave the memoir to General Marcus Wright who was collecting Civil War documents. Once edited for the *Official Records*, they were misplaced in the archives until relocated following enquiries by Australian historian Professor Ernest Scott in 1937.[10]

Some personal letters have come to light in recent years,[11] but with the exception of the leaked "mutiny" letter, not a single word of Waddell's regarding the *Shenandoah* appears to have been published after the ship's surrender in Liverpool.

Total silence is something he and Lilli Nichols had in common. People with something to hide generally keep quiet—but not so with Cornelius Hunt.

At the 1872 Claims Tribunal the *Shenandoah*'s share of the damage wrought was not assessed separately from that of the *Alabama* and the *Florida*. A total amount of $15,500,000 was awarded, payable in gold by Britain to the United States within one year. The Tribunal did not agree with American claims that the *Shenandoah* had been fitted out unlawfully in London, as she was then legally owned by Richard Wright, a British subject, and the sale of the vessel at sea was found to be within the law. But Britain was found "responsible for all the acts committed by that vessel after her departure from Melbourne on the 18th day of February, 1865." Too little had been done by local authorities to prevent British recruits violating the Foreign Enlistment Act. Police Commissioner Standish claimed the police had no power to stop people from going aboard "who would at once have urged that they were only going off to see their friends, and that they proposed returning before the vessel sailed." If Standish is correct, it would seem the ship being allowed to leave the slip after the arrest of illegal recruits was the mistake. In any case, it is estimated the Melbourne stay cost Great Britain $3,875,000.[12]

After her surrender the *Shenandoah* was handed over to the American authorities in Liverpool. An attempt to sail her to the United States ended when driven back to port by a furious storm. Put up for auction, she was purchased by the Sultan of Zanzibar and renamed *El Majidi*. This led to a racist newspaper story in the *Daily Telegraph*.[13] The writer found it a "ludicrous anticlimax" that the former *Shenandoah* should be manned by a black crew. He went on to say that she should have gone down fighting like the *Alabama* but instead would "cruise like a half-pay hulk about the mangrove swamps and steamy rivers of Zanzibar and the Somali country; if she carries anything, it must be gum copal and greasy palm oil; and from stem to stern she will be redolent of 'niggers, niggers, niggers, niggers.' ... nothing would astonish us less than to hear that the *Shenandoah* plays her black crew an ugly trick some day in Monsoon weather, to show that the old spirit is in her timbers yet."

The writer, with prophetic insight, suggested "the deep waters around Socotra" as a likely place for the ship to come to grief. No doubt he was gratified when his wish bore fruit in 1879. Australian newspapers in February of 1880 reported the ship "foundered off the island of Socotra, in the Indian Ocean, with most of her crew." Waddell's memoirs also state that she went down in a gale off Socotra with all on board "except one or more persons who were picked up by a passing vessel who told of her fate." James Bulloch recalled, "the teak planks were torn from her bottom by a rough scrape on a coral reef, and her iron ribs were left to rust and crumble on a melancholy island in the Indian Ocean."[14]

Another account in Stanley Horn's *Gallant Rebel*, however, states she was scuttled by a German skipper in 1872 as an inducement for the Sultan to purchase a vessel from Hamburg.[15] It seems unlikely this was the *El Majidi*; perhaps another ship with a similar name.

Waddell read the *Daily Telegraph* "half-pay hulk" article. Some of the content provided basis for text near the conclusion of his memoirs:

> When we see a great vessel rolling lonely at sea, her masts gone, her gear loose and adrift, and sheets of foaming sea pouring in and out of her helpless sides, who wants the fable explained? Many such a craft, once proud and capable, wallows among the screaming seabirds of destiny upon the waters of life.[16]

One gets the feeling James Waddell is talking about his own life here. He was basically a fine man, "courtly," "gracious" and "radiant with kindness," but like many others before and since, susceptible to innate passions; a burden he carried for the rest of his life.

Upon return to the United States, brother Charles described Waddell as fit and healthy and "one of the finest looking men in Maryland or any other

State." The commander of the *Shenandoah* would have taken pride in the fact that he finally made it to that elusive destination; Sydney, but as captain of the Pacific Mail Line steamer *City of San Francisco,* in 1876. The passengers commended him through a newspaper advertisement for his "skill, vigilance" and "unvarying courtesy and attention."[17]

But peacetime did not end confronting events for James Waddell. Whale men in San Francisco threatened violence if he docked there, stirred on by hostility in the press, and the Hawaiian authorities wanted to charge him with piracy. He had destroyed the whaler *Harvest* along with three Yankee vessels at Ascension Island in April 1865. The matter was dropped after intervention by an American government anxious to have the Civil War laid to rest. In May of 1877, however, during a voyage to Panama, the *City of San Francisco* foundered after striking an uncharted rock. The *New York Times,* which had once stated "No pirate ever more richly deserved hanging," now wrote:

> The captain behaved in the coolest and bravest manner, and saved the passengers and crew, with provisions, and landed them on the neighboring coast, from which the whole of them were safely taken. The highest Board of Inspectors in San Francisco exonerated Capt. Waddell from all blame.[18]

Waddell's naval training was eventually put to good use again when he took command of the Maryland Water Police. The oyster pirates of Chesapeake Bay were a constant menace and he was given the task of clearing them out. *The New York Tribune* wrote that Waddell:

> two weeks after his appointment, ran one of his little police steamers, carrying two howitzers, and manned by ten men, into a fleet of illegal dredgers in the Honga River. He called upon them to surrender, and was greeted with jeers. He immediately opened fire on the dredgers with both howitzers and rifles, and in fifteen minutes had sunk one boat, driven three ashore, and captured three others. The others escaped by flight, and no Chesapeake Bay oyster pirate ever laughed off the veteran fire-eater again.[19]

James Waddell died at Annapolis, Maryland on March 15, 1886, aged sixty-one. He was given a full state funeral, attended by numerous dignitaries including the governor. He was the only Confederate officer to be given this honor outside a former rebel state. His pall bearers included the CSS *Florida*'s last commander, Charles Morris, and his casket was saluted by officers and cadets from the U.S. Naval Academy as it passed to his last resting-place in St Anne's Cemetery.[20]

But the James Waddell story did not end there. Lieutenant Colonel James Waddell, a foremost hero of the French Foreign Legion, born in New Zealand, won the Croix de Guerre eight times during World War I. An article in the *New Zealand Herald* states:

19. The Crinoline Under Which Thou Hast Kindled an Incendiary Fire

Growing up in 19th-century Dunedin, the young Waddell was, in the words of his parents, "fair dinkum mad on soldiering as a boy," an obsession his surviving grandchildren say was helped by having an infamous great uncle in the American Civil War. James Iredell Waddell captained the Confederate cruiser *Shenandoah*, which controversially attacked the United States-flagged whaling fleet in the South Pacific weeks after the war had ended—because of poor communications at the time.[21]

And in 1964, one hundred years after the CSS *Shenandoah* sailed, the destroyer USS *Waddell* was launched, named after the "infamous" rebel commander.

For Lillias and William Nichols it was a case of "till death do we part." In nineteenth century Maine separation was untenable in good families, let alone divorce. To do so was to mire oneself and children in public scandal. Marriages between the Pendletons and the Nichols were everlasting, come what may. No doubt that biblical prophecy read by William Nichols before the *Delphine*'s capture came back to haunt him time and again,—the twenty-seventh chapter of Acts[22]—Paul saying: "Sirs, I perceive that this voyage will be with hurt and much damage, not only of the lading and ship, but also of our lives." A number of damaged lives emerged from this. Perhaps, however, William Nichols took solace in the fact that his wife's love affair had saved his next command. He became captain of the *David Brown*; his family saved from further financial strife.

In 1867 the *David Brown* docked in Adelaide, and the Nichols again made the news, but in a small story this time under much less dramatic circumstances. One William Lucas was charged with stealing a gray rabbit from the ship. The defendant claimed the pet, "jumped into his bosom when he was coming away" from the vessel, then some young men in a bar snatched it up and "went away with it." The prisoner appeared very sorry about the loss and said the "lady was very fond of it." No doubt Mr. Lucas was even more sorry when he was fined one shilling plus the rabbit's value, which William Nichols claimed was the princely sum of at least two pounds.[23]

In 1887 Captain Nichols was in the papers once more. He was put on trial after being charged by five sailors for tricing them up while "drunk at the time and has been ever since." The article, "Released on a doubt," appeared in *The New York Times* on April 16.

William Nichols died on board the *Frank Pendleton*, March 1893, in New York Harbor, a little short of his sixtieth birthday. Lilli lived until April 7, 1933, passing on aged 94 in Searsport. The only relative to outlive her out of eight siblings and two children was her younger sister Delphine, for whom the fateful vessel had been named. This seems appropriate, as the story of the destruction of the *Delphine* and the aftermath should live on far beyond Lilli's own lifetime.

She had lived through a period of astonishing change, from sailing ships and whale oil lanterns to a modern world of giant ocean liners, electric lighting, radio, movies, aircraft and automobiles. She had a powerful impact on those she came in contact with, being described as "a truly great lady."

Ransom Carver wrote of "Cousin Lill—Goodness knows, EVERYONE respected HER ... I looked upon her as one of the wonders of the world."[24]

What an intriguing story James Waddell and Lilli Nichols left behind, a love story enmeshed with romance and deception from 1864 to 1960, nearly one hundred years, to be pondered by later generations.

In his memoirs James Waddell had proud words for his ship:

> She was the only vessel which carried the flag of the South around the world, and she carried it for six months after the overthrow of the South.... The last gun in defense of the South was fired from her deck on the 22nd of June, Arctic Ocean ... she ran a distance of 58,000 statute miles and met with no serious injury during a cruise of thirteen months.... She never lost a chase, and was second only to the celebrated *Alabama* ... I claim for her officers and men a triumph over their enemies and over every obstacle, and for myself I claim having done my duty.[25]

Lillias Nichols' final home, Searsport, Maine. She never remarried after her husband's death in 1893, but a companion, Mrs. Annie Lowell, shared the home during her final six years (author's collection).

This book rewrites the history of the *Shenandoah*. Sometimes the truth takes many years to unfold: the Viking colonization of North America, and the discovery of ancient Troy come to mind. These stories were thought to be mere myths, until souls with open minds confirmed their truth.

Lillias Nichols, however, did not launch a thousand ships as did Helen of Troy. She merely launched the only Confederate warship to circumnavigate the globe.

Appendix: Victims of *the* Shenandoah

Bark *Alina* of Searsport, Maine. Value $95,000. Destroyed October 30, 1864.

Schooner *Charter Oak* of San Francisco, California. Value $15,000. Destroyed November 5, 1864.

Bark *D. Godfry* of Boston, Massachusetts. Value $36,000. Destroyed November 8, 1864.

Brig *Susan* of New York, N.Y. Value $5,436. Destroyed November 10, 1864.

Clipper *Kate Prince* of Portsmouth, New Jersey. Ransomed for $40,000, November 12, 1864.

Bark *Adelaide* of Baltimore, Maryland. Ransomed for $24,000, November 12, 1864.

Schooner *L. Stacey* of Boston, Massachusetts. Value $15,000. Destroyed November 13, 1864.

Bark *Edward,* of New Bedford, Massachusetts. Value $20,000. Destroyed December 6, 1864.

Bark *Delphine* of Bangor, Maine. Value $25,000. Destroyed December 29, 1864.

Bark *Pearl,* whaler of New London, Connecticut. Value $15,000. Destroyed April 3, 1865.

Ship *Hector,* whaler of New Bedford, Massachusetts. Value $58,000. Destroyed April 6, 1865.

Ship *Edward Carey,* whaler of San Francisco, California. Value $15,000. Destroyed April 6, 1865.

Bark *Harvest,* whaler of Honolulu, Sandwich Islands. Value $34,750. Destroyed April 10, 1865.

Bark *Abigail,* whaler of New Bedford, Massachusetts. Value $10,705. Destroyed May 27, 1865.

Bark *Jireh Swift,* whaler of New Bedford, Massachusetts. Value $61,960. Destroyed June 22, 1865.

Ship *William Thompson,* whaler of New Bedford, Massachusetts. Value $40,925. Destroyed June 22, 1865.

Ship *Euphrates,* whaler of New Bedford, Massachusetts. Value $42,320. Destroyed June 22, 1865.

Ship *Sophia Thornton,* whaler of New Bedford, Massachusetts. Value $70,000. Destroyed June 22, 1865.

Bark *Nimrod,* whaler of New Bedford, Massachusetts. Value $29,260. Destroyed June 22, 1865.

Brig *Susan Abigail,* sailing from San Francisco, California. Value $6,500. Destroyed June 23, 1865.

Bark *William C. Nye,* whaler of New Bedford, Massachusetts. Value $31,512. Destroyed June 26, 1865.

Bark *Catherine,* whaler of New Bedford, Massachusetts. Value $26,000. Destroyed June 26, 1865.

Bark *Gypsy,* whaler of New Bedford, Massachusetts. Value $34,300. Destroyed June 26, 1865.

Bark *Isabella,* whaler of New Bedford, Massachusetts. Value $38,000. Destroyed June 26, 1865.

Bark *General Pike,* whaler of New Bedford, Massachusetts. Ransomed for $34,000, June 26, 1865.

Bark *General Williams,* whaler of New Bedford, Massachusetts. Value $44,750. Destroyed June 26, 1865.

Bark *Favorite,* whaler of Fairhaven, Massachusetts. Value $57,896. Destroyed June 28, 1865.

Bark *Waverly,* whaler of New Bedford, Massachusetts. Value $62,376. Destroyed June 28, 1865.

Ship *Brunswick,* whaler of New Bedford, Massachusetts. Value $16,272. Destroyed June 28, 1865.

Bark *Nile,* whaler of New London, Connecticut. Ransomed for $25,500, June 28, 1865.

Ship *James Murray,* whaler of New Bedford, Massachusetts. Ransomed for $40,550, June 28, 1865.

Ship *Milo,* whaler of New Bedford, Massachusetts. Ransomed for $30,000, June 28, 1865.

Bark *Congress,* whaler of New Bedford, Massachusetts. Value $55,300. Destroyed June 28, 1865.

Bark *Hillman,* whaler of New Bedford, Massachusetts. Value $33,000. Destroyed June 28, 1865.

Ship *Isaac Howland,* whaler of New Bedford, Massachusetts. Value $75,112. Destroyed June 28, 1865.

Ship *Nassau,* whaler of New Bedford, Massachusetts. Value $40,000. Destroyed June 28, 1865.

Bark *Martha 2nd,* whaler of New Bedford, Massachusetts. Value $30,307. Destroyed June 28, 1865.

Bark *Covington,* whaler of New Bedford, Massachusetts. Value $30,000. Destroyed June 28, 1865.

The total number of prisoners taken was 1,052, plus one—Lilli Nichols, who considered herself a passenger.

Chapter Notes

Chapter 1

1. Waddell's commanding officer, James Bulloch, considered the war to have ended with the capture of President Davis on May 10. The battle of Palmito Ranch, May 12 and 13, 1865, is considered by the *Official Records* to be a post-war clash, the final conflict being the Battle of Columbus, April 16, 1865.
2. *Official Records of the Union and Conf. Navies*, p. 832. Waddell's reaction was typical of all officers on board, shattered by the final proof of the South's defeat. Whittle's reaction can be read in *The Voyage of the CSS* Shenandoah, *a Memorable Cruise*, p. 182.
3. *Official Records*, p. 754.
4. Journal of John Mason, Aug. 3, 1865.
5. Ibid.
6. Journal of Charles Lining, Aug. 3, 1865.
7. Hunt, *Last Cruiser*, reproduces Waddell's letter of Dec. 27, 1865, pp. 266–70.

Chapter 2

1. Waddell Notes, *Official Records*, p. 807.
2. Whittle, *A Memorable Cruise*, p. 98.
3. Journal of Charles Lining, Dec. 30, 1864.
4. Journal of John Mason, Dec. 30, 1864.
5. Nearly all accounts state that Dr. Lining crossed to the *Delphine*, but he makes no such claim in his journal. Assistant Surgeon Frederick McNulty, however, states that he crossed and spoke to Mrs. Nichols in his brief account supplied online by the Confederate Navy Research Center—Google "The CSS Shenandoah *Cruise by One of Her Officers, Dr. McNulty*." The misconception would appear to originate with a mistaken account by Midshipman Mason in his 1898 *The Century Magazine* article, p. 605.
6. Journal of Charles Lining, Dec. 29, 1864.
7. Affidavit of Lillias Nichols, *British Case and Papers*, p. 872 (first ed., p. 649).
8. Waddell Notes, *Official Records*, p. 808.
9. Journal of John Mason, Friday, Dec. 30, 1864.
10. Grimball, *Cruise of the Shenandoah*, *Sunday News*, Charleston, S.C., Feb. 3, 1895, pp. 121–2.
11. Hunt, *Last Cruiser*, p. 75.
12. Journal of Charles Lining, Dec. 30, 1864.
13. From the records of the Penobscot Marine Museum, 1991.
14. Waddell Notes, *Official Records*, p. 807.
15. Whittle, *A Memorable Cruise*, p. 98.
16. Journal of John Mason, Friday, Dec. 31, 1864.
17. Waddell Notes, *Official Records*, p. 808.
18. Lightoller would visit Australia himself in 1900, during the Boer War, when he and some prank-prone shipmates scaled the tower of the abandoned Fort Denison in Sydney Harbor. They raised an improvised Boer flag and fired a cannon shot that caused a panic, residents thinking the African War had arrived in Australia.
19. Grimball, *Cruise of the* Shenandoah, *Sunday News*, Charleston, S.C., Feb. 3, 1895.

20. John Mason's account as it appeared in the 1898 *The Century Magazine*, p. 606.
21. Journal of Charles Lining, Jan. 6, 1865.

Chapter 3

1. The original wording can be seen on p. 809 of the *Official Records of the Union and Confederate Navies*, and rewritten lines on p. 122 of the Horan version.
2. *Official Records*, p. 807, and missing from p. 120 of the Horan version.
3. *Official Records*, p. 809.
4. Horan version, p. 124.
5. *Official Records*, p. 801, and rewritten lines on p. 107 of the Horan version.
6. Clark was honored in 2010 for 40 years service on the Museum Board. He passed on in Searsport, in his late 90s, in 2013.
7. Charles Nichols Blanchard died on Jan. 6, 2004, age 81. An obituary can be read by Googling "Charles Nichols Blanchard—Searsport."
8. Lewene A. (Nichols) Blanchard—Death Cert. no. 8804190. June 12, 1890–27 April 1988.
9. The article is headed "Searsport in her 95th year ... remarkable woman," etc. Censorship of a sort started with this article, the word "him" replaced with "they" expunging her anger with Waddell personally when leaving the ship. A photocopy of the article has a handwritten addition talking about Lillias playing with a child called Billy and his red wagon—"A truly great lady!" adds the writer.
10. *Bay Chronicle*, Searsport, January 1980, Vol. 3, p. 3.
11. Hunt, *Last Cruiser*, p. 77.
12. Olivia at the time of writing is age 98, the last star of *Gone with the Wind* still living.
13. Flynn had a much-publicized trial for statutory rape in 1943—sex with underage females. He was acquitted.
14. A paperback version of this novel appears as what could be an exposé on the love affair, the cover showing a handsome Confederate officer with a beautiful girl in his arms, and the caption *An Epic Voyage ... An Impetuous Love Affair*. All true in reality, but the novel revealed nothing of the real love affair.
15. Forward of Horan version, p. 35.
16. Lillias P. Nichols, Social Security no. 147-36-1147, Jan. 15, 1895–Nov. 23, 1991.
17. The Horan version of Waddell's memoirs can be purchased online from Amazon and other outlets. Waddell's original notes can also be viewed online—*The Official Records of the Union and Confederate Navies in the War of the Rebellion*, Vol. 3. pp. 792–836.
18. The small, weathered 1862 headstone had (1991) inscribed upon it "Little Hanna, whose all of life a rosy ray, blushed into dawn, then passed away."

Chapter 4

1. Scharf, *History of the Confederate States Navy*, p. 21.
2. McPherson, *Battle Cry for Freedom*, p. 280.
3. Waddell, *Memoirs*, ed. James Horan, p. 66.
4. Scharf, *History of the Confederate States Navy*, p. 65.
5. Ibid., p. 93.
6. Ibid., pp. 71–7.
7. Bulloch, *The Secret Service of the Confederate States in Europe*, pp. 39–40.
8. Waddell, *Memoirs*, ed. James Horan, p. 189, based on a *Daily Telegraph* article republished in the *Brisbane Courier*, July 3, 1867, p. 3.
9. Bulloch, *The Secret Service*, p. 118.
10. Pearl, *Rebel Down Under*, p. 11.
11. Commager, *The Blue and the Gray*, p. 876.
12. Spencer, *The Confederate Navy in Europe*, p. 189.
13. Ibid., p. 114.
14. Bulloch, *Secret Service*, p. 269.
15. McPherson, *Battle Cry of Freedom*, p. 362.

Chapter 5

1. Pearl, *Rebel Down Under*, p. 15.
2. Ibid., pp. 16–17.
3. Baldwin/Powers, *Last Flag Down*, p. 48.
4. Bulloch, *Secret Service*, p. 405.
5. McKay, *The Sea King*, pp. 107–8.
6. Testimony of William Temple, *British Case and Papers*, pp. 968–9.
7. *Official Records*, p. 758.

8. Ibid., p. 752.
9. Pearl, *Rebel Down Under*, pp. 5–6.
10. Waddell Notes, *Official Records*, p. 796.
11. Pearl, *Rebel Down Under*, p. 23.
12. McKay, *The Sea King*, p. 22.
13. Maryland State Archives Online.
14. McKay, *The Sea King*, p. 88.
15. Bulloch, *Secret Service*, pp. 416–17.
16. *Official Records*, pp. 749–54.
17. Bulloch, *Secret Service*, p. 413.
18. Waddell Notes, *Official Records*, p. 798.
19. Whittle, *A Memorable Cruise*, p. 56.
20. Waddell Notes, *Official Records*, p. 800.
21. Whittle, *A Memorable Cruise*, p. 58.
22. Ibid., p. 22.
23. John Mason Journal, Nov. 5, 1864.
24. Chatwin, *Sea of Gray*, p. 74.
25. Whittle, *A Memorable Cruise*, p. 56.
26. Waddell Notes, *Official Records*, p. 803.
27. Whittle, *A Memorable Cruise*, p. 71.
28. *British Case and Papers*, p. 864.
29. Ibid., pp. 768–9.
30. McKay, *The Sea King*, p. 133.
31. Chatwin, *Sea of Gray*, p. 127.
32. Whittle, *A Memorable Cruise*, p. 93.

Chapter 6

1. Journal of John Mason, Friday, Dec. 31, 1864.
2. Gratwick, *Stories from the Maine Coast*, p. 30.
3. Hunt, *Last Cruiser*, pp. 87–8.
4. Whittle, *A Memorable Cruise*, pp. 86 and 105.
5. Bulloch, *Secret Service*, p. 401.
6. *Official Records*, p. 750.
7. Bulloch, *Secret Service*, p. 163.
8. Schooler, *The Last Shot*, p. 120.
9. Affidavit of Lillias Nichols, *British Case and Papers*, p. 872.
10. Whittle, *A Memorable Cruise*, pp. 105–6.
11. Journal of Charles Lining, Dec. 19, 1864.
12. Ibid., Jan. 21, 1865.
13. Lining and Whittle first mention the ship moving under steam on the morning of Jan. 22, so it was raised during the night. Mason gives no date.
14. Journal of John Mason, "At sea March 18th 1865."
15. Ibid.
16. Waddell Notes, *Official Records*, p. 809.
17. Maps of the voyage (e.g. Pearl, *Rebel Down Under*, p. 135) show a wide divergence to port at one time, but based on longitude readings this is would have been on about January 19th if it occurred. Based on latitude readings, however, no divergence of such magnitude occurred in Australian waters.
18. Curry, *The Officers of the CSS Shenandoah*, p. 125.
19. *Official Records*, p. 755.
20. Journal of John Mason, "At sea March 18th 1865."
21. *Official Records*, pp. 759–61.
22. Ibid., p. 761.
23. John Mason's abridged account as it appeared in the 1898 *The Century Magazine*, p. 606.
24. Lining's journal quotes the *David Brown* as first sighted on January 22, and another ship looking like "a Yankee" the following morning. Whittle's journal (*Memorable Cruise*, p. 107) says the *David Brown* was in sight on the January 23, Waddell still saying she was the *Nimrod*.
25. *South Australian Register*, Monday, January 30, 1865, p. 2 under "ARRIVED—Sunday, January 29. DAVID BROWN, Ship, 830 tons. Phineas Pendleton, master from Searsport, U.S. October 23. Passengers—Mrs. Pendleton, family, and servant. First voyage, cargo of lumber."
26. Whittle, *A Memorable Cruise*, p. 107.
27. Journal of Charles Lining, Jan. 23, 1865.
28. Whittle, *A Memorable Cruise*, p. 108.
29. Lillias' affidavit of Feb. 3, 1865, *British Case and Papers*, p. 872.
30. Journal of Charles Lining, Jan. 23, 1865.

Chapter 7

1. *Official Records*, p. 755.
2. Whittle, *A Memorable Cruise*, p. 108.
3. *Official Records*, p. 761.
4. Ibid., p. 759.
5. Waddell Notes, *Official Records*, p. 809.
6. Whittle, *A Memorable Cruise*, p. 109.
7. The history of the Jeannie W. Paine posted by the Department for Environment

and Heritage can be seen online by Googling "Kadina—possibly Angas Inlet."
   8. Bulloch, *Secret Service*, p. 416. The Melbourne newspapers also stated 48 hours as the time permitted for the *Shenandoah* to remain in port, e.g., the *Age*, Feb. 1, 1865.
   9. *British Case and Papers*, p. 852.
   10. Crompton, *The CSS* Shenandoah *in Melbourne*, p. 13.
   11. 1865 Sands and McDougall Melbourne Directory, p. 226. The building no longer exists and the both street name and numbering have been changed.
   12. *British Case and Papers*, p. 857.
   13. Books about the *Shenandoah* generally state her affidavit of Feb. 3 to have been sworn out on arrival at the consulate, Jan. 26, throwing an incorrect light on the contents.
   14. Ibid., pp. 856–7.
   15. Pearl, *Rebel Down Under*, pp. 191–2.
   16. *The McIvor Times and Rodney Advertiser*, Friday, Feb. 3, 1865, p. 3.
   17. *Brisbane Courier*, June 4, 1898, p. 9.
   18. Journal of Charles Lining, Jan. 27, 1865.
   19. Hunt, *Last Cruiser*, p. 103.
   20. Journal of Charles Lining, Jan. 26, 1865.
   21. Gratwick, *Stories from the Maine Coast*, p. 28.
   22. Brown-May, *Melbourne Street Life*, p. 108.
   23. Pearl, *Rebel Down Under*, p. 135.
   24. Journal of Charles Lining, Jan. 29, 1865.
   25. Frost, *A Face in the Glass*, p. 290.
   26. Waddell, *Memoirs*, ed. James Horan, p. 187.
   27. *British Case and Papers*, pp. 905–7, and Waddell's *Memoirs*, ed. James Horan, pp. 124–5.
   28. Whittle, *A Memorable Cruise*, p. 111.
   29. Journal of Charles Lining, Jan. 31, 1865.
   30. Journal of John Mason, "At sea March 2d 1865."
   31. *British Case and Papers*, p. 784.
   32. Fricke, *Ned's Nemesis*, pp. 32–3, 44, 59.

Chapter 8

   1. *British Case and Papers*, p. 197.
   2. Whittle, *A Memorable Cruise*, p. 106.
   3. *British Case and Papers*, p. 764.
   4. *Illustrated Melbourne Post*, Feb. 18, 1865, p. 25.
   5. *Brisbane Courier*, Dec. 14, 1865, p. 3.
   6. *Sydney Morning Herald*, Feb. 18, 1865, p. 7.
   7. Sadleir, *Recollections of a Victorian Police Officer*, p. 123.
   8. Pearl, *Rebel Down Under*, pp. 77–9.
   9. Waddell, *Memoirs*, ed. James Horan, pp. 127–8.
   10. *Creswick and Clunes Advertiser*, Feb. 1, 1863, p. 3.
   11. Hunt, *Last Cruiser*, pp. 110–11.
   12. Pearl, *Rebel Down Under*, p. 54.
   13. Waddell Notes, *Official Records*, p. 811.
   14. Ibid., p. 810.
   15. *British Case and Papers*, p. 852.
   16. Ibid., pp. 852–3.
   17. Sadleir, *Recollections of a Victorian Police Officer*, p. 129.
   18. Pearl, *Rebel Down Under*, pp. 35–6.
   19. Macfarlane, *The Kelly Gang Unmasked*, pp. 153–4.
   20. Pearl, *Rebel Down Under*, pp. 69–70.
   21. Waddell Notes, *Official Records*, p. 813.
   22. *Brisbane Courier*, March 7, 1865, p. 3.
   23. Pearl, *Rebel Down Under*, p. 123.
   24. Frost, *A Face in the Glass*, p. 241.
   25. *British Case and Papers*, p. 785.

Chapter 9

   1. This is a composite of two quotes from Mason, one from his journal and the other from his article in the *Century Magazine*, p. 606.
   2. *British Case and Papers*, p. 973.
   3. Sadleir, *Recollections of a Victorian Police Officer*, p. 22.
   4. *British Case and Papers*, p. 853.
   5. Ibid., p. 862.
   6. Ibid., p. 897.
   7. Ibid., p. 872. The original affidavit can be found in the *Shenandoah* papers of the Victorian Public Records Office. It has been misrepresented in books as having been sworn out by Lillias when she reached Blanchard's office on Jan. 26, exposing the ship's background, thus "she did not intend to hold her tongue," as in Lining's account. Due to being handwritten, her middle name "Lewene" has been mis-transcribed as "Lervene" in the *British Case and Papers*.
   8. Ibid., p. 890.

9. Ibid., p. 967.
10. Ibid., pp. 864–5.
11. Ibid., p. 873.

Chapter 10

1. Journal of Charles Lining, Feb. 3, 1865.
2. Ibid., Feb. 4, 1865.
3. *British Case and Papers*, p. 853.
4. Ibid., pp. 865–7.
5. Ibid., p. 853.
6. Journal of Charles Lining, Feb. 6, 1865.
7. Pearl, *Rebel Down Under*, p. 83.
8. Craig's Royal Hotel and the ballroom, in Lydiard Street, are still intact, and a display in the foyer commemorates the "Buccaneer Ball."
9. The *Argus*, Feb. 11, p. 5, recounting their correspondent's report of Feb. 10.
10. Whittle, *A Memorable Cruise*, p. 81.
11. Pearl, *Rebel Down Under*, pp. 66–7.
12. Journal of Charles Lining, Feb. 10, 1865.
13. Ibid., Feb. 11, 1865.

Chapter 11

1. Pearl, *Rebel Down Under*, p. 132.
2. Waddell Notes, *Official Records*, p. 810.
3. Fricke, *Ned's Nemesis*, p. 10.
4. Pearl, *Rebel Down Under*, p. 78.
5. The Alabama Claims Tribunal would find that the police had been lax in allowing recruits on board.
6. *British Case and Papers*, p. 873.
7. Pearl, *Rebel Down Under*, p. 183.
8. *British Case and Papers*, p. 788.
9. Ibid., p. 789.
10. Ibid., p. 853.
11. Ibid., p. 802.
12. Ibid., p. 191.
13. Ibid., p. 893.
14. Noble, *Port Phillip Pilots and Defences*, p. 84.
15. Journal of Charles Lining, Feb. 14, 1865.
16. Waddell Notes, *Official Records*, p. 810.
17. *British Case and Papers*, p. 854.
18. Minto's report, *British Case and Papers*, pp. 805, 807, 810, 838, 839.
19. As per Minto's police record in the Victoria Police Museum.
20. *British Case and Papers*, p. 839.
21. Ibid., p. 854.
22. Frost, *A Face in the Glass*, p. 290.
23. *British Case and Papers*, p. 886.
24. Ibid., p. 793.
25. Pearl, *Rebel Down Under*, pp. 104–7.
26. *British Case and Papers*, p. 803.
27. Ibid., p. 810.
28. Waddell Notes, *Official Records*, p. 811.
29. *British Case and Papers*, p. 856.
30. Ibid., p. 891.
31. Pearl, *Rebel Down Under*, p. 135.
32. Ibid., p. 136.
33. Anderson, *When Passion Reigned*, pp. 51–2, 102.
34. Minto's written account can be read in the Treaty of Washington, *British Case and Papers*, p. 810.
35. *British Case and Papers*, p. 854.

Chapter 12

1. Journal of Charles Lining, Feb. 17, 1865. The *Great Britain* was the forerunner of the modern ocean liner and can be seen today, restored, in Bristol, U.K.
2. Noble, *Port Phillip Pilots and Defences*, lists a John Nicholson as pilot at this time, and this is corroborated by Whittle's *A Memorable Cruise*, quoting the pilot as "Mr. Nicholsen" [*sic*] p. 108. At the time of writing a house built by Nicholson in 1855 is available as holiday accommodation at Queenscliff.
3. *British Case and Papers*, p. 855.
4. S. P. Lord's written deposition, *British Case and Papers*, p. 884.
5. *British Case and Papers*, p. 855.
6. Lyttleton's report, *British Case and Papers*, p. 817.
7. Kennedy's report, *British Case and Papers*, p. 819.
8. Journal of Charles Lining, Feb. 17, 1865.
9. *British Case and Papers*, p. 833.
10. Waddell Notes, *Official Records*, p. 812.
11. Ibid., p. 813.
12. Whittle, *A Memorable Cruise*, p. 123.
13. Waddell Notes, *Official Records*, p. 813.
14. *British Case and Papers*, pp. 816–817.
15. Pearl, *Rebel Down Under*, p. 185.
16. Ibid., p. 192.

Chapter 13

1. Waddell Notes, *Official Records*, p. 813.
2. *Hobart Mercury*, March 2, 1865, p. 2.
3. Bulloch, *Secret Service*, p. 416.
4. Whittle, *A Memorable Cruise*, pp. 116–19.
5. Birth and Death Records, ArlisHerring.com.
6. Hunt, *Last Cruiser*, p. 232.
7. Ibid., p. 77.
8. Ibid., p. 223.
9. Keneally, *American Scoundrel*, pp. 116–17, 203—biography of Dan Sickles, goes into the affair and its repercussions at some length. Sickles was the first person in American legal history to get off killing someone due to "temporary insanity."

Chapter 14

1. Whittle, *A Memorable Cruise*, p. 116.
2. Waddell Notes, *Official Records*, p. 814.
3. Whittle, *A Memorable Cruise*, pp. 119, 121.
4. Ibid., p. 122.
5. *South Australian Register*, March 9—*David Brown* departure from Adelaide for Callao, Peru—1865, p. 2. Also "captain and family reached Callao and went north on the steamer *Chile*"—extract from story in the *Panama Star* about the *Delphine*, May 6, as reported in the *Daily Alta California*, San Francisco, vol. 17, no. 5559, May 26, 1865.
6. Frost, *A Face in the Glass*, p. 272.
7. Sadleir, *Recollections of a Victorian Police Officer*, pp. 132–3.
8. *Launceston Examiner*, March 28, 1865, p. 2.
9. Whittle, *A Memorable Cruise*, pp. 124–5.
10. Hunt, *Last Cruiser*, p. 131.
11. Chatwin, *Sea of Gray*, pp. 207–8.
12. Waddell Notes, *Official Records*, p. 821.
13. McPherson, *Battle Cry of Freedom*, p. 849.
14. *Official Records*, p. 755.
15. Whittle, *A Memorable Cruise*, pp. 128, 147.
16. Ibid., p. 160.
17. Waddell Notes, *Official Records*, p. 823.
18. *Sydney Morning Herald*, Jan. 3, 1867, p. 6.
19. *Official Records*, p. 790.
20. Whittle, *A Memorable Cruise*, p. 182.
21. Ibid., p. 169.
22. Ibid., p. 170.
23. Horan's foreword to the edited version of Waddell's *Memoirs*, pp. 32–3.
24. Waddell Notes, *Official Records*, pp. 829–30.

Chapter 15

1. *Official Records*, p. 791.
2. Waddell Notes, *Official Records*, p. 831.
3. Whittle, *A Memorable Cruise*, pp. 175–6.
4. As reprinted in the *Argus* of June 17, 1865, p. 4.
5. Waddell, *Memoirs*, ed. James Horan, p. 175.
6. Bulloch, *Secret Service*, p. 420.
7. *Official Records*, p. 754.
8. Bulloch, *Secret Service*, p. 423.
9. Whittle, *A Memorable Cruise*, p. 179.

Chapter 16

1. Whittle, *A Memorable Cruise*, p. 182.
2. Journal of John Mason, Aug. 3, 1865.
3. Ibid.
4. Ibid.
5. Journal of Charles Lining, Aug. 3, 1865.
6. Hunt, *Last Cruiser*, p. 129.
7. Ibid., p. 223.
8. Ibid., pp. 261–2.
9. Ibid., p. 229.
10. *Official Records*, p. 750.
11. McPherson, *Battle Cry of Freedom*, pp. 775–7.
12. *Official Records*, p. 754.

Chapter 17

1. Journal of John Mason, Aug. 4, 1865.
2. Whittle, *A Memorable Cruise*, p. 185.
3. Journal of Charles Lining, Aug. 24–27, 1865.
4. Horn, *Gallant Rebel*, p. 243.
5. *Official Records*, pp. 779–82.
6. Hunt, *Last Cruiser*, p. 231.
7. Ibid., p. 244.
8. Hunt, *Last Cruiser*, pp. 219–21.
9. Ibid., p. 230.
10. *Official Records*, p. 783.

11. Whittle, *A Memorable Cruise*, p. 197.
12. Ibid.
13. Journal of Charles Lining, Oct. 2, 1865.
14. Whittle, *A Memorable Cruise*, p. 202.
15. Ibid., p. 203.
16. Ibid., p. 204.
17. Waddell Notes, *Official Records*, p. 832.
18. Morgan, *Recollections of a Rebel Reefer*, pp. 190–6.
19. Waddell Notes, *Official Records*, pp. 833–4.
20. Whittle, *A Memorable Cruise*, pp. 206–7.
21. Ibid., pp. 207, 209.
22. Ibid., p. 210.
23. Whether this was all cash or partly letters of credit is unclear, Waddell writing as though all in cash, but Bulloch had written to Mallory that 3,000 pounds was in letters of credit, 2,000 in cash. The only possible place to exchange letters of credit for cash during the voyage was Melbourne, leaving Waddell with no "letters of credit to fall back upon," as he stated, once that money was gone. Either way, both agree the total was 5,000 pounds, or $22,000.
24. Testimony of Seaman William Temple, *British Case and Papers*, p. 973.
25. Whittle, *A Memorable Cruise*, p. 211.
26. Hunt, *Last Cruiser*, p. 244.
27. Bulloch, *Secret Service*, p. 417.
28. Whittle, *A Memorable Cruise*, p. 159.

Chapter 18

1. Waddell Notes, *Official Records*, pp. 783–4.
2. Pearl, *Rebel Down Under*, p. 171.
3. Hunt, *Last Cruiser*, p. 243.
4. Pearl, *Rebel Down Under*, p. 166.
5. Hunt, *Last Cruiser*, p. 253.
6. Waddell Notes, *Official Records*, p. 835.
7. Hunt, *Last Cruiser*, pp. 262–3.
8. Whittle, *A Memorable Cruise*, p. 241.
9. *British Case and Papers*, p. 973.
10. Hunt, *Last Cruiser*, pp. 263–4.
11. *British Case and Papers*, pp. 967–77.
12. Ibid., pp. 969, 973.
13. Ibid., p. 996.
14. Hunt, *Last Cruiser*, p. 263.
15. *British Case and Papers*, p. 969.
16. Ibid., p. 973.
17. Hunt, *Last Cruiser*, p. 255.
18. *British Case and Papers*, p. 988.
19. Pearl, *Rebel Down Under*, pp. 173–7, and Bulloch, *Secret Service*, p. 433.
20. *British Case and Papers*, p. 1001.
21. McKay, *The Sea King*, p. 228.
22. Whittle, *A Memorable Cruise*, p. 247.
23. Hunt, *Last Cruiser*, p. 265.
24. Ibid., pp. 268–9.
25. Ibid., p. 223.
26. Whittle, *A Memorable Cruise*, pp. 196–7.
27. Hunt, *Last Cruiser*, p. 232.
28. Ibid., pp. 266–70.
29. McKay, *The Sea King*, p. 233.
30. Bulloch, *Secret Service*, p. 407.
31. Ibid., p. 416.
32. Waddell Notes, *Official Records*, p. 812.
33. Ibid.
34. Waddell, *Memoirs*, ed. James Horan, p. 183.
35. Waddell Notes, *Official Records*, p. 799.
36. Waddell, *Memoirs*, ed. James Horan, p. 185.

Chapter 19

1. Letter provided by Paige Lilly of Penobscot Marine Museum, Searsport, Maine, 1991.
2. *Dental Cosmos*, vol. 53 (May 1911), pp. 616–17.
3. *Maine Boats and Harbors* (Winter 1990), pp. 45–8.
4. *Chatham Crossroads*, April 2002, p. 4.
5. Journal of John Mason, Nov. 5, 1865.
6. Waddell Notes, *Official Records*, p. 812.
7. Waddell, *Memoirs*, ed. James Horan, p. 185.
8. McKay, *The Sea King*, p. 235.
9. Ibid., pp. 234–5.
10. *Argus*, April 3, 1937: "*Cruiser* Shenandoah: New Light on a Forgotten Episode," p. 28.
11. McKay, *The Sea King*, pp. 234–5.
12. Pearl, *Rebel Down Under*, p. 187.
13. *Daily Telegraph* article reprinted in the *Brisbane Courier* of July 3, 1867, p. 3.
14. Bulloch, *Secret Service*, p. 440.
15. Horn, *Gallant Rebel*, p. 291.
16. Waddell, *Memoirs*, ed. James Horan, pp. 188–9.

17. Pearl, *Rebel Down Under*, p. 189.
18. From an obituary in *The New York Times*, March 17, 1886.
19. As reprinted in the *Brisbane Courier*, May 31, 1886, p. 2.
20. McKay, *The Sea King*, p. 265.
21. *New Zealand Herald* article by Paul Charman, April 22, 2012.
22. Waddell Notes, *Official Records*, p. 808.
23. South Australian Advertiser, Oct. 9, 1867, p. 4, and Oct. 10, 1867, p. 2.
24. Letter provided by Paige Lilly of Penobscot Marine Museum, Searsport, Maine, 1991.
25. Waddell Notes, *Official Records*, p. 836.

Bibliography

Main Sources

Australian Dictionary of Biography Online. www.adb.online.anu.edu.au.

The Case of Great Britain as Laid Before the Tribunal of Arbitration. www.quod.library.umich.edu/cgi/.

Chew, Francis T. Unpublished journal. Typed transcription, Archer Memorial Library, American Civil War Round Table of Australia.

CSS *Shenandoah*. Trove, National Library of Australia, www.trove.nla.gov.au.

Lining, Charles E. Unpublished journal. Typed transcription, Archer Memorial Library, American Civil War Round Table of Australia.

Mason, John T. Unpublished journal. Typed transcription, Archer Memorial Library, American Civil War Round Table of Australia.

Naval History and Heritage Command. www.history.navy.mil.

Official Records of the Union and Confederate Navies in the War of the Rebellion. 31 vols. Washington, D.C.: U.S. Govt. Printing Office, 1894–1922. www.digital library.cornell.edu.

The *Shenandoah* papers in Victorian Public Records Office.

Treaty of Washington, The British Case and Papers, presented at the Geneva Arbitration Hearings, now contained within the *U.S. House of Representatives Executive Documents 1871–72*, 2d ed. This contains a voluminous amount of material regarding the cruise of the *Shenandoah* and her stay in Melbourne, including government reports, affidavits, police reports, court proceedings etc. Volumes are held in the State Library of Victoria, and also available online.

Newspapers and Periodicals

The Age
The Argus
Australasian
Ballarat Star
Bangor Daily News
Bay Chronicle (Searsport)
Bell's Life in Victoria
Bendigo Advertiser
Brisbane Courier
Charleston Daily News
Creswick and Clunes Advertiser
Daily Alta California
The Herald
Illustrated Melbourne Post
Launceston Examiner
Maine Boats and Harbors
McIvor Times and Rodney Advertiser
Melbourne Punch
Morning Post
New York Herald
New York Times
New York Tribune
New Zealand Herald
Pall Mall Gazette
Rockhampton Bulletin
Sacramento Daily Union

San Francisco Bulletin
South Australia Advertiser
South Australian Register
Sydney Morning Herald
The Times

Other Sources

Anderson, Patricia. *When Passion Reigned: Sex and the Victorians.* New York: Harper Collins, 1995.

Baldwin, John, and Ron Powers. *Last Flag Down: The Epic Journey of the Last Confederate Warship.* New York: Crown, 2007.

Black, Frederick F. *Searsport Sea Captains.* Searsport, ME: Penobscot Marine Museum, 1960.

Blainey, Geoffrey. *The Tyranny of Distance.* Melbourne: Macmillan, 1988.

Brown-May, Andrew. *Melbourne Street Life.* Melbourne: Australian Scholarly Publishing, 1998.

Bulloch, James D. *The Secret Service of the Confederate States in Europe.* New York: Modern Library, 2001.

Commanger, Henry. *The Blue and the Gray.* New York: Crescent, 1950.

Crompton, Barry. *The CSS Shenandoah in Melbourne.* Melbourne: Privately published booklet, 1993.

Curry, Angus. *The Officers of the CSS Shenandoah.* Gainesville: University Press of Florida, 2006.

Fricke, Graham. *Ned's Nemesis; Ned Kelly & Redmond Barry in a Clash of Cultures.* Melbourne: Arcadia, 2007.

Frost, Lucy. *A Face in the Glass: The Journal and Life of Annie Baxter Dawbin.* Melbourne: Heineman, 1992.

Goodheart, Adam. *1861: The Civil War Awakening.* New York: Vintage Books, 2012.

Gratwick, Harry. *Stories from the Maine Coast.* Charleston, SC: History, 2012.

Grimball, John. *Cruise of the Shenandoah. Sunday News* (Charleston, S.C.), February 3, 1895.

Gurner, John A. *Life's Panorama.* Melbourne: Lothian, 1930.

_____. *The Shenandoah Incident.* Victorian Historical Magazine, vol. 11, 1926.

Hackett, Frank Warren. *Reminiscences of the Geneva Tribunal of Arbitration, 1872: Alabama Claims.* Boston: Houghton Mifflin, 1911.

Hill, Jim Dan. *Sea Dogs of the Sixties.* Minneapolis: University of Minnesota Press, 1935.

Horn, Stanley F. *Gallant Rebel: The Fabulous Cruise of the Shenandoah.* New Brunswick, NJ: Rutgers University Press, 1947.

Hughes, Robert. *The Fatal Shore.* London: Collins Harvill, 1987.

Hunt, Cornelius E. *The Shenandoah; or the Last Confederate Cruiser.* New York: Carleton, 1867.

Hunt, O. E., ed. *The Photographic History of the Civil War, The Navies.* Vol. 3. Secaucus, NJ: Blue and Grey Press, 1987.

Keneally, Thomas. *Abraham Lincoln: A Life.* New York: Viking Penguin, 2003.

_____. *American Scoundrel: Murder, Love and Politics in Civil War America.* Sydney: Random House, 2002.

Lewis, Lloyd. *Sherman, Fighting Prophet.* New York: Smithmark, 1994.

Mason, John Thompson. *Last of the Confederate Cruisers. Century Illustrated Magazine*, no. 56, 1898.

Matzen, Robert. *Errol and Olivia: Ego & Obsession in Golden Era Hollywood.* Pittsburgh: Goodnight, 2010.

McKay, Gary. *The Sea King: The Life of James Iredell Waddell.* Edinburgh: Berlin, 2009.

McNulty, Frederick J. *The CSS Shenandoah Cruise* as told to James Riley. *Southern Historical Papers*, vol. 21, 1893, p. 165.

McPherson, James M. *Battle Cry of Freedom: The American Civil War.* New York: Penguin and Oxford University Press, 1988.

Morgan, James Morris. *Recollections of a Rebel Reefer.* Boston: Houghton Mifflin, 1917.

Morgan, Murray. *Dixie Raider.* New York: E.P. Dutton, 1948.

Nichols, Charles J. *James Nichols (Nickels) of Searsport and His Descendants, 1733–1943.* Portland, ME: Privately printed, 1944.

Noble, Captain J. *Port Phillip Pilots and Defences.* Melbourne: Hawthorn Press, 1979.

Pearl, Cyril. *Rebel Down Under: When the Shenandoah Shook Melbourne, 1865.* Melbourne: Heineman, 1970.

Perret, Geoffrey. *Ulysses S. Grant, Soldier and President.* New York: Random House, 1997.

Sadleir, John. *Recollections of a Victorian Police Officer*. Melbourne: Penguin, 1973.

Sandburg, Carl. *Storm Over the Land*. 1942. Old Saybrook, ME: Konecky and Konecky, 2009.

Scharf, J. Thomas. *History of the Confederate States Navy*. 1887. New York: Random House Avenel, 1996.

Spencer, Warren F. *The Confederate Navy in Europe*. Tuscaloosa: University of Alabama Press, 1983, 1997.

Thomas, Emory M. *Robert E. Lee*. New York: W.W. Norton, 1997.

Waddell, James I. *CSS Shenandoah: The Memoirs of James I. Waddell*. Ed. James D. Horan. New York: Crown, 1960.

_____. *Notes on the Cruise of the CSS Shenandoah, as Transcribed in the Official Records of the Union and Confederate Navies*. Washington, D.C.: U.S. Govt. Printing Office, 1896.

Wheelan, Joseph. *Terrible Swift Sword: The Life of General Phillip H. Sheridan*. Cambridge, MA: Da Capo, 2012.

Whittle, William C. *The Voyage of the CSS Shenandoah: A Memorable Cruise*. [Whittle's journal with introduction and annotation by D. Alan Harris and Anne B. Harris.] Tuscaloosa: University of Alabama Press, 2005.

Index

Numbers in ***bold italics*** indicate pages with photographs.

Adams, Charles F. 26–7, 31, 61, 160, 165
Adelaide, Australia 54, 59, 126, 177
CSS *Alabama* 4, 23, 25, 29, 31, 33, 35, 36, 41, 43, 47, 50, 59, 120, 126, 134, 142, 156, 161, 174, 175, 178
Alabama Claims Tribunal 112, 118, 174
Aleutian Islands 140–1
Alfred, Prince 94
Amukta Pass 141
Arctic Ocean 37, 131, 140, 142, 159, 178
Ascension Island (Pohnpei) 129–132
Aspinall, Butler C. 127–8
Astor, Mary 16, 18, 67
CSS *Atlanta* 23

Barker, Dr. Edward 64, 66, 76–7, 146
Barracouta (ship) 3, 145, 161
Barron, Samuel 52–3, 58
Barry, Justice Redmond 66–7, 127
Beauregard, Gen. Pierre G.T. 20
Beaver, Inspector S. 96, 98
Behnck, Charles 95, 104, 108
Bering Sea 135
Berry, Graham 82, 108
Bill, William 157
Black Eagle (tug) 101
Blacker, Capt. John 117, 137, 151, 156
Blanchard, Charles Nichols 13–4, 17, 60
Blanchard, Clara E. 13, ***14***, 45, 60
Blanchard, Lewene A. 14
Blanchard, Scott 14
Blanchard, U.S. Consul William 59–62, 73–5, 75, 78, 80–88, 94–7, 98, 99, 104, 108, 109, 111–6, 119
Blanchard, Capt. William H. 14, 60

The Boy Pirate (novella) 111
Bracket, George 84
Braveheart (film) 17
Brayton, E.C. 90
Browne, Midshipman Orris A. 152, 161
Bruce, William 83
Buccaneer Ball (Ballarat) 89–90, ***91***, 92
Bulloch, Sailing Mast. Irvine S. ***6***, 36, 87, 89, 90–2, 111, 112, 126, 147, 152
Bulloch, Cmdr. James D. 1, 22–6, 28, ***29***, 30–1, 33, 35, 36, 43, 47, 56, 121, 122, 125, 143, 146, 147–9, 158–63, 168, 169, 175

Calcutta (ship) 66
Call, Magistrate F. 108, 111–2, 114
USS *Camanche* 142–3
Canning, George P. 117, 157, 158
Canning, Henry 117
Cape Horn 48, 152
Cape of Good Hope 36, 40, 43
Cape Town 4, 148, 150, 152–4, 162, 167, 169–70
Captain Blood (film) 15–7
Carver, Ransom 172
Carver, Wealthy 8
Cashmore, Michael 112
HMVS *Cerberus* 119
Chambers, Enoch 80, 89, 98, 101, 105
Charley *see* Davidson, James
Chew, Lt. Francis T. 7–8, 11, 36, 38, 43, 59, 62–3, 90, 106, 116, 118, 129, 139, 142, 144, 152–6, 169–70
Chili (ship) 126
City of San Francisco (ship) 176
Clara (ship) 45

Clarendon, Lord 160, 165
Colby, George 41, 81, 84
Colton, Lodge Mast. Mate 136
USS *Congress* 23, 40
Copper Island 136
Corbett, Capt. Peter S. 29, 31-3
Craig's Royal Hotel 90
Criterion Hotel 104 107
USS *Cumberland* 23
Curtiz, Michael 17

Damita, Lili 16
Darling, Sir Charles H. 58-62, 74, **75**, 80, 86, 95-8, 104-6, 111-2, 115, 118
David Brown (ship) 53-5, 77, 123, 125-6, 166, 177
Davidson, James (Charley) 96-7, 100-2, 104, 105-8, 110-2, 118, 126-8
Davis, Jefferson 3, 20, 22, 28, 132-3, 137, 143, 145, 175
Dawbin, Annie B. 64, 79, 104, 127
de Havilland, Olivia 16-7
Delphine (ship) 6-10, 14, 17, 31, 45, 48-9, 60, 63, 74, 83, 84, 172-3, 177
HMS *Donegal* 159, 165
Drummond Island 129
Dudley, Thomas H. 25, 163, 165
Duffett, Joseph G. 81-3, 88

Edward VIII, King 16
Elder, Capt. Douglas 71, 98
Eli Whitney (ship) 95
Eureka Stockade 71, 91
Eves, William 90

Favorite (ship) 138
Ferguson, Capt. Charles 113
CSS *Florida* 4, 23-5, 29, 35, 41, 56, 65, 156, 174, 176
Flynn, Errol 15-7
Forbes, Andrew 114
Fort Sumter 20-2
Francis, James G. 60, 65-6, 74, 80, 99, 101, 103, 105, **106**, 107-10, 112-3
Frank Pendleton (ship) 14, 46, 177
Fraser, Sarah 94

Gage, Simeon 96
Gilman, Capt. Samuel J. 39, 40, 47-8
Glover, Frank 111-2
Gone with the Wind (film) 16
Grant, Gen. Ulysses S. 9, 28, 132, 141
Grattan, Henry C. 33
Gravesend, England 6, 31
Great Britain (ship) 81, 111, 113
Grimball, Lt. John 7, 10, 36, 42, 49, 51, 52, 57, 58, 62, 89-90, 96-7, 101, 112, 136, **137**, 141, 153, 161
Gurner, Henry F. 95, 114
Gurner, John 76
Guy, Gunner Peter 87

Hall, Ben 71
Harrocke, Thomas 129, 130
Higinbotham, George 76, 82, 88, 95, 105, 113-4, 117, 128
CSS *H.L. Hunley* (submarine) 24
Horan, James D. 12-3, 17-19, 169
Horn, Stanley 151-2
USS *Housatonic* 24
Hunt, Mast. Mate Cornelius E. 7-8, 15, 46, 62, 73, 90, 121-2, **123**, 128-31, 135, 137, 141, 146-56, 158-71, 174; accuses Waddell of theft 161-3; background 122; Ballarat Ball 90; blackmails Waddell 122; character 90; publishes book 15, 167

USS *Iroquois* 42, 157

Jackson, Thomas 96
Jeannie W. Paine (ship) 59-60
Jireh Swift (ship) 136
USS *John Adams* 21, 35
John Fraser (collier) 107, 111
Jones, Edward 6

USS *Kearsarge* 25
Kell, Lt. John M. 25, 41
Kelly, Ned 76, 94
Kennedy, Detective D.S. 95, 117-8
Kennedy, George 93
Key, Phillip B. 124, 166
King, Comm. Henry. 68

Ladd, Allan 17
Lalor, Peter 71
Las Desertas 32, 53
Laurel (ship) 30-3, 48, 59, 61, 82-3, 88
Lee, Gen. Robert E. 9, 64, 132, 141
Lee, Lt. Sydney S. 36, 64, 76, 101, 126, 151- 4
Lillias (ship) 14
Lilly, Paige 13
Lincoln, Abraham 20-2, 71, 136-7, 140, 148
Lindborg, Frederick 83
Lingo, Edward 9, 83
Lingo, Mary 7, 60, 109
Lining, Charles, E. 6-8, 10-11, 36, 38, 43, 51, 55-8, 62-4, 66, 76, 85, 87-92, 99, 101, 115-6, 135, 147, 151-4, 156, 159, 173
Liverpool Sailors' Home 163, **164**, 165
Lohd Harbor 129-132
Lord, Samuel 95, 114, 119

Index

Lucas, William 177
Lyttleton, Superintendent Thomas H. 78–80, 94, 96–99, *100*, 101, 104, 108, 115, 127

MacFarlane, Tide Inspector James 66, 74, 111
Mackenzie, William 111–2, 126, 128
Madden, Walter 95–6, 104, 108
Maffitt, Lt.-Comm. John N. 35
El Majidi (*Shenandoah* renamed) 175
Mallory, Stephen R. 28–9, 52, 58
Manning, Thomas S. 134–5
Maria Ross (ship) 114–5
Mason, Midshipman John T. 4–7, 9–10, 37, 39, 42, 45, 48, 51–3, 56, 64–6, 72–3, 76, 81, 87, 93–4, 116, 130–3, 136, 140, 145–6, 150, 152, 154, 159, 161, 173
McCready, Maud 172
McCulloch, Premier James 82, 104, 109
McDougal, Lt. Charles J. 142–3, 145
McNulty, Asst. Surg. Frederick J. 6, 135, 154, 156, 161
Melbourne Club 65–6, 76–8, 117, 146
Metcalf, Eliab W. 7
Minor, Mast. Mate John 6, 43, 88, 129, 136, 155
Minto, Sr. Const. Alexander 100, 108, 111, 117
Mitchie, Archibald 76, 88, 105
Molesworth, Henrietta 127
Molesworth, Justice Robert 126–8
USS *Monitor* 23–4
Monroe, U.S. Consul James 42
Morris, Lt. Charles M. 35, 176
Morton, Charles 163–5
Mustang (ship) 78

CSS *Nashville* 30
HMS *Nelson* 119
Neutrality Proclamation 23
USS *Niagara* 31
Nichols, Clark 13
Nichols, Edward P. 45–6, 63, 83
Nichols, Hannah 9, 19, *50*
Nichols, John McCready 15, 171
Nichols, Lillias Lewene (née Pendleton) 6–7, *8*, 9–20, 45–6, 48–55, 58–60, 65–7, 69, 82–4, *85*, 86, 88, 111, 120–4, 126, 139, 141, 157, 166, 168, 170–4, 177, *178*, 179; affidavit 84–5; altercation with Smith 55, 84–5; assignation 51, 65; background 8–9; cajoles Whittle 48–9; captured 5–7; character and appearance 7–8, 45; death 13, 177; departs Australia 126; deserts cruiser 59
Nichols, Lillias Pendleton 15, 17–9, 171
Nichols, Phineas 7–9, 15, 60, 172
Nichols, Capt. William Green 6–8, 10, 12, 14, 45, *46*, 50–1, 60, 54–55, 58, 83, 168, 173, 177–8
Nicholson, John 113, 116
Nickle, George 100
Nicolson, Inspector Charles C. 95, 114
Nye, Capt. Ebenezer 134

O'Brien, Chief Engineer Matthew 25, 36, 46–7, 51, *52*, 152

Palmerston, Lord 26
Payne, Capt. Charles B. 68
Paynter, Capt. John 159, 161, 165
USS *Peacock* 129
Pendleton, Delphine 177
Pendleton, Capt. John G. 48
Pendleton, Capt. Phineas II 8, 20
Pendleton, Capt. Phineas III *54*, 126
USS *Pennsylvania* 34
Penobscot Marine Museum 13
Pirate Party (film) 19
Powell, Mr. 93
The Proud Rebel (movie) 17
Pussy (ship's cat) 142

Ramsay, Lt. John F. 31, 33, 59
USS *Release* 34
Rio de Janeiro 40, 42
Robbins, George W. 115, 117
Rodgers, Lt.-Comm. Christopher R.P. 42
Ross, Captain 115
Russell, Lord John 26, 59

USS *Sacramento* 31
Sadleir, Supt. John 76, 79, 94
USS *Saginaw* 34, 137
St. Paul's Island 7, 10, 46
San Francisco 34, 137–8, 142–6, 176
Scales, Lt. Dabney M. 36, 43, 62, 76, 94, 126, 134, 151, 153–4
Sclopis, Count 118
Scott, Prof. Ernest 174
Scott, Mrs. 66–7, 127
Scott, William 83
Scott's Hotel 62, 66, 73
Sea of Okhotsk 134
Searsport, Maine 6, 8, 13–9, 38, 48, 141, 171–2, 177, *178*
Seek Out and Destroy (novel) 17
Semmes, Capt. Raphael 22, 25–6, 35, 59, 62
Seward, William 42, 165
CSS *Shenandoah*: armament 36; construction 29, 68; discipline 38–9, 41, 81; prop damage 46–47, 51–3, 72, 80; financial situation 158–159; officers list 36; purchased as *Sea King* 29

USS *Shenandoah* 156–7
The Shenandoah Affair (novel) 18
Sheridan, Gen. Phillip H. 13, 109
Sherman, Gen. William T. 9, 13, 28, 84
Shirley, Capt. Paul 48
Sickles, Gen. Dan 123–4
Sickles, Teresa 123, *124*, 127, 166
Sibley, Captain 40
Simpson, Wallis 16
Smith, Capt. 136
Smith, Paymaster William B. 36, 55, 76, 84–5, 89–92, 101, 112, 147, 152, *155*, 161–2
Solferino (ship) 48
Standish, Police Comm. Frederick W. 65, 94–5, 98, 114, 117–8, 174
Stanton, Edwin M. 48
Staples, Everett 38
CSS *Stonewall* 26
Sturt, Magistrate E.P.S. 114
CSS *Sumter* 22
USS *Suwanee* 48, 157
Sydney, Australia 3, 36, 52, 66, 71, 75–6, 104, 122, 129, 146–8, 150, 154, 162, 167, 170, 176

Temple, William 81, 117, 163–5
Theatre Royal 72
Tristan da Cunha 42, 102
Tucker, Capt. Moses 137

Van Dorn, Gen. Earl 123
Verdon, George F. 71, 119, 127
HMCS *Victoria* (ship) 98
Victoria, Queen 23, 50, 123
Violetta, Jacob 34
CSS *Virginia* 23–4

USS *Wachusett* 157
USS *Waddell* 177
Waddell, Anne H. 34, 50
Waddell, Anne S. 34, *35*, 48, 50, 125, 165
Waddell, Charles 173–5

Waddell, Lt.-Col. James 176–7
Waddell, Lt.-Comm. James I. 1, 3, *4*, 5–10, 12–9, 21–2, 24, 29–62, 64–6, 69–70, 72–4, 76–80, 82–7, 89, 94–7, 99–102, *103*, 105, *106*, 107–18, 120–3, 125–6, 128–33, 135, 137–65, *166*, 167–178; accused of theft 161–3; appearance and character 34; argues with Whittle 43–4; arrives in Melbourne 56; assignation 51, 65; assumes command 32; background of 34; blackmailed 122; Bulloch's orders 1, 18, 36, 125, 143, 148–9, 160, 168; Cape Town petitions 153–4; contacts *Barracouta* 3, 145; death 176; departs Melbourne 116; depressed 121, 128; marriage 34; meets Mrs. Nichols 7; Melbourne Club dinner 66, 76–7, 117; resigns 21; ship surrounded 99; surrenders 159
Walmsley, Arthur 111
Welles, Gideon 42, 48, 142
Whicker, Herman 95–6
Whitcher, Sr. Cons. 117
Whittle, Lt. William C. 5, 9, 18, 30–1, 35–44, 46–8, *49*, 50–1, 53–4, 56, 58, 63, 65, 68, 81, 84, 88, 90, 101, 112, 115–7, 121–3, 125–6, 128–30, 133–8, 140–2, 144, 146–7, 151, 153–9, 162, 167, 169, 173
Wiggins, Qtm. Louis P. 162–5
Wilding, Henry 160
Wilkins, J.P. John 97
Williams, Capt. 136
Williams, John 23, 40, 94–96, 111–2
Winslow, Capt. John A. 25
Wiseman, Sir W. 115
Wright, Gen. Marcus 174
Wright, Richard 31, 174
USS *Wyoming* 157

Young, Capt. Thomas 138

Zanzibar, Sultan of 175

www.ingramcontent.com/pod-product-compliance
Ingram Content Group UK Ltd.
Pitfield, Milton Keynes, MK11 3LW, UK
UKHW042007140426
5217IPUK00015B/1032